HEALING SOUNDS

"*Healing Sounds* is a great gift for humankind."

KITARO, GRAMMY AWARD–WINNING COMPOSER

"Jonathan Goldman, a visionary and master teacher of sound healing, has now released a 30th anniversary edition of his classic *Healing Sounds.* In it you'll find explanations and exercises, including audio downloads that allow you to experience the magic of vibrational sound healing. You will treasure this book and find inspiration for the value of vibrational sound healing. I highly recommend it!"

STEVEN FARMER, PH.D., AUTHOR OF *EARTH MAGIC*

"How did the ancients know of sound healing? Jonathan Goldman has the answers in his powerful book *Healing Sounds.* It offers proof that sound healing really works. He has struck gold with this book."

GEORGE NOORY, HOST OF *COAST TO COAST AM*

"Jonathan Goldman's *Healing Sounds* is a very important book. It contains information and understandings on sound that will always be relevant to anyone wanting to know more about how sound affects our mind and body. That is why *Healing Sounds* is a classic and always at the top of my bookshelf."

JOHN BEAULIEU, N.D., PH.D, AUTHOR OF *HUMAN TUNING*

"The processes, exercises, and meditations in this book entrain ancient wisdom with a modern-day application for healing our mind, body, and spirit through sound and, in so doing, change our lives. In this 30th anniversary edition of master teacher Jonathan Goldman's classic, *Healing Sounds,* we are once again gifted with a comprehensive guide for raising consciousness through vibrational activation. I love this book!"

DR. DARREN R. WEISSMAN, AUTHOR OF *THE POWER OF INFINITE LOVE AND GRATITUDE* AND DEVELOPER OF THE LIFELINE TECHNIQUE

"After 30 years, Jonathan Goldman's groundbreaking book *Healing Sounds* remains an essential classic in the field of sound healing. It's the best introduction to the magical world of harmonics. It belongs in the library of everyone interested in the therapeutic and transformative powers of sound."

Alec W. Sims, coauthor of *Sound Healing for Beginners*

"This book (and Jonathan's music!) played a big role in my early education on sound healing. Thirty years after its first publication, *Healing Sounds* is still fresh and relevant and a must-read for anyone interested in the healing power of sound and music!"

Eileen McKusick, author of *Tuning the Human Biofield*

"Jonathan Goldman is a powerful advocate for the voice as an instrument for healing. The rich background and the lucid explanation of harmonics in all its beautiful complexity given in *Healing Sounds* will enrich your practice and your connection to the world of sound."

Roger Nelson, Ph.D., director of the Global Consciousness Project

"An imperative for our time. *Healing Sounds* provides an essential pathway into the medicinal power of sound for true health and transformation in the twenty-first century."

Chloë Goodchild, author of *The Naked Voice*

"This work of Jonathan Goldman presents a mastery of knowledge about sound healing that keeps giving and giving and giving. *Healing Sounds* is a legacy of its own. These principles work today, just as they have for centuries. Celebrate this 30th anniversary edition!"

Lee Carroll, publisher of Kryon Writings, Inc.

30TH ANNIVERSARY EDITION

HEALING SOUNDS

THE POWER OF HARMONICS

JONATHAN GOLDMAN

Healing Arts Press
Rochester, Vermont

Healing Arts Press
One Park Street
Rochester, Vermont 05767
www.HealingArtsPress.com

Text stock is SFI certified

Healing Arts Press is a division of Inner Traditions International

Copyright © 1992, 1996, 2002, 2022 by Jonathan Goldman

First and second editions published in 1992, 1996 by Element Books under the title *Healing Sounds: The Power of Harmonics*
Third edition published in 2002 by Healing Arts Press
30th anniversary edition published in 2022 by Healing Arts Press

All rights reserved. No part of this book may be reproduced or utilized in any form or by any means, electronic or mechanical, including photocopying, recording, or by any information storage and retrieval system, without permission in writing from the publisher.

Note to the reader: *This book is intended as an informational guide. The remedies, approaches, and techniques described herein are meant to supplement, and not to be a substitute for, professional medical care or treatment. They should not be used to treat a serious ailment without prior consultation with a qualified health care professional.*

Cataloging-in-Publication Data for this title is available from the Library of Congress

ISBN 978-1-64411-582-4 (print)
ISBN 978-1-64411-583-1 (ebook)

Printed and bound in the United States by Lake Book Manufacturing, Inc.
The text stock is SFI certified. The Sustainable Forestry Initiative® program promotes sustainable forest management.

10 9 8 7 6 5 4 3 2 1

Text design and layout by Priscilla Harris Baker
This book was typeset in Garamond Premier Pro with Aviano Copper, Copperplate, Futura, and Tide Sans used as display typefaces

To send correspondence to the author of this book, mail a first-class letter to the author c/o Inner Traditions • Bear & Company, One Park Street, Rochester, VT 05767, and we will forward the communication, or contact the author directly at **healingsounds.com**.

Contents

Acknowledgments

Healing Sounds has been a special work for me. The use of overtones as transformative and therapeutic tools has been a major focus since I first became aware of them over three decades ago. I have met, worked with, and learned from some of the great pioneers who are using sound and music for health and change. Many of these people are cited in this book, but others are not. I would like to dedicate this book to the Masters of the Sound Current, who have allowed this work to manifest, and to Shamael, Angel of Sacred Sound, whose continued guidance is a blessing. I would also like to dedicate it to the various pioneers, musicians, teachers, and scientists whose work has been an important contribution to the field of sound and music for health and transformation. In addition, this book is dedicated to my beloved wife Andi Goldman, whose gifts of love and compassion continue to inspire and amaze me; to my son, Joshua Goldman, great friend and teacher, whose very essence brings joy into my life; and to Karen Anderson, for manuscript editing of the original project.

Thanks to John Beaulieu; Sarah "Saruah" Benson; Joachim-Ernst Berendt; Don Campbell; Rinchen Chugyal and the lamas of the Drepung Loseling Monastery, including Chant Master Ngawang Tashi Bapu; Kay Gardner; Steven Halpern; Barbara Hero; David Hykes; Peter Guy Manners, D.O.; the Gyume and Gyuto monks; Alec Simms; and Alfred Tomatis, M.D., for their harmonic transmissions.

To my parents, Rose and Irving Goldman, and my brothers, Richard and Peter Goldman, I give thanks for all the love and support you gave me while you were on this planet and for that which you still give me from afar.

In addition, I'd like to thank the many extraordinary beings working with the energy of light and love through sound, whether through their writings, teachings, music, assistance, or simply by being. The list of those who have influenced and affected my life and my work during the decades is too numerous to truly contemplate. Following are some who have assisted this work and therefore have my gratitude: Gregg Braden, Bruce Lipton, Margaret Horton, Steve Brown, Thea Beaulieu, Charles Eagle, Christian Bollmann, Chloe Goodchild, Reb. Zalman Schachter-Shalomi, Daniel Levitin, Jeralyn Glass, Steve Koral, Alice Cash, Jason Stillwell, Joshua Leeds, Kathleen Riley, Lee Carroll, Monika Muranyi, Roger Nelson, Sam McClellan, Lynn McTaggart, Rabbi Auri V. Ishi, Kenneth Garret, John and Aly Galm, James Ford Wright, Jim Albani, Tae Darnell, Tom Kenyon, Laraaji, Arji, Nasiri Suzan, John Stuart Reid, Glenn Kamamura, Katharine and Makasha Roske, Donald Beaman, Akshara Weave, Paul Temple, Paul Pena, Steve Farrell, Amy Strombotne, Tim Wheater, Jim Berenholtz, Susan Lenox, Simon Heather, Molly Scott, Steve Stone, Tony Davis, Marcia Guntzel Feldman, Rollin McCraty, Arthur Harvey, Bruce Paley, Barbara Marciniak, Dik Darnell, Howard Martin, Barbara Lee, Jeff Volk, Barry Oster, Mandara Cromwell, James D'Angelo, Fabien Maman, Kitaro, Dean and Dudley Evenson, Kimba Arem, Robert Gass, John Adams, David Gibson, Louise Hay, Iasos, Paul Utz, Jill Purce, Daniel Statnekov, Alex Theory, Vickie Dodd, Eric Neurath, Ed Wilson, Patrick Bernhard, Lyz Cooper, Buddha Bomb, June Leslie Wieder, Raja and Moira StarDove, Tierro Malloy, Andy and Bette Pullman, Light Technology, Jay Nelson, Lesa Sneider, Gene S. Jones, Nestor Kornblum, Beverly Kempt, Pat Paulson, Meredith McCord, Rollin Rachel, Joe Dispenza, Kenji, Michael Noll, Sheila Attig, Hay House, Joseph Rael, Dan Furst, Joan Vann, Stephen Mehler, Deepak Chopra, Linda MacKenzie, Gay and Kathlyn Hendricks, Warren Klausner, Leonard Laskow, Peter LeVine, Donna Eden, David Feinstein, George Noory, Darren Weismann, Todd Ovokaitys, George L. Lindenfeld, Ranjie

Singh, Jill Schumacher, Jay Cruz, Fred Grover Jr., Dr. Bea, Phil Weber, Nelson Trujillo, Kathy Mason, Aaron Pyne, Wayne Perry, D. N. Shukla, James Rick, Harlan Sparer, Igor Smirnov, Bob Margolin, Ola Aloha, David Ison, Barry Goldstein, Shelley Snow, Jim Atwell, Kay Mora, Gary Malkin, Kayla Toher, Cannon Labrie, Sharon Reed, co-creators of World Sound Healing Day, Healing Sounds Intensive attendees, and all of those who have studied with me and carried on the tradition of sound healing on this planet.

Special thanks to Debbie and Eddie Shapiro for the impetus to write the first, original edition of this book and to Jon Graham and Inner Traditions • Bear & Company for recognizing the importance of *Healing Sounds*.

Prelude to the 30th Anniversary Edition

Welcome to the 30th anniversary edition of *Healing Sounds.* It is extraordinary that, so many years after the first publication of this book, I should have the honor and ability of being able to write a new beginning. I am calling this piece, for the sake of its relationship to music, "prelude" because, in music, that means "something that serves as an introduction." It is my intention to provide something short and sweet.

Healing Sounds has changed my life. So have harmonics. They have both been the foundation upon which all my other work has been based. As such, there is literally nothing I would change from the text of the very first edition. Everything in it continues to be true and correct and is relevant now more than ever.

Every book, every teaching, and, in fact, all the recordings that I have created and released have utilized the information, techniques, and materials in *Healing Sounds* as their core. This is now thirty years' worth of material that I am talking about, and has included activities and manifestations from all sorts of media—radio, television, internet, recordings, magazines, newspapers, books, and much more including lots of live and in-person appearances whether they were teachings, performances, or presentations—and they all utilized *Healing Sounds.*

There is information in this book that, gratefully, has now become a sort of mainstay in the field of sound healing, so much so that often people are not aware of *Healing Sounds* as the source when they repeat information or exercises from it. This is really a blessing because it means that *Healing Sounds* has been a foundation not just for me, but for the field of sound healing.

I always hoped that sound healing would be publicly accepted and recognized as more than a fringe area of activity. This has occurred in a greater fashion than I could have ever believed. Sound healing has grown and grown—it well may be considered the staple for much of new, modern thought and the human potential movement. Today, if the subject somehow involves the field of meditation, alternative healing, or any of a number of different topics, you'll often find some sort of reference to "everything is vibration," "we need to raise our frequency," or something like that. These are the basic tenets of sound healing, and they are here for you to encounter and explore.

Most of the above references did not originate with *Healing Sounds,* but they're most certainly found within these pages and were most likely popularized through this book. These and many other concepts are abundant in our world now. When I first wrote *Healing Sounds,* there might have been perhaps a few dozen books that had manifested—throughout the ages—with information about sound as a therapeutic and healing modality. Now there are hundreds, if not thousands. I give thanks for the current abundance of information.

I would suggest that within the pages of this book is so much more information that has yet to be incorporated into the consciousness and awareness of those working with sound for health and transformation. *Healing Sounds* contains a treasure trove of material—it is a cornerstone of sound healing, and it has within it many more jewels of information and techniques yet to be mined.

There is a smorgasbord of information in this book. A potpourri of techniques that can be utilized. A plethora of essential topics and teaching—from Pythagoras and sacred geometry to Tomatis and the power of the ear and listening, from Kabbalastic God Names chanting to chakra/vowel sound resonance, from the Tibetan "Deep Voice" tonality to neuro-resonance with harmonics. Perhaps one of the most important concepts that manifested uniquely in *Healing Sounds* is the creation of the formula "Frequency + Intention = Healing." It is more relevant now than ever.

Nothing in this book is stale. Nothing in it needs to be replaced. When I recently reread it, it simply reminded me of all the amazing things about sound, and of the experiences of my life in this field, that continue to be resonant. It's all still relevant. It's all still accurate. As I reread it, I was amazed at the extraordinary information in it. I trust that as you delve into these pages, it will be a great learning experience for you.

Knowledge and understanding of harmonics is incredibly useful, particularly for those interested in the use of sound as a healing modality. As attention to the therapeutic and transformational ability of sound continues to grow, it is now time for those with interest in this subject to begin to explore the fundamental and yet oh-so-intricate world of harmonics. The subject, like harmonics themselves, will continue to unfold into infinite new permutations and possibilities.

As you will discover within these pages, harmonics provide an underlying framework of not only sound, but the structure of the universe. Harmonics are part of a natural manifestation of sound that can provide insight that can be adapted throughout all octaves of vibration.

Every sound that we hear in nature is actually a composite sound, composed of a fundamental frequency and the subsequent harmonics that are simultaneously generated at the same time. These harmonics are mathematically related and may well be responsible for the signature vibration of each and every sound that we make and that we hear. Harmonics are also responsible for the timbre or tonal color of different sounds, including instruments and our voice. They literally color our sonic world.

Harmonics have been described in mystical literature as providing a stairway to heaven. Through awareness of them, we are able to alter our hearing and our consciousness and open up to higher realms of being. The universal principles displayed by harmonics are one of the foundational aspects that modern quantum physicists perceive are responsible for manifesting the creation of reality.

Harmonics can change your life as they've changed mine. If you think about it, we experience much of reality through our senses, of which there are said to be five main ones. The sense involved with making and perceiving sound—the sense that many of the ancient mystics as well as our modern physicists suggest may be the most sensitive and most important—can be shifted and changed through opening our awareness to sound.

Being able to understand and experience harmonics will shift your consciousness. You will be able to perceive in a new, different, and expanded way. As this occurs, your perception of reality will change, and you will be enhanced. It's almost like a superpower!

While there have been no changes to the content of the original text besides the addition of recent research to the end of chapter 7 and a much-enhanced bibliography for further exploration, there has also been one other important addition to the material in this book. In order to further enhance your ability to understand and perceive harmonics, actual sounds—audio files—are included in this new, 30th anniversary edition.

This inclusion of sounds was the only thing missing when *Healing Sounds* originally came out in 1992. Yes, you could seek out some of the recordings mentioned in it, but oftentimes that was difficult. Now, through the magic of the internet and the phenomenon of audio downloads, you can hear many of the different sounds described in the original text, and you can experience some of the important exercises described within.

As you'll find out, in order to become aware of specific harmonically related sounds (and to learn to vocalize and create them), it's really important to be able to hear them—and now you can. Being able to listen to some of the examples that are provided, will, I believe, enhance your interaction with the material in this book.

Shortly after *Healing Sounds* first came out, I created a recording that was available separately and featured two of the essential exercises from chapter 8 and chapter 9 of this book. It's now my great privilege to be able to include those recordings as part of these downloads. I've also included other recordings that will enhance your experience. I trust that these additions will only add to the life-changing abilities of *Healing Sounds* and harmonics. At the end of this book is an appendix that describes the different recordings and provides the links so that you may download and listen to them.

Once again, dear reader, I welcome you to these timely pages of sound healing information and materials. If this is new territory and you have never before encountered them, they have been waiting for you for three decades. They will provide a landscape of sonic riches that are precious beyond belief. And if by chance you have passed through these pages before, they await you with new vigor and vitality.

What a blessing it is for me to be able to present this 30th anniversary edition of *Healing Sounds* to what I trust will be a new audience and to old friends as well. Enjoy! *Healing Sounds* is not only a great introduction to the world of sound healing, it is so much more. Within these pages you will find a Merkaba—a spiritual vehicle that will take you into a world of vibration that can shift and change the very way that you perceive reality. How extraordinary!

You are about to go on a journey into the realms of sound that will mystify and illuminate you and more—much more! Here is your passport. Welcome aboard, and bon voyage.

JONATHAN GOLDMAN

BOULDER, COLORADO (2022)

Preface to the Third Edition (2002)

It's been over a decade since *Healing Sounds: The Power of Harmonics* was first published. Since that time the awareness of the uses of sound and music as healing modalities continues to expand. The psychic Edgar Cayce predicted that "sound would be the medicine of the future." We are indeed now in the future.

When it was first published, *Healing Sounds* was one of the first of a handful of books on the subject of sound healing. It continued to gain recognition and audiences throughout the planet, being published in numerous editions and foreign languages. Now, in this new millennium, it again emerges into the sound healing arena.

Not having done so in a very long time, I recently took the opportunity to reread *Healing Sounds.* Quite frankly, I was a bit surprised. Not only was the information and material in the book as relevant, fresh, and important as the day it was first published, but there were things in the book that I had forgotten. It was quite startling to be reintroduced to my creation in such a powerful manner. I give thanks.

Healing Sounds keeps resonating with readers desiring knowledge and exercises on the uses of sound and music for health and transformation. These readers have been neophytes who want a little taste, having heard that there actually might be something to the idea of sound healing, and world-renowned specialists in sound or healing, who received an idea or a concept that they could add to their already extensive sound work.

As I am composing this preface the phone rings. It is a writer who is coauthoring a book of inspirational stories on the healing power of music. Would I like to contribute? What an interesting synchronistic occurrence this phone call is—particularly because my next sentence was to be, "More and more people are writing books on the healing and transformational power of sound and music." What a blessing that the world is now reawakening to sound!

I truly believe that one of the key ingredients with regard to the longevity of *Healing Sounds* is that it incorporates both the scientific and spiritual aspects of sound; it ignores neither element and at times combines both, creating a unified field theory of sound healing with formulas such as Frequency + Intention = Healing or Vocalization + Visualization = Manifestation. These original formulas that I created have influenced and affected so many.

Contained within the pages of this book is not only material about the scientific and spiritual aspects of sound healing but also exercises that you can learn and apply to your daily life. Through this book the world of sound healing becomes more than merely a good idea. Sound as a healing and transformational tool becomes a reality, and an important one at that. The combination of both the scientific and the spiritual approaches to sound is mandatory for true discovery and exploration of the ability of sound to heal and transform. In order for us to truly resonate with the immense and important subject of sound healing, it is important that information about sound is coupled with personal experiences with sound. I do not believe I've ever encountered a scientist or doctor working to discover and validate the power of sound to heal and transform (as opposed to merely measuring some aspects of sound) who has not become somewhat of a mystic as he or she progressed on the journey through sound. And rarely have I encountered someone using sound as a spiritual discipline who has not absorbed some knowledge of the physics of sound as he or she continued along the path.

I am blessed to be able to report that literally thousands of people have had their lives changed by reading this book—and this continues to be true. I give thanks for this and am grateful that you have chosen to be one of those who has undergone a genesis through sound to become part of those who have received transformation. Sound really will change your life.

Enjoy this new edition of *Healing Sounds*.

JONATHAN GOLDMAN (2002)

PREFACE TO THE SECOND EDITION

(1996)

NEW HORIZONS

Welcome to the second edition of *Healing Sounds*. The original edition was published by Element in 1992 and has since become a landmark in the field of sound healing. It has been translated into German, Portuguese, Dutch, Spanish, and a number of other languages. The publishers have requested that I contribute a new introduction to this edition. It is with pleasure that I do so.

Since the first printing of this book, it has been my great honor to travel the world presenting *Healing Sounds* seminars. I continue in wonderment at the power of sound and its ability to transform people's lives. Sometimes this transformation occurs through physical healing. Sometimes it is through mental, emotional, or spiritual changes. Through these seminars, individuals are empowered by sound. They explore new horizons in human potential. They realize a new aspect of their being. They experience themselves as vibration, as being sound. Through this, they experience transformation.

Since the first publication of *Healing Sounds,* the field of sound and music for healing has greatly expanded. This is in part due to the pioneering efforts of many who are initiating others into the experience of sound. It is also due in part to the great changes in consciousness that we are now undergoing.

SHIFTING FREQUENCIES

We are living in extraordinary times; times of enormous shifts in awareness, times of great changes in culture and society, times of planetary evolution. Some would say that vibrational modulations are occurring. Others would say that it is Earth changes. And yet others would say that it is the end-of-the-millennium blues. I like to talk about frequency shifts and their relationship to people and the planet. For many different reasons, we are waking up, becoming aware. About ourselves. About human potential. About creating a better world. About changing reality. Sound plays a key role in these times, for sound is helping us adjust to the frequency shifts that are occurring on so many levels.

In the many different traditions and cultures of this planet, our connection to the source is through sound. "In the beginning was the Word." The sound! The harmonics. This understanding is both spiritual and scientific. Everything is in a state of vibration. Everything is frequency. Sound can change molecular structure. It can create form. We realize the potential of sonic energy; we understand that virtually anything can be accomplished through vibration. Then, the miraculous seems possible. Through practice and experience with sacred intent, we can learn to shift our own frequencies using harmonics. These sounds can resonate our body, our brain, and our etheric fields. We can change our vibrational rate through our own self-generating sounds. These sacred sounds, made with a specific intention, and with the energy of love, can interface with the different planes of consciousness, invoking and evoking different levels of awareness. This is particularly true when harmonics are made with conscious intention in a group.

One of the most powerful ways of consciously using vocal harmonics and overtoning is to create sacred sound together in a group. Sounding in a group can create a morphic field resonance through a unified consciousness. Fields created through group sounding have potentials far greater than we've dreamed. On our own, we can consciously interface and affect our own vibratory levels. In groups, sacred sound can influence not only ourselves and those around us but can adjust the planet to a new level of consciousness. It is the throwing of a tiny pebble into a still lake. The ripples and waves created by the pebble spread to reach to the farthest ends of the lake. This rediscovery of our own ability to shift frequencies through harmonics is a gift that we are given.

HARMONICS AND HEALING SOUNDS

Harmonics are there and yet not there, tangible and yet not tangible. They are present and yet not noticed, until the shift begins to occur. First our hearing changes—we can perceive things that are hidden. Next, our voices change—we can create sounds that were not previously there. Then our consciousness changes and other realities come into our awareness.

Healing Sounds focuses on the ability of harmonics to create vibrational changes. These changes may occur in the physical body, or in the mental, emotional, and etheric bodies. When these changes occur, they initiate transformation and healing. The purpose of the book is to link interdisciplinary, multicultural, sacred, and scientific approaches to sound through harmonics.

Harmonics display universal principles and are a constant in the various traditions and societies that use sound for healing and self-transformation. Through experiencing harmonics, we can learn a great deal about ourselves and the worlds around us. I trust you will find a resonance with them. I trust they will awaken something in you. They can be sacred, magical, and truly transformational. I trust that in time you will "read between the lines" and see the possibilities within possibilities in using sound. Some of the potentials are described in this book. I trust you will discover the other potentials yourself.

Harmonics have been and always will be a great inspiration to me. It is now apparent that many others also share this interest. Since the completion of this book, there continues to be a tremendous reawakening of interest in sound as a healing and transformative modality. In particular, a large portion of this interest has focused upon harmonics. Awareness and use of harmonics are truly expanding. This would not have occurred without the openness of the masters of vocal harmonics: the Tibetans, Mongolians, and Tuvans.

Members of the different Tibetan monasteries have toured throughout the United States and Europe, sharing their sacred chants and much of their knowledge of Tibetan overtone chanting. A number of different Mongolian and Tuvan overtone singing ensembles have also toured and given workshops in the extraordinary vocal techniques of *hoomi.*

NOUVEAU EUROPEAN VOCAL HARMONICS

It has become apparent that there is now a new form of vocal harmonics that I and other Western teachers of sound are imparting to audiences. It is different from the Tibetan "One Voice Chord" and the Mongolian and Tuvan hoomi style. It is primarily this new vocal harmonic style that is being taught and practiced in the United States and Europe. I call this new style Nouveau European Vocal Harmonics. Nouveau European Vocal Harmonics is based upon some of the techniques utilized in the Tibetan, Mongolian, and Tuvan traditions. However, this new style does not require years of practice nor does it present the possibility of straining the voice in order to create vocal harmonics. You will be learning about this in chapter 9, "The Fundamentals of Vocal Harmonics." Nouveau European Vocal Harmonics are easily learned and can produce powerful results. This style of creating vocal harmonics represents a new form of sounding that is accessible to those in the West. As the awareness of sound continues to expand, we now have a new way of sounding that incorporates this awareness. This could not have occurred if the Tibetans and Tuvans had not shared their techniques with us.

It is my pleasure to continue to meet amazing people who are working with vocal harmonics and to have wondrous encounters with them. Some have been musicians, others have been scientists, healers, and meditators. I have received teachings through my experiences with masters of vocal harmonics from the Tibetan and Tuvan traditions. I will share several recent adventures with you. I trust they are appropriate to the spirit of sacred sound and harmonics.

DREPUNG LOSELING MONKS

After the first edition of *Healing Sounds* was published, I was empowered by the chant master of the Drepung Loseling Monastery to teach Tibetan overtone chanting. This is what transpired:

On Sunday, December 15, 1991, monks from the Drepung Loseling Monastery gave a performance of sacred Tibetan music in Boulder, Colorado. These monks have developed a chanting style that is as deep and resonant as that of the Gyuto and Gyume monasteries. I had the privilege of spending the next day with these monks, sharing my work with sound with them. That night, the Drepung Loseling monks gave a special workshop in Boulder on their chanting techniques. This was a transformative experience, which I realized in retrospect I had been awaiting since I first heard the Tibetan "One Voice Chord" many years before.

In this workshop, the monks demonstrated their extraordinary chanting. Then they openly discussed the creation and use of their chanting techniques, which they called the "Deep Voice" or "Voice of Melodious Tones," said to be the embodiment of the fully developed speech of the Buddha. There were nine monks in this group. Of these nine monks, three were considered "chant masters," deeply skilled in the ability to create and project the "Deep Voice." These chant masters worked with the audience encouraging those in attendance to try to create their own "Deep Voice" sound.

The Empowerment

Among those present that night was Rinchen Chugyal, the chant master of the entire Drepung Loseling Monastery. Rinchen Chugyal spent time with me, helping to further refine and develop my Tibetan chanting techniques. Of the fifty in attendance, I was the only one who was able to create the "Deep Voice." After Rinchen Chugyal was satisfied that I had absorbed his refinements, he looked at me and said: "Teach!"

"Are you empowering me to teach the 'Deep Voice'?" I asked in amazement.

"Yes!" he said. "You teach!"

Since I had developed the "Deep Voice" on my own (with no

supervision on the physical plane), I had not felt it appropriate to attempt this before. Indeed, as I relate later in this book, my first experience attempting the voice was not entirely successful. I still believe that improper methods of learning the voice may be damaging. Until that time with Rinchen Chugyal, I had never consciously tried teaching anyone the Tibetan chanting techniques. However, with the empowerment from the Drepung Loseling chant master, I was encouraged to begin teaching the "Deep Voice."

Teaching the Tibetan Voice

I taught my first class in the "Deep Voice" two months later to a group of Buddhist men who had attended the Drepung Loseling monks' workshop. One third of the class was able to produce minimally the "Deep Voice" during my workshop. Others received the "Deep Voice" later.

Since then, I have become more proficient at understanding the physiological mechanism of the "Deep Voice." I have also realized the extraordinary power and sacred responsibility of the voice and reserve the actual teaching of the voice for higher levels of the *Healing Sounds* seminars. It is, however, not unusual for a student at my opening seminars to receive the "Deep Voice" simply by hearing me sound and by being around me. These students have been both men and women! It is quite an experience and a remarkable example of "harmonic transmission." I believe that the "Deep Voice" is a gift that I received through association with the Gyuto and Gyume monks and that has now been amplified through the Drepung Loseling monks. Almost two years later I had another profound experience with Tibetan overtone chanting and sacred sound that I would now like to share.

IN CONCERT

The extraordinary musician and composer Kitaro invited me to perform with him in an ensemble at a benefit concert for Tibet that was to take place in New York. One week prior to the concert I was informed that the Drepung Loseling monks would be performing with us! As there are now several groups of Tibetan monks who perform on tour, I found this occurrence rather synchronistic.

The night of October 9, 1993, was one of the most sacred sonic experiences I have ever had. The concert took place at the Church of St. John the Divine in New York City. Five thousand people attended this performance. The "Voices of Tuva" began the concert, performing folk songs from Tuva in the hoomi voice. Next, the Drepung Loseling monks sounded forth with their powerful chanting. Then Kitaro's ensemble came on stage.

Kitaro performed on synthesizer and taiko drums. There was also a guitar player, a tabla player, another keyboard player, and a didjeridoo player. I played Tibetan bowls, bells, bamboo flute, and percussion, and chanted in the "Deep Voice" as well as in the Nouveau European Vocal Harmonic style. Then, the Drepung Loseling monks performed a final sacred chant in which I took part.

It was a wonderful evening of old and new harmonic music, honoring the sacred sounds from many different traditions. I trust in some small way, through my part in the performance, I was able to return to the Tibetan monks some of the extraordinary gifts that they have dispensed throughout the planet.

ONE LAST NOTE

As the final note for this book, I would again thank the Masters of Sound Current. They continue to assist in my teaching and in this work. They have helped in the creation of this book and to assure that *Healing Sounds* has found its way into the right hands. I would also thank you for showing a mutual interest in sound with me. I trust that I will have the opportunity of creating and sharing vocal harmonics with you. May sacred sound flow through you for the harmony of all.

JONATHAN GOLDMAN (1996)

My First Introduction to Harmonics

PIR VILAYAT KHAN

It was November 6, 1981. I was in Washington, D.C., at a conference entitled "Healing in Our Times" sponsored by the Sufi Healing Order. Thousands of people filled the lecture hall watching well-known teachers and pioneers of the spiritual and scientific communities speak on topics related to alternative healing: Elizabeth Kübler Ross spoke on death and dying; Robert O. Becker on electromagnetism and healing; Dolores Krieger on therapeutic touch; Hiroshi Motoyama on the chakras; and Thelma Moss on Kirlian photography.

This was at the beginning of the holistic health movement, which has grown to monumental proportions in the 1990s. It was the first conference I had attended on a subject that had already begun to interest me. I had recently taken a workshop on healing with sound and music and, coming from a family focused on traditional allopathic medicine (my father, grandfather, and brother are all M.D.s), this new approach to wellness was very exciting.

I had not followed in my father's footsteps. I had been a musician playing the guitar in commercial rock 'n' roll bands. Until my introduction to holistic health, I had seen no possible connection between music and healing. That was why I was so pleased to be at this conference waiting for the next speaker: Pir Vilayat Khan, spiritual head of the Sufi Order of the West. His topic was "Healing with Light and Sound."

Pir Vilayat Khan spoke on using sound and light to stimulate the body and the auric fields. I was intrigued by the concepts of the chakras and their relationship to sound, and now specifically wanted to hear about this. I listened carefully to Pir Vilayat and I waited for the information I was seeking. It did not come, and throughout most of the lecture I sat excitedly in my seat, waving my hand wildly, trying to ask a question about the subject. Pir Vilayat took a number of questions from the audience, but not mine. At the end of his talk, I found myself in a crowd that surrounded him. Suddenly, I was facing this white-haired spiritual master. He looked at me and nodded.

"Pir Vilayat," I began. "Is there a relationship between tones and the chakras?"

He thought for a moment and then replied, "Yes. I believe there is. But I think the true healing power of sound is to be found in harmonics."

"Harmonics!" I said. "Yes! Harmonics! Thank you!" and I walked away triumphantly, feeling that my most important question had been answered at last!

THE HARMONIC CHOIR

The problem was that I had no idea what Pir Vilayat was talking about. As a musician, I knew that harmonics were part of a technique of tuning the guitar. You would dampen the string so that a muffled tone was produced when the string was struck and you then tuned another string to this muffled tone. But that was all I knew about harmonics.

Nevertheless, I was in a sort of daze from this encounter with a spiritual master who surely was an authority on healing with sound. Somehow, I ended up in a little bookstore outside the conference auditorium. This bookstore had been set up for the conference and sold books and tapes on subjects related to alternative healing. Almost as though I were being led by unseen forces, I found myself in front of a table that had a number of audiotapes. I looked down at a tape entitled

"The Harmonic Choir," thinking "Yes! This is what I want." I had not heard of this recording and had no idea what was on it. But it did contain that magical word "harmonic" and something inside of me said "Buy it!"

With tape in hand, I went into the lobby of the hotel where the conference was being held. Inside the briefcase I had been carrying was a cassette player with headphones. I took out the cassette player, put on the headphones, popped in this mysterious tape and began to listen. The first thing I heard was a powerful human voice singing one single note. Then this note began to expand with extraordinary bell-like sounds that seemed to come out of nowhere. It was ethereal and unearthly and it was gorgeous. I do not normally have transformative experiences in crowded hotel lobbies, but almost instantly I became entranced. The next thing I became aware of was the click of the cassette player as it shut itself off.

I had had powerful experiences while listening to music, but never before had I totally lost consciousness and been transported to some other realm as had happened with this tape. Then and there, I vowed that I would find out all I could about harmonics. I listened to that cassette almost continuously. The more I listened, the more I became entranced by it. It was the most heavenly sounding music I had ever heard, and I played it for practically everyone I met. Their responses were similar to mine, though perhaps not as obsessive.

The notes on the Harmonic Choir tape explained that the voices on the cassette really were human, unenhanced by any studio effects. The members of the choir had learned an ancient technique found in the sacred music of Mongolia. It enabled singers to sing two or more notes at the same time. This was called "harmonic singing."

For months in Boston, I tried imitating the sounds on the tape. Through trial and error I actually began to create some rudimentary harmonics. Then in 1983 I went to New York to hear the Harmonic Choir in concert and take a workshop on harmonic singing. From the workshop I was able to refine my harmonic singing techniques, and I became more proficient at creating two notes at the same time. After months of practice, I had my techniques down well enough so that I could begin to show others how to create some basic harmonics.

My reasons for doing this were simple. In my experience of using sound and music for healing I had encountered some excellent sounds and techniques, from the music of Steven Halpern to the toning exercises of Elizabeth Laurel Keyes. But nothing was as powerful or as profound as creating vocal harmonics. I would be relaxed and at the same time energized when I produced these double voices. I could feel the sound resonating in my head and body unlike anything else. I wanted to share this experience with others.

THE SONG OF THE SOUL

There was also an interesting phenomenon that I had begun to observe regarding harmonics and toning, which was the use of the voice as a healing instrument. My initial teacher in toning was a woman named Sarah Benson from the New England area. Sarah taught the transformative and healing uses of sound and in particular the voice. One exercise that was effective involved using the voice in order to scan the auric field of another person and then project sound into that person. I began working with this technique and, as I did, I would observe extraordinary results. There were emotional, mental, and even physical imbalances that were immediately released through the use of this technique.

My first real transformational experience with sound had occurred several months before the Washington conference during a workshop with Sarah Benson in an exercise called "The Song of the Soul." In it, a person is put in the middle of a circle of people who then chant and sing the person's name. I was conscious during this exercise and remember being transported from the circle to the inside of a purple pyramid made of crystal. I sat inside this pyramidal structure being bathed by green light. When the group stopped chanting my name, I gently returned to my body. It was one of the most extraordinary experiences of my life, and it had been due solely to the power of sound.

When my own personal studies and sound work developed to the point where I felt confident, I began teaching toning in workshops. I became aware that after a person had scanned another with their voice and was projecting sound into that person, I would hear harmonics. I could close my eyes and listen to the sounds that were coming from the person doing the toning and know when they had found the right location. Though none of my students knew about the creation of vocal harmonics, these harmonics would occur naturally when they were being used for healing.

I intuitively felt that there was something very special about this ancient singing technique, but there was virtually no available information on the subject. I found a paragraph in one book and a page in another, but there was no substantial writing on the relationship between vocal harmonics and healing. This was at the very beginning of the reemergence of harmonic singing in the West, in the early 1980s.

THE LAMBDOMA AND CYMATICS

I began to read books on the physics of sound to find out about harmonics as a phenomenon of vibration, hoping that science would provide some answers, and then I met Barbara Hero. Barbara had been working with a Pythagorean formula—called the Lambdoma—for healing with sound and created the Lambdoma frequencies of this formula with a synthesizer. I realized that the Lambdoma was based upon the harmonic series and could be applied to the voice.

In 1983, through my acquaintance with Barbara, I was introduced to Dr. Peter Guy Manners, a British osteopath who had invented a machine called the Cymatic Instrument, which utilized the direct application of sound into the body for healing and used harmonically related tones that resonated imbalanced parts of the body, restoring their natural frequency. I asked him if it was possible to do the same thing with the human voice and he replied affirmatively. This confirmed for me that my intuitive feelings about harmonics as a tool for healing were correct. I began to study and learn about cymatics and the principles of resonant frequency healing.

TIBETAN MONKS AND THE "ONE VOICE CHORD"

Next, I came in contact with the sacred music of Tibet. The Dalai Lama's chanting Gyuto monks sang a fundamental tone that was so deep and low it sounded like the growl of a wild animal. It was inhumanly low, impossibly deep, and there were other tones along with this that sounded like a schoolboy choir singing in falsetto. It was an unearthly sound.

I now wanted to be able to duplicate this sound, but it seemed impossible. From the little material available on the subject I learned that it took the monks ten to fifteen years to learn this "One Voice Chord." Nevertheless, I was determined to create this voice myself. In 1984 I had a teacher of sound who was a singer of Hindustani music. He was able to imitate nearly any vocal sound and was fairly adept at chanting the hoomi-style voice utilized by Mongolian shamans. He also seemed able to duplicate the sound of the Gyuto monks. He could do this for only fifteen seconds at a time and then he would have to stop because the sound strained his throat. I asked him if he could teach me this technique and he asked why anyone would want to learn it, since it created a terrible strain on the vocal cords.

At the time, I did not know that he was not creating the One Voice Chord correctly. It had sounded similar to the sound of the Gyuto monks to me but I later learned that it was different—the placement of the sound was wrong, and it did indeed damage your vocal chords. Unaware of this, I asked him to show me his technique for creating the growl tone, which he did. But when I tried to duplicate it I really strained my voice. I had a sore throat for nearly a month and gave up attempting to learn the One Voice Chord.

A year later, the Gyuto monks went on a tour of the United States. It was my privilege to spend some time with the monks while they were in Boston and to attend a number of performances and chanting sessions that they gave. I thought perhaps that I might learn how and why they created their incredible sound. However, the monks were understandably guarded about the technique and purpose of the One Voice

Chord. It was a profoundly sacred tool to them and nothing they would share with the uninitiated.

Some time later, the Dalai Lama's chanting Gyume monks of Tibet, who also sing in a similar voice, came to Boston. Gyuto and Gyume are both tantric colleges originally located in Tibet. The names describe the geographical location of the tantric colleges in Lhasa, the capital of Tibet. It was my honor to help bring the Gyume monks into a recording studio for the first time in order to record their sacred chants.

That night, after the recording session, I went home with a cassette copy of their chanting and fell asleep in my meditation room listening to these sounds. The next morning upon awakening I found a sound emerging from myself that I had never before produced. It was the One Voice Chord of the monks. Astounded, I walked into the studio where the monks had recorded and demonstrated the voice to David Collett, who had recorded the monks with me. He laughed and then opened his mouth. The same sound came out of him! Somehow, we had both been given this extraordinary vocal ability. The Gyume monks returned to Boston to do a performance that we were arranging, and when they walked into the recording studio, my partner and I smiled at them and sounded out with a One Voice Chord. The Rinpoche laughed and said something to the interpreter who said, "Rinpoche says 'Best in the West.'"

It was an extraordinary example of what I call "harmonic transmission" in which the sacred knowledge and techniques of masters are transferred simply by their presence. I had heard stories of similar experiences occurring when students would sit with gurus. I had never, however, heard about sonic abilities being transferred in this manner.

My experience with the Gyume monks only amplified my fascination with sound and harmonics. At times, during sacred soundings, I would utilize this powerful One Voice Chord. There were often people around who wanted to learn this voice, but it was nothing I could teach. I discovered later that one of the ways in which the younger Tibetan monks learned to do the One Voice Chord was to simply be around the older monks who had perfected it.

TRANSFORMING SOUND INTO LIGHT

The next year another experience occurred that radically altered my concept of what harmonics were doing. It was during the Harmonic Convergence, August 16 and 17, 1987, a time when many people believed a shift in planetary consciousness would occur and were working to open themselves to these transformational energies through meditation and chanting. I journeyed to Mexico, first to the Tule Tree where Mayan prophecies had foretold that Quetzalcoatl, the plumed serpent God, would spring forth to issue a new era of consciousness on the planet. Next I went to Palenque, where the Maya had built a city with structures reminiscent of ancient Egypt.

Late one night a guide took me and five traveling companions on a tour of Palenque. He said he would show us a Palenque that we would not otherwise experience and took us into one temple that had been closed to the public, leading us down into a subterranean level using his flashlight. He pointed to a doorway and said to me, "Make sound here." He had known about my interest in sound, but I could not figure out why he wanted me to do this.

Then, he turned out his flashlight, and we were immersed in total darkness. I had never been in a place so black. There was no light anywhere.

"Make sound," he urged.

"Sure," I said, shrugging my shoulders, a futile gesture since nobody could see a thing.

I began to tone harmonics toward the area he had indicated before the light went out. As I did so, the room began to become illuminated, but it was not like the light from a flashlight. It was more subtle, but it was definitely lighter in the room. You could see the outlines and figures of the people there. Everyone was aware of this, and after I stopped toning, the room was filled with exclamations. Then the guide turned on his flashlight again and we continued our tour.

The full implications of this experience did not occur to me until I arrived back in the United States. Somehow, I had been able to use sound to create light. This was not the same phenomenon as sound turning into light, a scientific hypothesis in which a sound wave, when speeded up, becomes light. This was different, having to do with creating fields of light through sound and, in particular, vocal harmonics.

ABOUT THIS BOOK

Healing Sounds is about the extraordinary potential of vocal harmonics to be a tool for health and self-transformation. We will look at the science and mathematics of harmonics and how all things are harmonically related; we will examine sound as the primary creative force in the universe in relation to harmonics. We will explore the esoteric uses of harmonics in shamanic and magical practices, from the hoomi singing of Mongolia to the Kabbalistic Tree of Life, learning more about the Tibetan practice of harmonics and its use in sacred rituals. We will work with harmonics as tools for meditation and transformation, exploring the sonic yoga of listening. In focusing upon harmonics and healing we will begin to realize the full potential of this force.

We will learn exercises and techniques for creating vocal harmonics. After all, if we do not experience harmonics for ourselves, this is all merely food for the brain. Without experiencing the wonderment of vocal harmonics, we cannot know about the powers of harmonics. Enabling us to know this power is what this book is all about.

Several years ago, it was my pleasure to do a presentation for a group of about 150 medical doctors and scientists in Germany. The group was the International Society for Music in Medicine, and the presentation was on harmonics. For the first hour of this presentation, I talked about what harmonics were and their use in esoteric traditions. Then, for the second hour, I gave them step-by-step instructions on how to create vocal harmonics. As I concluded, I said to them, "I have shared with you information and techniques on what I consider to be one of the most powerful tools for sound healing in existence. I am unable to do the research that you can. I don't have the equipment or the expertise. But now, instead of having to travel to Mongolia and to bring back a shaman who can do this form of sounding, you can do it yourselves. Perhaps you will take the next step in this work and begin the experimentation that may prove to have enormous impact. Thank you."

I had allowed time for questions and answers and awaited them. The first hand that went up was a doctor whom I had observed at other presentations. He was always finding fault with the presenters and their material. Nothing was ever good enough; there was always something wrong. I took a gulp and called on this man, positive that he was going to say, "How can you have wasted our valuable time with this nonsense?"

Instead, he said, "Mr. Goldman, how do you feel about sharing such a powerful and sacred tool with us?"

I smiled and replied, "I feel this is most important work, and I am honored to have shared it with you. It is now time for the spiritual and the scientific communities to work alongside each other so that together we can discover the extraordinary gift of sound to heal and transform."

That is why I share the information and exercises in this book, so that we may all discover this extraordinary gift of sound.

Sound has been the major transformative energy in my life. It has taught me about meditation and healing and many other important aspects that have contributed to my health and happiness. Harmonics have been my greatest teacher. I trust that harmonics will be as great a teacher to all of us.

ONE
Hermetic Harmonics

HERMETIC PHILOSOPHY

Myths in many cultures speak of the universe having been created by way of sound. The Egyptian God Thoth was thus believed to have accomplished the work of creation by the sound of his voice alone. The Greeks knew this master of occult wisdom as Hermes Trismegistus, "Thrice-Greatest Hermes," the scribe of the Gods. The sacred writings of the ancient Mystery Schools were attributed to him as mediator of Divinely revealed wisdom.

Healing Sounds is all about esoteric music. The relationship between occult wisdom and sound may at first seem far removed. Yet, in the ancient Mystery Schools of Egypt, Rome, Greece, Tibet, India, and other centers of learning, knowledge of sound was a highly refined science based upon an understanding of vibration as the primary causative form of the universe.

In the ancient Mystery Schools, the priests and magicians were often also the musicians. Many of the great scientists of ancient times (such as Pythagoras) were also versed in esoteric knowledge. Their wisdom stemmed from an understanding of the universe that is only now being quantified in arenas such as quantum physics, where the scientific and the spiritual can become one.

While there are many mystical and spiritual paths, the principles laid out by Hermes Trismegistus seem to be incorporated in all of these paths. There were seven principles upon which the entire Hermetic philosophy was based. Described in *The Kybalion: A Study of Hermetic Philosophy,* these are:

I. The Principle of Mentalism: "All is mind"
II. The Principle of Correspondence: "As above, so below"
III. The Principle of Vibration: "All is in vibration"
IV. The Principle of Polarity: "Everything is dual"
V. The Principle of Rhythm: "Everything flows"
VI. The Principle of Cause and Effect: "Everything happens according to Law"
VII. The Principle of Gender: "Everything has its Masculine and Feminine Principles"

Upon examination of these seven principles, it becomes immediately apparent that two of these principles involve sound: the Principle of Vibration and the Principle of Rhythm. A third principle, the Principle of Correspondence, will also be seen to apply to sound.

In order to understand the meaning of these principles, it is first necessary for us to understand more about sound. In the next chapter, we will examine more specifically some scientific aspects of sound and, in particular, harmonics. For the moment, let us look at some of the basic principles of sound as an energy and how sound may be used as a tool for health and transformation.

RESONANCE

As the ancients seemed to know, everything in the universe is in a state of vibration. The chair you may be sitting on is in a state of vibration, as are the pages of this book. Sound may be understood as being vibration. "Resonance" is the frequency at which an object most naturally vibrates. Everything has resonant frequency, whether or not we can audibly perceive it. From the orbits of the planets around the sun to movement of the electrons around atoms, everything is vibrating.

It is also important to understand that, in alignment with this concept of sound, every organ, bone, and tissue in your body has its own separate resonant frequency. Together they make up a composite frequency, a harmonic that is your own personal vibratory rate. Through resonance, it is possible for the vibrations of one vibrating body to reach out and set another body into motion. This can easily be observed, for example, when a singer breaks a glass with his or her voice. What happens is that the singer is able to match the resonant frequency of the glass and set that glass into vibration. Then, when too much sound energy is used and the glass is overamplified, it breaks.

There are numerous examples of resonance with which we may be familiar. You may have seen footage of a bridge that has been vibrated by a heavy wind: the bridge begins to sway and then starts to vibrate and soon it breaks apart and falls into the water. This phenomenon is well-known to architects who now create structures that are not easily resonated by external vibrations such as wind.

This concept of resonance may explain how Joshua was able to bring down the walls of Jericho as relayed in the Old Testament. Joshua and his men began marching around the walls of Jericho beating drums and blowing trumpets. They marched around the wall seven times. Then they stopped and suddenly "The people gave a great shout!" and the walls came tumbling down. Is it possible that Joshua had knowledge of using resonance to collapse the walls of the city?

These images of the glass shattering, the bridge collapsing, and the walls crumbling are all examples of the destructive use of resonance. Yet, as sound can be used to destroy, it can also be used to heal and transform. Just as it is possible to set an object into its own natural motion through resonance, so it is possible to restore the natural vibratory frequencies of an object that may be out of tune or harmony. When an organ or another portion of the body is vibrating out of tune, we call this "disease."

Let us conceive of the human body as a wonderful orchestra that is playing this marvelous symphony. When we are in a state of health, the entire orchestra is playing together. However, when disease sets in it is as though a player—the second violin, for example—

has lost their sheet music and begins to play in the wrong key and the wrong rhythm. First it begins to affect the rest of the string section. Ultimately this person causes the entire orchestra to sound poorly.

Traditional allopathic medicine currently has several approaches to the problem we have just described. One solution is to drug the violinist, sometimes to death, in hopes of getting this person to stop playing. Another more frequently utilized solution is to cut out the offending organ, as occurs in surgery. But what if it were possible to give this suffering musician back their sheet music and let the whole orchestra return to normal? Analogously, what if it were possible somehow to project the proper resonant frequency back into the organ that was vibrating out of tune and harmony?

When an organ or another part of the body is in a state of health, it will be creating a natural resonant frequency that is harmonious with the rest of the body. However, when disease sets in, a different sound pattern is established in that part of the body that is not vibrating in harmony. Therefore, it is possible, through use of externally created sound that is projected into the diseased area, to reintroduce the correct harmonic pattern into that part of the body that is afflicted and effect a curative reaction. Through the principle of resonance, sound can be used to change disharmonious frequencies of the body back to their normal, healthful vibrations.

ENTRAINMENT

The different rhythms of the body may also be changed through sound. This is known as "entrainment" and involves the ability of the more powerful rhythmic vibrations of one object to change the less powerful rhythmic vibrations of another object and cause it to synchronize its rhythms with the first object. Through sound it is possible to change the rhythms of our brainwaves, as well as our heartbeat and respiration.

Different brainwave rates have been equated to different states of consciousness. There are four basic categories of brain waves, based upon cycles per second (hertz or Hz), the measurements given to sound. They are:

1. Beta waves—from 14 to 20 Hz, which are found in our normal waking state of consciousness
2. Alpha waves—from 8 to 13 Hz, which occur when we daydream or meditate
3. Theta waves—from 4 to 7 Hz, which occur in states of deep meditation and sleep, as well as in shamanic activity
4. Delta waves—from 0.5 to 3 Hz, which occur in deep sleep and have been found in very profound states of meditation and healing

The use of music in sacred ceremonies and shamanic rituals has occurred since ancient times. It has recently been verified that sound can be used to affect and change our brainwaves. The changing of these rates creates changes in consciousness, allowing mystically altered states to be induced.

These principles of using resonance and entrainment are the fundamental concepts behind the use of sound to heal and transform. They are found in every practice that uses sound, regardless of the tradition, belief system, or culture. Many times those utilizing sound for spiritual or magical purposes may not be aware of them. But examination of these practices, from the Hindu use of mantras to shamanic use of chanting and drumming, reveals a commonality in these principles of resonance and entrainment as the basis of sonic transformation and healing.

CORRESPONDENCE

In 1988 the following headline appeared in a newspaper: "Sound Shaped in Dazzling Tool with Many Uses." The subheading read: "Ultrasonic beam can make, break, or rearrange molecules and levitate objects in midair." A source of energy that can rearrange molecular structure and levitate objects? This surely sounds like something from *UFO Digest,* but it is actually from the Science section of the *New York Times* in February 1988. While the article focuses upon the use of ultrasonic beams that are many thousands of hertz higher than any frequencies that we can actually hear, the extraordinary power demonstrated can just as easily be applied to those frequencies within our normal realm of hearing.

Everything in the universe vibrates and is in a state of flow. The Hermetic Principles of Vibration and Rhythm are correct. But what about the Principle of Correspondence? The Principle of Correspondence may also apply to sound, particularly with harmonics. When, for example, a string is plucked, there is that single note that sounds, called the "fundamental." There are other notes that also sound, called "harmonics" or "overtones." These harmonics are mathematical ratios of that first note. The first harmonic that occurs vibrates twice as fast as that first note, the second harmonic vibrates three times as fast, the fourth harmonic vibrates four times as fast and so on.

If we examine a piano we find there are eight octaves. The note C, for example, occurs eight times. The lowest note C on the piano is very deep, while the uppermost note C is very high. These notes are not the same and yet they are interrelated. If you were to strike that lowest C on the piano, you would also set into resonance all the other Cs on the piano. They are harmonics of each other.

It is possible with sound to set into resonance and entrainment frequencies that may be much lower or higher than the frequency that we are sounding because of these principles. If we use our imagination, we can understand that conceptually the vibrations of the Earth may reach all the way to the heavens and vice versa: "as above, so below." As an example, if we take a planet's rotation period and reduce it to seconds of time, then divide one by this number for the inverse proportion, the frequency corresponding to the resulting number is well below a sound that we can hear. However, when doubled many times, it becomes an audible frequency. For example, the Earth has a rotational period of 23 hours, 56 minutes, and 4 seconds, totaling 86,164 seconds. By taking the reciprocal value of this by dividing one by this number, a frequency of 0.000011605775 Hz is obtained. If this number is raised by 24 octaves (doubled 24 times), the result is a frequency of 194.71 Hz, which we perceive as the tone of a note found within the range of an audible G.

If we listen to the audible frequency of this planet, it may be possible for us to resonate and entrain with it despite the fact that the actual vibratory resonance created may be thousands of times faster or slower than the frequencies to which we are listening. This same principle applies to the frequencies of the human body, which may be far removed from those sounds that we can hear but that can be affected by audible vibrations. Through the Principle of Correspondence, we may use harmonically related sounds to influence the vibrations of atoms or the stars.

SOUND AND HEALING

The use of sound as a healing modality is nothing new. It is probably as old as the first sound ever made by a man or a woman. The first humans are believed to have used sounds in sacred and ritualistic ways to promote fertility, to aid at birth, to facilitate the growing of crops, to accept death, and for many other occasions. Using sound, they would summon spirits and ancestors to cure sickness and rid a body of disease.

As humankind developed in its understanding and knowledge of sound, the masters of the ancient Mystery Schools realized the true power of sound to bring healing and transformation. While little of the exact knowledge of these ancient Mystery Schools remains, it is, however, quite probable that the major instrument used in those times was the human voice.

For all the instruments available on this planet, the most powerful is the human voice. This is especially true when the voice is used for healing. Electronic instruments can make louder sounds with more amplitude and decibel levels than the human voice; these machines can also create tones that are well above or below the ability of any human. This does not mean, however, that great loudness or frequency range are any more effective than the volume and frequencies of the human voice. Bigger is not necessarily better. Louder does not necessarily mean more healing.

SOUND AS A "CARRIER WAVE OF CONSCIOUSNESS"

When I first began working with sound and music for healing, I understood that everything was based upon frequency. As the Hermetic Principles tell us, the universe is nothing, more or less, than an endless number of vibrations and rhythms. Yet, as I began to pursue and study this work more, I began to notice another interesting phenomenon. Sometimes different people apparently used different frequencies or different sounds to heal the same problem. "How could this be?" I wondered, unless there was something else besides the frequency. There must have been something equally important in sound that I had been ignoring.

It was my friend and fellow colleague Steven Halpern, Ph.D., who first brought my attention to the missing area in question. "Sound is a carrier wave of consciousness," Steven said. This means that depending upon where an individual's awareness is placed when he creates a certain sound, the sound will carry information on that state to the person receiving it. If, for example, you are angry and you create a sound, even though it may be a pleasant sound, you will be sending anger that is incorporated into that sound. This will be perceived on some subtle level by those receiving the sound.

I like to think of this as the intent or purpose behind the sound. With this word *intent,* we are really talking about the consciousness of the sound being created. This encompasses the overall state of the person making the sound and involves the physical, mental, emotional, and spiritual aspects of that person. The initial understanding of intention involves our conscious mind. Is the conscious intent of the sound to heal or to hurt, or is there no specific intent or purpose there at all?

A more advanced understanding of intent involves what may be understood as alignment with the purpose of our higher selves, or the "Divine Will." It is that aspect of consciousness that is able to align with the sacred energy of sound. It is "thy will," not "my will." When we have reached this level, our intent is to become a vehicle for sacred sound, and we are able to bypass the lesser aspects of self that may be out of balance. For many people, the initial understanding of intent is a major stepping-stone in using sound as a transformative and therapeutic tool, for most of us have never created sound with conscious awareness and purpose. Once I began to bring the concept of intent into the area of healing with sound, answers appeared for me. The concept of intent relates to the Hermetic principle that all is mind, for intent stems from the mind of the creator of sound. All is vibration and rhythm, but what is the intent behind the energy?

John Diamond, M.D., worked for years with behavioral kinesiology, a method of muscle testing. With kinesiology you would test a person to determine if his muscle was strengthened or weakened by an external force or stimulus. For example, when someone held a cigarette and you pressed his arm down, his arm would be much weaker than before he held the cigarette. Cigarettes, among many other things, tend to rob us of our life energy.

Dr. Diamond spent many years demonstrating that not only would certain substances make us strong or weak, but that music could do the same thing. The main aspect of what made the music positive and strengthening or negative and weakening depended upon the intention of the person creating the music.

An example of this was demonstrated when I listened to a classical piece performed by an orchestra with a well-known conductor. While I listened to this piece of music, I had my muscle tested for strength or weakness. I was also asked just to observe my respiration and my heartbeat: both of these were slow; I was breathing deeply and regularly.

Then I listened to the same piece of classical music performed by the same orchestra with a different conductor. The music went on and before I was muscle tested, I was again asked to observe my heartbeat and respiration. Much to my amazement, I found that I was breathing shallowly and that my pulse was faster. When I was muscle tested, I tested weakly. What was different? It was the same piece of music with the same orchestra! How could such a dramatic change have taken place within me? The answer lay with the conductor.

The first conductor was a man who was loved and revered by the classical community. He really seemed to be in touch with the flow of music that was being created and acted as a conduit for the music. His music made me strong. The second conductor was a very strict and regimented man who created fear in those with whom he worked. His music always had to be perfect. His reputation and his ego were committed every time he picked up the baton. His music made me weak. Here was a perfect example of intention creating the difference in the effect of the music. The sound had been the same, and yet the influence it had had upon me was very different.

THE HUMAN VOICE

The major focus in this book is the human voice. There are two reasons for this. First, the human voice is the most accessible of instruments. We do not have to go out and buy a piece of scientific machinery or a musical instrument in order to experience harmonics. Second, the easiest instrument through which intention can be focused and channeled is the human voice. It is a bit more difficult to pick up an instrument and project your intent. It is more difficult to turn on a machine and project your intention, especially if the machine is designed for healing and all you have to do is turn it on and leave the room.

Because of this understanding of the importance of intention within the use of sound as a modality for healing and transformation, I have created a formula that is important for us to comprehend. It is this:

Frequency + Intention = Healing

It means that the intention of the person working with the sound is as important as the frequency that is being projected at a person to create resonant frequency healing. Since the concept of intention is, at present, a scientifically immeasurable quality, it is extremely difficult for many in the medical community to understand it. Nevertheless, I am convinced that this formula is correct and that without the aspect of intention, working with pure frequency alone is not the answer.

This is another reason why I have been working more closely with the human voice. When we have learned techniques for harmonic toning, the human voice is able to create nearly every frequency, at least within the bandwidth of audible hearing. Due to the Principle of Correspondence, these sounds can potentially relate to any vibrating object. We therefore have the resonance and entrainment aspects of sound within our own capacity.

Try this for yourself. Take a little phrase such as "I really like you" and project different qualities onto this. For example, say "I really like you" and imagine saying this to a loved one such as a parent, a child, a brother, or a good friend whom you haven't seen in a long time. Close your eyes and see this person and say "I really like you." Now imagine that you are with a person whom you find sexually attractive. It may be a husband, wife, boy- or girlfriend. Whoever it is, imagine your attraction to this person and then say "I really like you" and perceive the difference in the way you felt it from the first time you said it.

Now imagine that you are with a person who is a dreaded enemy. This is someone you really don't like and really can't stand to be with. Now close your eyes, feel the disharmony in the situation, and say "I really like you" to this imagined person. It may sound very different or it may sound very similar. But the energy behind this "I really like you" is certainly different from the other two. Even if you use the exact tone of voice with all three "I really like yous," do you think the different people receiving these sounds would be able to perceive the differences in intention in them? They are the same words (the same frequency), but with different intentions they will affect us very, very differently.

We can learn to use our voices for positive means or we can create the opposite effect. The human voice seems to be the most potent creator of sound frequencies that can be coupled with intention.

An additional formula that uses the same principles of frequency and intention is:

Visualization + Vocalization = Manifestation

This formula developed through an examination of the creation myths from many different traditions. In many of these myths, the Creator God would manifest the world and all its objects through sound. This

God would visualize or first think of the object to create, placing intention upon this. Then the God would vocalize the sound for the object, creating its frequency and bringing it into being.

In Genesis, 1:3, for example, we have: "And God said, Let there be light: and there was light." The creator, God, speaks the name "light" and through this creates light. Similarly, the ancient Egyptians believed that the God Thoth would speak the name of an object and bring it into being. Other examples of this creation through sound are:

> "In the beginning was the Word." (John, 1:1)
> "In the beginning was Brahman with whom was the Word." (Vedas)

The Hopi legends tell of the Spider Woman who sang the song of creation over the inanimate forms on the Earth and brought them to life. And from *Popul Vuh* in the Mayan tradition, the first real men are given life by the sole power of the voice.

Through the principles related in this chapter, we can understand how the voice may be used to heal and transform. We can embody the mystical and sacred power of sound and rediscover our own innate ability to use our voices as extraordinary instruments of health and well-being. As we do this, we will discover one of the most sacred and mystical aspects of sound, the magic and mystery of harmonics.

TWO
The Science of Harmonics

WHAT IS SOUND?

The universe is alive with sound, and within all sounds are harmonics. Harmonics, also known as "overtones," are a phenomenon that occurs whenever sound is created. Normally we perceive what seem like single tones when we hear a note struck on a musical instrument like a violin or a piano. However, nearly all tones that are produced by musical instruments, our voices, or other sound sources are in reality not pure tones, but mixtures of pure tone frequencies called "partials." The lowest such frequency is called the fundamental. All partials higher in frequency than the fundamental are referred to as overtones.

Before we begin our exploration of harmonics as a phenomenon of sound, let us first examine sound. Sound is a vibrational energy that takes the form of waves. These waves are scientifically measured in units called hertz (Hz), which measure the cycles per second that this energy creates. This rate is objectively known as the "frequency." It is subjectively experienced as "pitch."

Frequency

A string that vibrates back and forth one hundred times per second will create a sound that can be measured at 100 Hz. This would be its frequency. One that vibrates one thousand times per second would be measured at 1,000 Hz.

We hear within a range limited to vibrations between 16 and 25,000 Hz. This may vary dramatically, depending upon the individual and their age. While the upper limit for young people with perfect hearing may sometimes reach 25,000 Hz, there is a large percentage of the population who cannot hear tones above 10,000 Hz. Sounds above 25,000 Hz are called ultrasonic. Sounds below 16 Hz are called ELFS (extremely low frequencies). The slower a sound vibrates, the lower we perceive it. The faster it vibrates, the higher we perceive it. On a piano, the lowest note vibrates at a frequency of 27.5 Hz. The highest note on a piano vibrates at 4,186 Hz.

Different frequencies that have specific measurements create the different notes that make up the musical scale we use today. If we examine the notes on a piano, we find they have been divided into seven white keys and five black keys. The seven white keys represent the notes of what is called the "diatonic" scale. This is the major scale in Western music. Starting from C, the notes are C, D, E, F, G, A, and B, ending with another C. The black keys represent the sharped (or flatted) notes that represent the steps between the white keys on the piano. They are C# (or D♭), D# (or E♭), F# (or G♭), G# (or A♭) and A# (or B♭).

If a note on a piano vibrates at 261 times (cycles) a second, we say its frequency is 261 Hz. This 261 Hz frequency creates a note whose pitch is called C. In the key of C, we refer to this as *do* in the solfege system of notation (*do, re, mi, fa, sol, la, ti, do*). On a piano, a note that vibrates at 293 Hz is a D; one that vibrates at 330 Hz is called E; at 349 Hz it is an F; at 392 Hz it is a G; at 440 Hz it is an A, at 494 Hz a B and at 523 Hz it is called a C once again.

Tuning

In the different systems of tuning musical instruments, different frequencies for particular notes occur. The note C, for example, may vary from 251 Hz to 264 Hz, and the other notes of the scale may also vary a great deal. This depends upon where you are tuning an instrument (concert pitch differs in Europe and the United States, for example), the instrument you are tuning (a piano tunes differently than a violin), and the system of tuning you are using.

The subject of tunings is quite complex. Differences in tunings have to do with mathematics. If we call a note vibrating at 256 Hz the note C and a note vibrating twice as fast at 512 Hz an octave above that C, there are many different ways to divide up the other notes between those two Cs. Some tunings are based upon the harmonic series and have to do with harmonic ratios. Other tunings are based upon equal division between the notes. It is an intriguing and complicated subject.

Overtones

With our example of a string that is struck and vibrates at 256 Hz and that we refer to as a C, when we listen to that string we usually hear, first and foremost, the C note. This is referred to as the "fundamental" tone. However, when that string is vibrating at 256 times a second and that C is sounding, many other notes besides the fundamental tone are also sounding. These are the overtones.

While in many cases we cannot individually distinguish the different overtones that are sounded, these overtones contribute to the overall sound color or timbre of an instrument. Different instruments will all sound overtones, but each instrument will have specific overtones that are most prominent. These prominent overtones are called "formants." They are the area of the sound spectrum where the sound energy is most highly concentrated.

Overtones are responsible for shaping the individual sounds that we hear, and for giving instruments their uniqueness. In an electronic laboratory, the harmonics were removed from three instruments using special filters. Upon listening to these instruments without their harmonics, it became impossible to tell them apart. Yet under normal circumstances, it is not difficult to distinguish between a violin, a trumpet, and a piano. Overtones are also present in our voices, and, in fact, they are responsible for our own unique speaking and singing qualities. Each voice is different and has its own specific formants that sound when we speak.

Overtones are mathematically related to each other. Remember the example of the string that vibrated at 256 and created the note C? As that string vibrates 256 times, other sound waves are also being created that are vibrating as geometric multiples of 256 Hz. The first of these overtones to sound is vibrating twice as fast as that fundamental, at a ratio of two to one (2:1), at 512 cycles a second. This creates a note that is referred to as the interval of an octave of the fundamental and is also called a C.

THE FIRST SIXTEEN HARMONICS

Table 2.1 shows the first sixteen harmonics created using C vibrating at 256 Hz as the fundamental. It also shows the solfege name of the overtone being created, its frequency, and the interval created.

The first column represents the note name given to the harmonic. The second column shows the interval within the octave created by the harmonic. The third column is the solfege name given for the harmonic (the parenthesis represents the number of times it appears). The fourth column represents the partial names for the harmonic. The fifth column shows the frequency of the harmonic.

Table 2.1. The First 16 Harmonics Created Using C Vibrating at 256 Hz as the Fundamental

Note	Interval	Solfege	Harmonic	Frequency
1. C	Unison	*do* (1)	1st partial	256 Hz
2. C	Octave	*do* (2)	2nd partial	512 Hz
3. G	Perfect fifth	*sol* (1)	3rd partial	768 Hz
4. C	Octave	*do* (3)	4th partial	1,024 Hz
5. E	Major third	*mi* (1)	5th partial	1,280 Hz
6. G	Perfect fifth	*sol* (2)	6th partial	1,536 Hz
7. B♭-	Minor seventh	ti ♭ (1)	7th partial	1,792 Hz
8. C	Octave	do (4)	8th partial	2,048 Hz
9. D	Major second	re (1)	9th partial	2,304 Hz
10. E	Major third	mi (2)	10th partial	2,560 Hz
11. F♯-	Augmented fourth	fa ♯ (1)	11th partial	2,816 Hz
12. G	Perfect fifth	sol (3)	12th partial	3,072 Hz
13. A-	Minor sixth	la ♭ (1)	13th partial	3,328 Hz
14. B♭-	Minor seventh	ti ♮ (2)	14th partial	3,584 Hz
15. B	Major seventh	ti (1)	15th partial	3,840 Hz
16. C	Octave	do (5)	16th partial	4,096 Hz

An interval is the difference in pitch between two tones. An example of this is the hitting of any two keys on a piano. The difference between these two keys is called an interval. The second overtone that sounds is vibrating three times as fast as the fundamental, at a ratio of three to one (3:1), at 768 cycles a second. This creates a note that is referred to as the interval of an octave and a fifth above the fundamental. The name we give to this note is G.

The third overtone that sounds is vibrating four times as fast as that fundamental, at a ratio of four to one (4:1), at 1,024 cycles a second. This note also creates an interval that is an octave of that first note. It is two octaves above the fundamental and creates another note C.

The fourth overtone to sound is vibrating five times as fast as that fundamental, at a ratio of five to one (5:1), at 1,280 cycles per second. This note creates an interval that is two octaves and a third above the fundamental. This note is an E. The fifth overtone vibrates six times as fast as that fundamental, at a ratio of six to one (6:1), and yields another G, an octave above the second overtone.

The sixth overtone is vibrating at seven times the speed of the fundamental, at a ratio of seven to one (7:1), and creates a note not normally to be found on a keyboard instrument. This is a note that is somewhat lower than a B♭ (often notated as a B♭-).

The seventh overtone, vibrating eight times as fast as the fundamental, at a ratio of eight to one (8:1), will create another C that is three octaves above the first.

The eighth overtone vibrates nine times as fast as the fundamental, at a ratio of nine to one (9:1). It will create a D.

The ninth overtone, vibrating at ten times the speed of the fundamental at a ratio of ten to one (10:1), will yield an E, an octave above the fourth overtone, which also created an E.

The tenth overtone, vibrating eleven times faster than the fundamental at a ratio of eleven to one (11:1), will create another note not normally found on the keyboard. This is a note somewhat flatter than an F# (notated as F#-).

The eleventh overtone, vibrating twelve times as fast as the fundamental at a ratio of twelve to one (12:1), creates another note G, an octave above the fifth overtone.

The twelfth overtone, vibrating thirteen times as fast as the fundamental at a ratio of thirteen to one (13:1), creates another note not found on the keyboard, a note somewhat lower than an A (notated as A-).

The thirteenth overtone vibrates fourteen times as fast as the fundamental, at a ratio of fourteen to one (14:1), and yields another B♭-, an octave above the last.

The fourteenth overtone, vibrating at fifteen times the speed of the fundamental at a ratio of fifteen to one (15:1), yields a note that is called a B natural (B♮).

The fifteenth overtone, which is vibrating sixteen times as fast as the fundamental at a ratio of sixteen to one (16:1), creates yet another C that is four octaves above that first C that sounded.

These are the overtones of the first four octaves that are created from that first C, which we called the fundamental and which was actually struck on the instrument. This is not, however, the completion of the overtones to be created. In theory the overtone series goes on infinitely, with each overtone being a geometric multiple of the fundamental, going faster and faster, higher and higher.

SCIENCE AND MUSIC

What is most important to realize about harmonics or overtones is that they are mathematically interrelated. For example, the proportions of the second and third overtones create a ratio of three to two (3:2). This is an interval called the fifth. This relationship may have profound effects upon the harmonious and healing aspects of sound.

These are the notes created by the harmonics of striking C. The same harmonic ratios arise regardless of the fundamental tone that is struck, though different pitches are created depending upon the fundamental. If we were to take these notes sounded by that fundamental C and put them together to create a scale from them, we would have a scale composed of C, D, E, F-, G, A-, B♭-, and C. In India, where the art of music has been developed to the point of being a science, there are thousands of scales, called ragas, which are designed to have particular effects on the emotions. The scale that arises from the harmonic series of the first four octaves is known as "raga Saraswati." It is named after Saraswati, the Indian goddess of both music and science.

In different cultures, science and music have not been separated as in the West. The ancient Mystery Schools of Greece, India, Tibet, and Egypt had a vast understanding of the relationship between music and healing, based upon vibration as the basic creative force in the universe.

Pythagoras and the Monochord

In ancient Greece, Apollo was god of both music and medicine. There were healing temples that focused upon music as the main force for harmonizing the body and spirit, thus effecting cures. One of the foremost Greek thinkers whose teachings continue to influence us today was the sixth-century BCE philosopher Pythagoras, who is best known to our civilization as the father of geometry. He is also responsible for being the first person in the West who correlated the relationship between musical intervals.

The key to this discovery was a simple instrument called the monochord that was composed of a single string stretched over a piece of wood. Using the monochord, Pythagoras was able to discover that the man-made division of this string created ratios. By examining the intervals created by this division, Pythagoras found that whole-number ratios could be observed. These whole-number ratios, such as 2:1, 3:2, 4:3, were archetypes of form, demonstrating harmony and balance that could be observed throughout the world.

If, for example, a string is divided into two even portions, the note that is created is an octave of the open string. The two even portions vibrate at a ratio of two to one (2:1). Then when the string is divided into three equal portions, the string vibrates at a ratio of three to one (3:1). When the string is divided into four equal portions, this creates a ratio of four to one (4:1). Looking back at the ratios created from the harmonic series, it is noted that the man-made division of strings exactly follows these ratios of the harmonic series.

It is quite possible that our understanding of ratios and the system of mathematics that grew from this was based upon Pythagoras's observation of music. "Study the monochord," he is credited with saying, "and you will know the secrets of the Universe." In the study of one vibrating string, one could understand the microcosmic aspects of sonic vibration and, through this, the macrocosmic laws of the cosmos could be observed.

Pythagoras believed that the universe was an immense monochord, an instrument with a single string that stretched between the heavens and the Earth. The upper end of the string was attached to absolute spirit, while the lower end was connected to absolute matter. Through study of music as an exact science, one could become familiar with all aspects of nature. He applied his law of harmonic intervals to all the phenomena of nature, demonstrating the harmonic relationship within the elements, the planets, and the constellations. Pythagoras spoke of "the Music of the Spheres." He taught that the movements of the heavenly bodies traveling through the universe created sounds. These sounds could be perceived by those who had been consciously trained to hear them. The Music of the Spheres could then be sounded in the intervals of plucked strings.

To Pythagoras and his students, the Music of the Spheres was more than a metaphor. The Greek master was said to have actually been able to hear the sounds of the planets as they vibrated in the heavens. The relationship between this movement of the heavenly bodies and sound has been hypothesized by scientists for centuries. Recently, scientists using advanced mathematical principles based upon the orbital velocities of the planets have equated different sounds with different planets. Amazingly, they seem to be harmonically related. Perhaps this ancient master had hearing that could perceive these astronomical movements as sound.

In the musical example of harmonics, the creation of harmonics was explained through observing the ratios of a plucked string. However, harmonics are a manifestation of all forms of vibration. And although hearing is limited to objects vibrating between 16 Hz and 25,000 Hz—vibrations within this range are perceived as audible sound—the mere fact that we cannot hear above or below this range does not mean that there are not multiple unperceived waves of sound vibrating everywhere. Anything that vibrates creates harmonics. Since the universe is composed of nothing but vibrations, everything creates fundamental tones and harmonics, ranging from electrons orbiting around atoms to the planets orbiting around the sun.

Pythagoras had a school in the city of Crotona where he taught his understandings of the mysteries of the universe. This Mystery School operated at three levels of initiation. The first level, the *acoustici,* learned to recognize and then apply the various musical proportions demonstrated to them through the use of the monochord. The second level, the *mathematici,* dealt more specifically with knowledge of numbers, as well as individual purification and mental self-control. Before going on to the next level, it was necessary that the disciple be as clear in mind and body as possible for the responsibilities of the sacred information then received. The third and highest level of initiation, the *electi,* were taught the secret processes of psychic transmutation and of healing with sound and music.

Little of the knowledge Pythagoras taught at the highest level of initiation in his school has survived. His teachings of geometric theorems and musical proportions are part of our everyday understanding of the numerical and acoustical sciences. His philosophical concepts, such as the Music of the Spheres, continue to find their place in esoteric doctrines. Yet until recently those secrets of using sound and music to heal have been all but lost. Pythagoras is said to have met his end when his school in Crotona burned to the ground. Some of his disciples claimed to have carried his secret teachings to other lands and other students.

THE LAMBDOMA

The search for the Pythagorean secrets of sound have continued until this day. In particular, the secrets of a curious diagram called "The Pythagorean Table" or the "Lambdoma" have been the subject of much discourse among scientists. The discovery of the Lambdoma is credited to Pythagoras and was passed on by the neo-Pythagorean Iamblichus.

The Lambdoma is an ancient musical mathematical theory which relates music to ratios.

Mathematicians and scientists have studied the Lambdoma since its discovery. It is said to hold the many esoteric secrets of the relationship between matter and spirit, including being a numerical representation of the World Soul.

Figure 2.1 is a reproduction of the Lambdoma diagram. The Lambdoma is composed of two series. One represents the division of a string, which indicates frequencies. The other series represents the multiplication of it or the harmonic series.

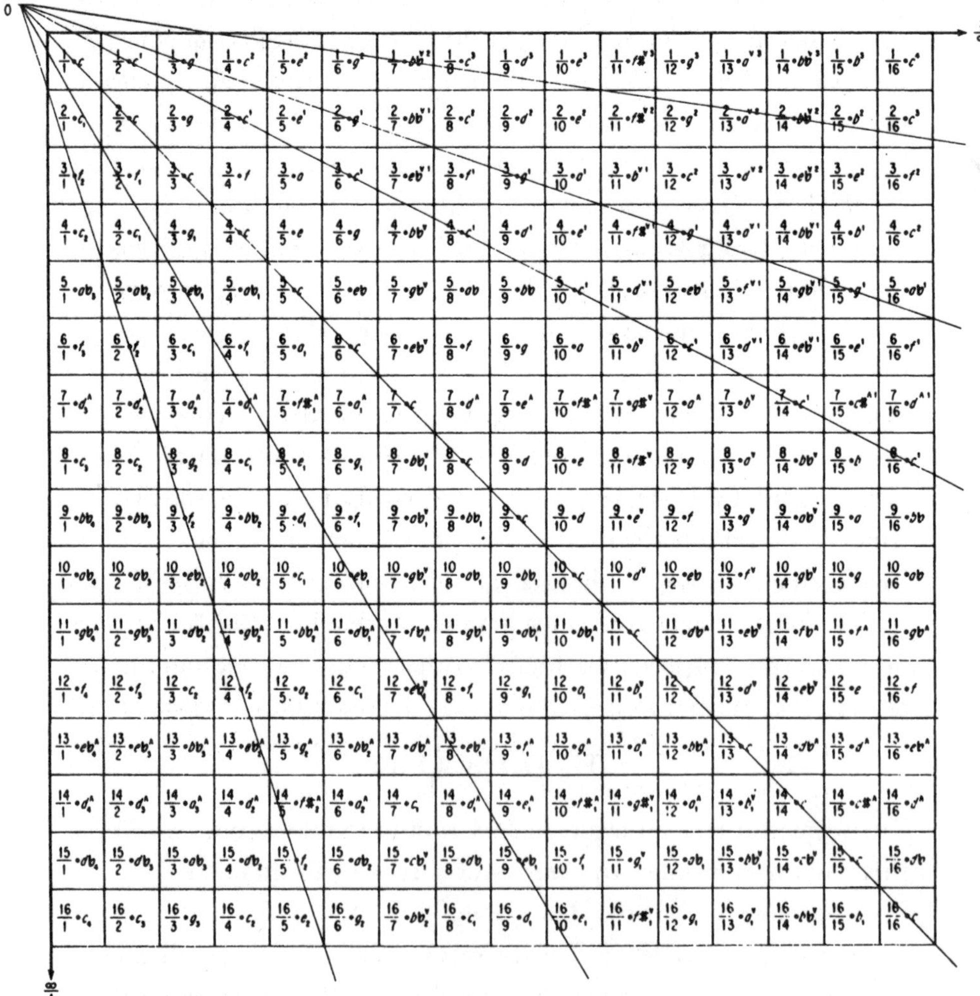

Figure 2.1. The Lambdoma diagram

Kayser and the Lambdoma

In the 1920s Hans Kayser, a German scientist, developed a theory of world harmonics based upon the Lambdoma. He found that the principles of harmonious structure in nature and the fundamentals of harmonics were essentially the same. Kayser called himself and others who adhered to this philosophy "harmonicists." He devoted much of his life to restoring to the sciences knowledge of the importance of harmonics. He believed that through understanding the connection between music and mathematics, it would be possible to create an understanding of the relationship between tone and numbers. Thus qualities (tonal sensations) could be derived from quantities (numbers) and quantities could be derived through qualities. In his book *Akroasis* (from the Greek word for "hearing"), he wrote:

> With the discovery of the relation between pitch and string length, which could be established numerically, western science was born. Qualities (tones) were derived from quantities (string or wave lengths) in an exact way.

Kayser believed that this knowledge of harmonics had become lost and had created a major schism between science and the spirit. He hoped that a true understanding of this relationship would create a bridge between matter and the soul.

According to Kayser, the whole-number ratios of musical harmonics correspond to an underlying framework existing in chemistry, physics, crystallography, astronomy, architecture, spectroanalysis, botany, and the study of other natural sciences. The relationship expressed in the periodic table of elements, an understanding of the formation of matter, resembles the overtone structure in music.

In *Akroasis,* he describes the relationship between the leaves of a plant and the harmonics series:

> If one projects all tones within the space of one octave (the same octave operation that Kepler applied in his *Harmonices Mundi*)

with their angles sketched in a specific way, one obtains the prototype of leaf form, which means that the framing interval of the octave, being the very basis for any music making and sensation, contains within itself the form of the leaf. This lends a new "psychological" support to Goethe's metamorphosis of plants, which, as we know, seeks to derive the development of plants from the leaf form. The many forms of blossoms, 2 (4, 8 . . .), 3 (6, 12 . . .), 5 (10 . . .), can be understood harmonically as morphological parallels to the numbers of the triad. . . . Just consider what it means that one blossom within a single plant exhibits an exact division into three and at the same time five. If one does not want to accept a logically reasoning intelligence, nevertheless, one must admit that in the soul of plants certain form-carrying prototypes—here, musical thirds and fifths—are at work, which as in music, shape the blossom forms as intervals.

Harmonics and Architecture

Kayser also describes the relationship between architecture and harmonics. This relationship was seen a century earlier by Goethe, the German man of letters and scientific investigator, who declared: "Architecture is frozen music." By this, Goethe was describing the relationship between ratios and their application to form and structure. While not all the forms found in geometry and nature are harmonic in their relationship, according to Kayser those we find most beautiful do indeed adhere to the harmonics series. In particular, forms that express ratios based upon the octave (2:1), fourths (4:3), fifths (3:2), and thirds (5:4) create forms that are extremely visually harmonious. The knowledge of these harmonic ratios to create architecture was basic to the ancient Mystery Schools. Thus, the most beautiful of the temples found in Athens, Rome, and Egypt are all based upon these proportions.

Table 2.2 lists the whole-number ratios that are found in the harmonic series.

Table 2.2 Whole-Number Ratios in the Harmonic Series

octave	1:2
fifth	2:3
fourth	3:4
major sixth	3:5
major third	4:5
minor third	5:6
minor sixth	5:8
minor seventh	5:9
major second	8:9
major seventh	8:15
minor second	15:16
tritone	32:45

The Golden Section

In architecture, a particular proportion known as the "Golden Section" was extremely important to ancient architects. Also known as the Phi Ratio, as well as the Divine Proportion, the Golden Section is a geometric proportion in which the ratio of the whole to the larger part is the same as the ratio of the larger part to the smaller. Thus $(a + b) : a = a : b$. The Golden Section often involves proportions that relate to the ratios found in the major sixth (3:5) and minor sixth (5:8). The proportions of the human body adhere to these ratios.

The entire length of the body can be viewed as adhering to the Golden Section if we first divide the length of the body into the proportions of the Golden Section at the navel. These proportions are then found at the nipple, dividing the entire width of the human body if the arms are stretched out. The loins divide the distance from the ground to the nipples in the proportions of the Golden Section. These proportions are found in many other aspects of the body: where the knee divides the entire leg; where the eyebrows divide the head; where the elbow joint divides the entire arm. These proportions of the major sixth (3:5) and minor sixth (5:8) can be found in other bodies, such as those found in the plant, insect, and animal kingdoms.

JENNY AND CYMATICS

Dr. Hans Jenny, a Swiss scientist, spent ten years of his life observing and photographing the effects of sound upon inorganic matter. He would put water and other liquids, plastics, paste, and dust on steel plates and then vibrate these plates with different frequencies. Much of this work was originally inspired by the work of Ernst Chladni, an eighteenth-century scientist who put grains of sand on glass and vibrated them with a violin bow. The sand would take on the most beautiful and symmetrical shapes. The experiments of Jenny took this understanding of the relationship between sound and form a quantum leap ahead.

Dr. Jenny spent thousands of hours experimenting with the effects of different frequencies upon the various inorganic substances he was using. Among the hundreds of photographs that he and his staff took are pictures that look like starfish, human organs, microscopic bacteria, and underwater life. In reality, these shapes are nothing more or less than lifeless mounds of plastic, dust, and other inorganic material that had been exposed to sound.

Cymatics is the name that Dr. Jenny gave to his work. The name comes from the Greek *kyma*, a word that means wave. Cymatics is the study of wave-form phenomena. It is proof positive that sound has the ability of creating form. Once they are exposed to sound waves, the inanimate materials in Dr. Jenny's experiments begin to undulate and move. Slowly, as the sound continues to affect them, they begin to take form. No longer shapeless blobs, these forms pulse and vibrate with the sounds that course through them, looking for all the world like living, breathing creations. They are, however, not alive but merely assume the features of life through the extraordinary power of sound. Once the sound is stopped, these shapes cease and the inorganic creations again become formless blobs.

Dr. Jenny, in volume II of *Cymatics* wrote:

> Now it is beyond doubt that where organization is concerned, the harmonic figures of physics are in fact essentially similar to the harmonic patterns of organic nature. . . . In the first place, we have the certain experience that harmonic systems such as we have visualized in our experiments arise from oscillations in the form of intervals and harmonic frequencies. That is indisputable. . . . If biological rhythms operate as generative factors at the interval-like frequencies appropriate to them, then harmonic patterns must be necessarily forthcoming.

According to Dr. Jenny, harmonics and harmonious patterns are interrelated. The intervals created by the frequencies and their harmonics were responsible for giving shape to the different substances with which Dr. Jenny experimented.

Barbara Hero has demonstrated a similar effect of harmonics using a laser and scanner system. Barbara placed a mirror under a speaker system that vibrated the mirror when two different frequencies were created. She then projected a laser at the mirror, and the laser was reflected onto a screen, revealing the images created by the sounds. Barbara found that those intervals that were created by the harmonic series created shapes that were geometrically perfect. These shapes, such as a circle, remained stationary as long as the intervals were sounding. Intervals that were not harmonically related created shapes that were not geometrically perfect and their shapes decayed.

Barbara experimented with the human voice using this laser and scanner system. The results were the same. When two people sang notes that were harmonically related, the perfectly symmetrical geometric shapes appeared. This was especially true when the people created vocal harmonics. When the voices created sounds that were not harmonically related, the shapes were not symmetrical.

The potential of the voice as a healing and transformative instrument intrigued Dr. Jenny, whose experimental focus consisted of recording the effects of sine wave frequencies upon inorganic substances. He concluded *Cymatics* with the statement:

> But the real work on what might be called *melos,* or speech, is still to be done. This brings the larynx and its action in the scope of our studies. And at the same time, we are confronted with origination of vibrations effects, the generative element; we must learn about the larynx as a creative organ which displays a kind of omnipotent nature.

The science of harmonics has revealed a phenomenon of sound that has application in the fields of mathematics, physics, and many other natural sciences. The universe is harmonically related, and this relationship may be found in the sounds of the voice. The voice may be the key to understanding sound as a tool for transformation and healing. The effects of our words and sounds, according to Dr. Jenny, need to be scientifically studied. The power of our words and sounds have been studied for many centuries in spiritual and esoteric studies.

THREE
Harmonics in the Occult

THE OCCULT

The word *occult* means "hidden or obscured from view." It can also describe something that is working at a more subtle level than can normally be observed on the physical level. With sound, we can apply this term to harmonics, which may often be hidden or undetected by our normal sense of hearing. The word *occult* is often utilized in conjunction with various systems of magical practice that may be found as offshoots of the world's religions. These magical practices feature esoteric rituals that may be the basis of those observed by the public in various services conducted by churches and synagogues. However, unless one has been initiated into one of these esoteric orders, the information and practices taught by these groups remain arcane and hidden, and thus are "occult" to most outsiders.

THE KABBALAH

The use of vowel sounds is the foundation of many magical formulas and incantations of these occult practices. In fact, the word *enchant* comes from the Latin *incantare* meaning "to sing or chant magical words or sounds." One of the most far-reaching occult practices is that of Kabbalah, a magical system that initially seems to have come from the esoteric study of Judaism. Kabbalah has since been incorporated into many forms of Western ritual, including gnostic and Christian groups.

The study of Kabbalah reveals an intricate understanding of the universe, based upon an archetypal structure known as the Tree of Life. There are ten different spheres of existence, or *sefirot,* in the Tree. These spheres have different attributes and deities and represent different levels of consciousness. The Hebrew word *kabbalah* means "to receive." Kabbalah is the esoteric, inner teachings of Judaism. Its basis is the Old Testament as well as the Talmud, and the latter-day works of the *Zohar.* It is speculated that the esoteric foundations of Christianity and Islam lie in the Kabbalah.

THE TREE OF LIFE

The Tree of Life is a geometric structure with which one can overlay a tree. The roots of the tree reach down into the domain called

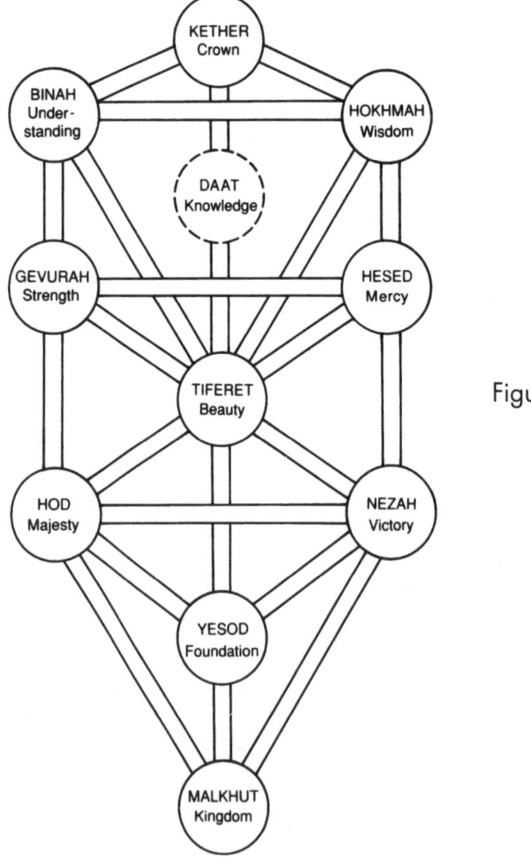

Figure 3.1. The Tree of Life

"Malkhut," which may be perceived as the physical plane, and the branches reach up to the region called "Kether," or Crown. Crown is the symbol used to describe the dimensionless point that is between the Manifest and Unmanifest. From the Crown, all things spring forth into the realms of creation.

Figure 3.1 illustrates the Tree of Life, giving the name of spheres (or sefirot in Hebrew) as well as the attribute for each.

There are many books written on Kabbalah and the Tree of Life. Using the Tree as a holographic model, it is possible to overlay practically all other models of consciousness and reality onto it. Certain esoteric groups have been able to align the physical body and chakras with the spheres. Different writers have assigned different vowel sounds, musical notations, and intervals to these sefirot. The form and shape of the Tree of Life seems to have universal appeal to philosophers and thinkers from many different traditions who have worked unceasingly to try to understand the Tree and fit their conceptual model of the universe into it.

VOGEL'S QUARTZ CRYSTALS AND THE TREE OF LIFE

Marcel Vogel, who was a head research scientist for IBM, spent years investigating the healing attributes of quartz crystals. In the mid 1980s, he began cutting quartz crystals to a specific shape that apparently aided and empowered the crystals' healing energy. I received one of these crystals cut by Marcel himself. A short time later, I became introduced to Kabbalah and the form of the Tree of Life. I remember staring breathlessly at this image that was represented on a poster on the wall of a friend's room. At the time, I was unfamiliar with Kabbalah, but I knew the form: it was the exact same dimensions as the crystals cut by Marcel Vogel.

Quartz crystals act as transducers of energy. That is, they have the ability of taking one form of energy, such as pressure waves, and converting it to a higher form of energy, such as electricity. They have the property of being "acousto-luminescent," which means that they can convert sound waves into light. Sound into light.

After my revelation looking at the Tree of Life on my friend's wall, I called up Marcel Vogel. We had spoken before about the relationship between sound and quartz crystals, and in particular, the ability of the specific harmonics to resonate them.

"Marcel," I began. "I was looking at the Kabbalistic Tree of Life and saw that it was in the exact same form as your cut crystals. Are you aware of this?"

"Certainly," he responded. "I received that shape from a dream and applied it to cutting crystals."

"Is that shape a universal form for energy conversion?"

"Yes," Marcel replied. "And I'll tell you something else. It's also the shape of the water molecule."

In traditional Hebrew Kabbalah, there are certain sacred names associated with specific spheres. These are names that, when chanted like a mantra, will cause the reciter to resonate to the frequency of the sphere. This is another aspect of sacred sonic entrainment similar to the practices of tantra, utilized by the Tibetan monks, in which the practitioner, working with vocalization and visualization, recites a specific mantric form designed to invoke a particular entity. While visualizing this entity, the practitioner unites with it.

VOWEL SOUNDS AND THE KABBALAH

One practice utilized by many different Kabbalistic groups is to work with the vowel sounds to manifest the energy of these different spheres. This is done through stressing the vowel sound of the sacred names associated with specific sefirot.

William Grey, one of the greatest Western magicians of this century, writes of vowels in *The Talking Tree:*

> The vowels were "extras" in Hebrew, and fitted in with consonant-formed words in order to give those words their real meaning according to the spirit in which they were intended. The vowels were originally very special sonics indeed, being mostly used for

> "God-names" and other sacred purposes. Consonants gave words their bodies, but vowels alone put soul into them.
>
> Taken together in combination, the vowels will "spell" the Name of the Living One: IAO; IEOA; HU; YAH; etc. Whichever way they are connected, they signify Divinity enlivening Existence, and hence were sacred in all Magical practices. . . . Thus the vowels are to language what Life and Consciousness are to Existence.

In this magical Kabbalistic practice, it is believed that, as Grey stated, the chanting of particular vowel sounds has the ability of connecting the chanter with the energies of the Divine. Through chanting the vowel sounds keyed by what Grey called "The Master-Code of the 'Word' A.E.I.O.U.," one could effect a "fully cosmic consciousness." Each of the vowel sounds chanted in specific combinations could create resonance with particular Divine aspects.

In Grey's work, the vowel *A* (AH) is equated with the element of Earth and the direction of the north; the vowel *E* (EEE) is equated with the element of Air and the direction of the east; the vowel *I* (EYE) is equated with the element of Fire and the direction of the south; the vowel *O* (OH) is equated with the element of Water and the direction of the west; and the vowel *U* (OOO) is equated with the element of the Aether (which he called the element of universal truth) and the direction is "around and about."

The use of the vowel sounds as magical formulas is apparently very ancient. Edgar Cayce, the "sleeping prophet," while in trance, talked of the ancient Egyptians using the seven vowel sounds to activate the energy centers of the body. Similar information is obtained from a totally different source. Yale University professor James Anderson Winn discusses the uses of vowel sounds in Egypt in his book *Unsuspecting Eloquence:* "In Egypt the priests, when singing hymns in praise of the gods employ the seven vowels, which they utter in due succession."

The relationship between vowel sounds and harmonics is not observed in the various books on Kabbalah and magic. Perhaps this information is intentionally absent. However, Professor Winn does not let this slip by. He continues:

> The different shaping of the mouth cavity and placement of the tongue necessary to produce different vowels actually gives each vowel a distinct overtone which will be present whether the vowel is sung or spoken, whether the speaker is male or female. If you speak this sequence of words—beat, bit, bet, bat, boat, bought—you should hear those overtones descending in pitch; if you take away the sound of the vocal cords by whispering, the effect will be even clearer.

Certain scholars have traced aspects of the Kabbalah to the ancient Egyptian temple ceremonies. It is not surprising, therefore, that William Grey's and other magical groups' work with vowel sounds may be similar to those practices utilized in the Egyptian temples.

GOD NAMES IN THE TREE OF LIFE

A difficulty that lies with investigation into occult and magical practices is simply that unless one is initiated into a magical order, it is highly unlikely that much exoteric information will be readily available regarding esoteric practices. An example of this may be found in the "God Names" of the different spheres from the Tree of Life. These "God Names" are now available to the public in various books on Kabbalah. As we have stated, the chanting of these God Names is said to act in a manner that resonates the chanter and unites them with the energy of the God Name.

Figure 3.2 represents the Tree of Life with the God Names of each of the sefirot provided, along with the name of the Archangel said to preside over the particular plane. Recitation of the Angelic Names is said to invoke the named angel.

William Grey writes that the chanting of the various vowel sounds and sacred names will not "accomplish anything by themselves for those who do not know and have not practiced all the prerequisites needed to make them what they are—major controls of living consciousness." A major prerequisite with any sound work of this manner lies in an understanding of the relationship between vocalization and visualization.

In both the ancient Egyptian and ancient Hebrew traditions, the Creator deity would speak the name of something and that something would come into being. For example, in Genesis God said, "Let there be light and there was light." By uttering the word *light,* light is created.

Naomi Janowitz, author of *The Poetics of Ascent,* theorizes that in order for Divine Language to create manifestation, this language must be encoded with a certain deed or content. Thus, added to the process of vocalization of a specific sound in order to create a particular "something" is the additional factor of the Creator God thinking of that "something" while speaking it. We therefore bring into focus the concept of "visualization." A formula that seems to embody this is:

Vocalization + Visualization = Manifestation

This formula seems to hold true in the sacred practices of nearly every tradition I have investigated. For example, a practitioner will both vocalize

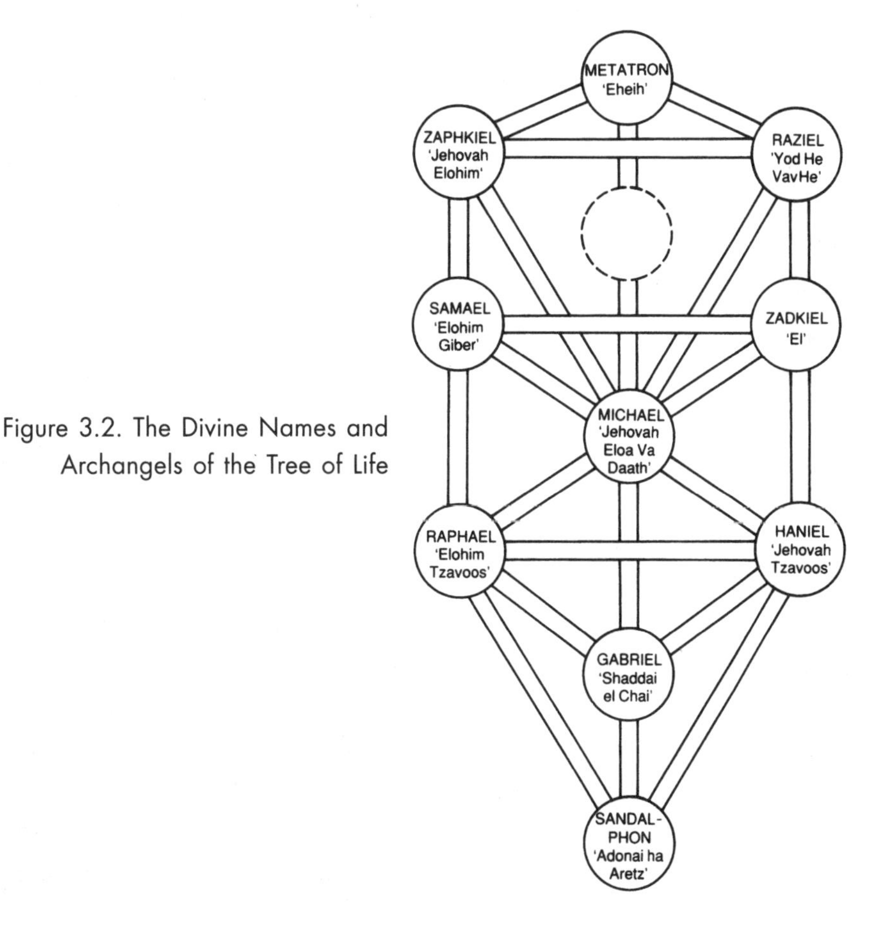

Figure 3.2. The Divine Names and Archangels of the Tree of Life

a specific sound to resonate with a particular entity but will also visualize this particular entity. With regard to the Kabbalah, a practitioner would visualize a sefira and then chant the God Name.

As we have stated, gaining information and insight into esoteric practices can be quite difficult. Often the uninitiated are simply not allowed to experience the true "inner" nature of ceremonies. Thus, as William Grey points out, the chanting of the Sacred Names of the Tree of Life without proper knowledge may not be effective.

REGARDIE'S CHANTING OF GOD NAMES

It has been my great privilege to have certain "inner" workings of sacred sound shared with me by students, friends, and teachers, despite the fact that I may not have been formally initiated into an order. One such sharing involved the Kabbalah. A friend of mine, a musician and practicing magician, allowed me to hear a recording of a secret Kabbalistic ceremony. I had taught him how to sing harmonics and, as a practicing magician, he then utilized harmonics in the magical ceremonies he took part in and taught vocal harmonics to others. An enthusiast in harmonics like myself, he looked for these sounds in sacred ceremonies.

The recording, made many years ago, was of a very famous Western magician, Israel Regardie, a member of the Order of the Golden Dawn, as he chanted the "God Names" of the different planes. This recording has now been made available to the public, though at the time it was quite a discovery of esoteric sound practices. As I listened to Regardie chanting these "God Names" such as "Yah Way" (chanted "Yod-He-Vav-He"), I immediately became aware that the vowel sounds in these names were elongated and focused upon. In other words, it was not simply "Yod-He-Vav-He" but "Yoooooooood-Heeeeeeeey-Vaaaaaaaahv-Heeeeeeeey." As I listened more intently, I realized that the harmonics found in these vowels were strongly stressed.

It was not as though the overtones were merely a by-product of this sounding. In this recorded ceremony, Regardie was consciously trying to create and then amplify and enforce the harmonics as he toned the "God Names." The technique was called "tonal chanting." This recording was apparently done before the awareness of vocal harmonics techniques, and the overtones are not nearly as powerful as they could have been. Nevertheless, upon hearing this recording it immediately became apparent to me that overtone chanting was one of the highest and most secretive levels of magical work.

While I have not found this in any book, it is my belief that the use of harmonics with these "God Names" creates a magical sonic formula for manifesting different aspects of Divine energy. My friend the musical magician is in agreement on this. Since each vowel sound has a particular set of overtones inherent in its creation, each different "God Name" would have a specific sonic formula that would occur when it was intoned properly.

SUFI CHANTING

This understanding of the sacred aspect of vowel sounds may be exoterically found in a number of different traditions, including the Sufis, who attribute different Divine qualities to the vowels. It is only upon hearing certain Sufi chanting that the importance of the harmonics within the vowels becomes obvious.

Peter Michael Hamel, in *Through Music to the Self,* writes of this chanting technique:

> In the Islamic sphere a special technique was likewise developed, in which the voice is altered beyond all recognition. From time immemorial the "muezzin," who intones the Holy Koran from the minaret, has placed both hands on his temples and sung the call to Allah in an unnaturally high tone with his head-voice, the falsetto. The notes, which in quiet areas can be heard miles away, sound in the distance like a soft woman's voice, and only in the vicinity of the singer does one become aware of his exertions in forcing and straining his voice. Here, too, tradition has it that the singer with divine powers is in direct touch with the Prophet's message.
>
> In Sufi chanting this jump into the head-voice has developed even further. In ecstatic moments, the singer of the Holy Scriptures brings off a kind of hiccup or very rapid yodel which, as with an

> overblown flute, switches the voice to a higher pitch. Via this powerful form of chanting, the mystic message of the texts, or ecstatic prayers, is conveyed to the initiate by direct means. This is a technique which reflects the mystic Islamic combination of austere power and loving devotion.

The Sufis are an esoteric branch of Islam. They have great knowledge of vowels, which they utilize in their healing work. In *The Book of Sufi Healing,* Shaykh Hakim Moinuddin Chishti writes:

> The three basic sounds are the long vowel sounds of "A," "I," and "U." These are what the Sufis call the universal harmonic constants, and they are used in all mystic paths that utilize sounds. . . . The long vowel sound of "A" (as in "father"), as a vibratory tone travels downward and slightly to the left from the throat and centers in the heart. . . . The long sound of "I" (as in "machine") moves in the opposite direction, up the nasal septum, and vibrates at the point of the pineal gland. . . . The long sound of "U" exists when uttered exactly at the point on the pursed lips, the point of connection between the in- and out-breaths.

The author also points out that, for example, the name "Allah" is just an elongation of the long vowel sound of "AH" and activates the heart. Another example of a prayer that uses the "AH" sounds to open up the heart chakra is the Lord's Prayer. ("Our Father, which art in heaven . . . Amen.")

Pir Vilayat Khan, head of the Sufi Order of the West, is greatly aware of the uses of harmonics as spiritual and healing modalities. In *Toward the One,* he utilizes the relationship shown in figure 3.3 between the vowel sounds and the chakras.

OVERTONES IN RELIGIOUS TRADITIONS

Hazrat Inayat Khan was the father of Pir Vilayat Khan. A musician himself, he was extremely aware of the power of sound and music to

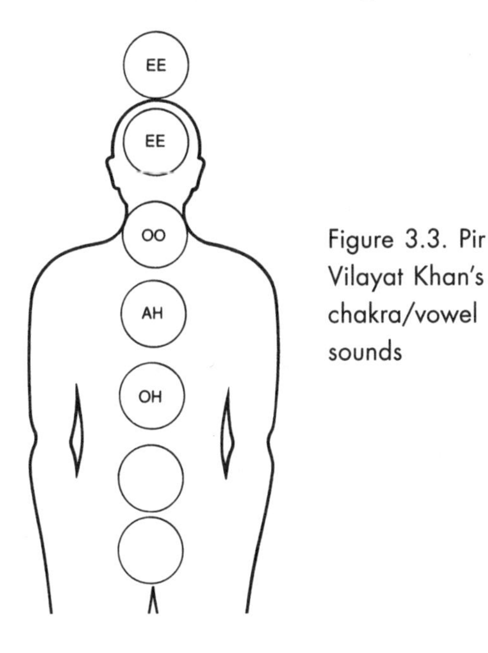

Figure 3.3. Pir Vilayat Khan's chakra/vowel sounds

heal. In *Healing and Music: The Viewpoint of Hazrat Inayat Khan,* author Sarmad Brody writes:

> The basic attunement for harnessing the will in healing with sound is the intoning of a single pitch on an open vowel sound. There is a secret to getting the right sound and that is to be able to hear the different overtones in the harmonic series of the tone you are producing. . . . Different overtones come out more clearly through different vowel sounds so intone slowly "OO-AH-EE" and hear the various overtones in a different emphasis with each vowel.

Brody then specifically describes the fourth overtone, which is two octaves and a major third above the fundamental. This is the harmonic stressed by the Gyuto monks during their tantric chanting:

> If you can be conscious of that fourth overtone, you can begin to heal yourself through sound since this brings one's whole being into tune and raises consciousness to a high pitch. Also, if you can sing very softly and send this sound, while being conscious of this fourth

> overtone, into an area where energy is blocked or tensed, you can release the tension.

The assignment of particular overtones to particular qualities and abilities may be found in other traditions. Robert C. Lewis, a student of the Rosicrucian Fellowship, covers much Christian mysticism in relationship to harmonics in *The Sacred Word and Its Creative Overtones.*

According to Lewis, the fundamental is a physical sound that is a projection of the Holy Spirit. Harmonic octaves of this fundamental also align to this energy. Lewis uses the note C for this and assigns it the geometric shape of a square. The next overtone that creates the interval of the third is assigned to the Christ Spirit. Lewis uses the note E for this and assigns it the geometric shape of a five-pointed star or the pentagram. The next overtone that creates the interval of the fifth is assigned to the Supreme Being. Lewis uses the note G for this and assigns it the geometric shape of a six-pointed star or the hexagram.

Rosicrucians such as Lewis and Max Heindel focus upon Christian mysticism. Yet, as in many esoteric teachings, they find universal principles of sound found elsewhere in this chapter. Lewis writes:

> Everything that exists in the universe was first a thought, that thought then manifesting as a word, a sound, which built all forms and itself manifested as the life within those forms. . . .
>
> The overtones of all musical sounds progress from the physical world into the spiritual world. That is why music is practically always part of religious services. Whether it be a Hindu mantra, the chant of a Jewish cantor, the call to prayer of a Moslem muezzin, a simple Christian hymn or a Bach cantata, the purpose of music in a religious service is to raise the vibratory rate of a congregation upward through a series of overtones to a spiritual level.

GREGORIAN CHANTING

While the Gregorian chanting of the Catholic Church may at first seem far removed from our subject of vowel sounds and vocal harmonics, there are many similarities to be found in this form of chanting. Christian hymns have existed since the earliest times of worship. Saint Augustine defined it as "the praise of God by singing." As a musical form, Gregorian rite won universal acceptance in Europe, where it was considered to have reached its apogee in the eighth century. According to Joscelyn Godwin, author of *Harmonies of Heaven and Earth:*

> The Christian tradition, while recognizing the great psychological value of music, has seldom used it for esoteric or initiatic purposes. The reason lies in the situation under which early Christianity, both esoteric and exoteric, developed. Under the Roman Empire music was associated with all things the Christians shunned: the ecstatic worship of pagan divinities, frivolous entertainment by virtuosi, sexual license and the horrors of the circuses. The Church Fathers allowed the singing of hymns but could not conceive of anyone listening to music except for mere sensual enjoyment.

While the sensual pleasures of music may have been shunned by the Church, the beauty of Gregorian chant, complete with audible overtones, has echoed for many centuries in various cathedrals. Gregorian chant was initially sung in unison, with all the monks singing the same musical line using elongated vowel sounds. This was called "plainsong." These elongated vowel sounds created overtones that seemed like a ghostly voice accompanying the monks. During that time of the eighth and ninth centuries, overtones were pursued in a number of different monasteries much more consciously than in today's Gregorian singing.

At some point, probably in the ninth century, music made a radical new departure. This was the performance of the music of the liturgy with two voice parts. The new style was termed "organum" and at its most primitive consisted simply of one voice singing the plainsong melody, being accompanied step-by-step at the interval of a fourth below by another voice.

Please bear in mind that if we were using modern notation, for example, in the key of C, the plainsong would be in the key of C while the accompanying voice would be in the key of G. Gradually the plainsong was relegated to the lower voice. The upper voice combined with this plainsong to create together what sounded like a series of long-drawn-out pedal notes. When heard in the acoustically resonant chambers of many of the cathedrals in Europe, one becomes aware of the clarity of specific harmonics that resound during the chanting. The spiritual and physical benefits from Gregorian chanting were so little recognized by the Catholic Church that after Vatican II chanting of the sacred texts in Latin was discontinued. The effect of this is illustrated by the story in our chapter on meditation about Dr. Alfred Tomatis and the Benedictine monks he treated for exhaustion and depression due to their lack of chanting.

Dr. Tomatis believes that the sacred chants from different traditions are rich in high-frequency harmonics and have a neurophysiological effect that charges the brain. This may be a scientific explanation for some of the transformative abilities of harmonics. Yet, there is more.

THE LANGUAGE OF HARMONICS

In the various esoteric and occult traditions, harmonics and vowel sounds are utilized for ceremonial and magical work. They are "God Names" and "chakra sounds" and contain within them some inherent energy that has mystified mankind since the first sound. There are legends that before there was a spoken language of words, there was a harmonic language. This language allowed humankind to communicate with all the creations of nature. It utilized the concept of information being encoded on the pure tone frequencies of harmonics. It was different from telepathy in that it used sound, but it was similar to telepathy in that the thoughts and information were sent on the sound wave and were received by the listener. This may be one of the ways by which dolphins communicate with each other, transmitting three-dimensional holographic thought-forms of sound. Eventually this harmonic language separated. The consonants combined with the tones to create words. The tones combined with other sounds to make music. Perhaps we may one day again rediscover this harmonic language.

FOUR

HARMONICS IN SHAMANISM

INTRODUCTION

In western Mongolia there is a very special waterfall that feeds into the Deer River. This waterfall is said to be very sacred, for legend has it that it was through this waterfall that the shamans of Mongolia were able to learn to sing harmonics. They did this by listening to the sounds of the waterfall, which sang harmonics itself. Slowly, they began to attempt to duplicate the sounds of the waterfall using their own voices, and thus mastered the ability to create vocal overtones. This waterfall was said to be a gift from the spirit world to mankind in order to give them the gift of harmonics.

The word *shaman* comes from the Siberian *saman.* It has been utilized by anthropologists to refer to persons who were previously known by such terms as "witch doctor," "witch," "medicine man," "sorcerer," "wizard," "magician," "seer," and "magic man." Michael Harner, in *The Way of the Shaman,* defines a shaman as a man or woman who enters an altered state of consciousness to contact and utilize an ordinarily hidden reality in order to acquire knowledge and power and to help other people.

According to Jeanne Achterburg in *Imagery and Healing:*

> Shamanic practice involves the ability to move in and out of a special state of consciousness, a notion of a guardian spirit complex and has the purpose of helping others.

Shamanism is thought to be the oldest form of healing known to mankind. In shamanism, shamans communicate with the spirit world in order to do their work. Most commonly, they utilize sound as a means of achieving this and, naturally, the voice is a most common instrument for invoking spirits and traveling to the spirit realms. Dr. Achterburg calls this "Auditory Aids to Altered States."

In this chapter, we will examine the use of harmonics and their sonic counterpart, vowel sounds, as they may be utilized in different shamanic traditions.

MONGOLIAN OVERTONE CHANTING

Perhaps the most highly developed use of vocal harmonics is the tradition of hoomi (*choomig, xoomij*) or throat singing, found in the Tuvic region of Mongolia. This is the Mongolian name for a solo style of overtone singing where two distinct pitch lines are sounded throughout. One of these is a nasal-sounding drone of relatively constant pitch and corresponds to the fundamental. The other pitch consists of piercing, whistle-like tones that form a melody line above the drone utilizing the 5th through the 13th partials. The singing style is reminiscent of the sound of the mouth harp.

Working with a fundamental tone of, for example, about 100 Hz, a Tuvic singer would create a melodic line working with the 5th through the 13th partial, vibrating at what would be between 600 through 1,300 Hz. These singers also create extremely high nasal harmonics utilizing the 16th through 23rd partials, creating tones that would vibrate between 1,600 and 2,300 Hz. Of course, singers working with a higher fundamental nearer a middle A, of 440 Hz on a piano, might be able to create frequencies up to 10,120 Hz, a sound that is almost supersonic in its scope.

Ethnomusicologists have analyzed Mongolian overtone chanting in terms of the frequencies and harmonic partials that are created by this style. However, little has been written about how the Mongolians are able to create these sounds and why they would want to create such extraordinary sounds in the first place.

We cover some of the techniques utilized for vocal harmonics in chapter 6. As for the particular reasons for and uses of hoomi, we can only speculate. It is my hypothesis that the Mongolian style of singing that is now found in the secular music of that region is the exoteric version of an extremely shamanic esoteric sacred sounding utilized by shamans to heal and transform. These shamans would utilize these sounds to communicate with nature spirits and various kinds of entities.

Peter Michael Hamel, in his book, *Through Music to the Self,* writes of the "magico-animistic" musical language found in Mongolia, which was a center of shamanic power. Hamel believes that the Mongolians listened very carefully to the sounds created by the bowing and plucking of their singing bows. From this they were able to "appreciate the secret of music, the physical basis of sound-production and learnt to realize vocally this original archaic phenomenon of the 'monotone.'" Through this, the Mongolians developed the hoomi or throat-singing technique. Hamel offers us a description of an individual Mongolian able to sing in two voices at once:

> He hums or sings nasally a note of medium pitch and alters the volume of his mouth-cavity by opening and closing his mouth, thus varying the harmonic spectrum of this single, long-drawn-out note. Suddenly, at a very high pitch, a shrill melody rings out, though consisting solely of the amplified harmonic of the single bass-note. . . .

The ghostly and almost supernatural effect of this singing technique makes it easy to understand the legend that singers able to master such overtone melodies were in touch with the spirits and possessed supernatural powers. It is said that there have been shamans who showed such mastery of this technique that they could be heard loud and clear over great distance.

Certain ethnomusicologists believe that throat-singing techniques, found in Mongolia and in southern Siberia among the Tuvans and Khakassy, were learned from the sound of the mouth harp, for the sound is quite similar. Others believe it may have been learned from the singing bow. Perhaps it was learned from the sounds of the Deer River. Regardless of its origin, these ethnomusicologists feel that the technique did not arise as a matter of mere vocal acrobatics. The songs that were performed and notated by these scientists were secular, but their traditional connection with the mouth harp, an important shamanic instrument in those regions, suggested a different derivation to them.

The ethnomusicologists believed that the guttural, whistle-like sounds that are part of the songs seem more likely to constitute an extreme example of voice masking, such as is used ritually in different forms in many cultures. It is interesting to note that older Mongolian traditions connect both this kind of singing and the mouth harp with supernatural communication. The probability of such a link gains strength from the occurrence of a related phenomenon in Tibet. There the singing of partials is not found in a secular context at all, but as a form of chanting associated with the Tantric rituals practiced by the monasteries of Gyume and Gyuto.

There are validations about the shamanic origins of overtone singing as demonstrated in the Tuvic region of Mongolia, from both Hamel's mystical approach and the scientific approach of ethnomusicologists. A problem that many ethnomusicologists encounter is an inability to perceive the mystical and shamanic aspects of the music they are investigating, and even when the mystical is encountered by them, it is not recognized as such.

Ted Levin, founding member of the Harmonic Choir, traveled to Tuva to record the hoomi singers there. While Levin's approach to these sonic phenomena is quite scholarly, he writes of hoomi in the notes of *Tuva: Voices from the Center of Asia:*

> These styles might well represent vestiges of a proto-musical sound world in which man sought through mimesis to link himself to beings and forces that most concerned him: in the case of the Tuvans, domestic animals, the physical environment of mountains and grasslands, and the elemental energies of wind, water, and light.
>
> In the traditional sound world of present-day Tuva, throat-singing is still intimately connected to nature. . . . Throat-singing seems to have served traditionally as a means of responding to states of heightened feelings brought on by exaltation at the beauty of nature. Walking alone on the grasslands, herders sang not for one another, but for themselves, for the mountains and for the steppe.

Interestingly enough, Levin writes in Tuva, throat singing is almost exclusively the province of men. Women are physiologically able to produce the same sounds, though at higher pitch levels. There is, however, a taboo against women throat singers based upon the belief that such singing may cause infertility. This belief is gradually being abandoned as newer cultural values are replacing the old, and some girls are now learning hoomi. Levin notes that the Tuvan herders are poised between old cultural values and new ones:

> In many arenas of material and spiritual culture, the once strong voice of traditions is now only a faint echo. For example, shamans, the traditional healers, are all but non-existent, and shamanism has been officially consigned to the non-threatening status of an historical artifact amenable to theatrical recreations.

We can understand Levin's thoughts about this. On the extraordinary recording *Tuva: Voices from the Center of Asia* is an example of a shamanic ceremony, performed not by an actual shaman but an actor "who has long and convincingly acted the role of a shaman in plays." Perhaps there were no shamans who existed. However, it is quite possible that while there were shamans in the region, they did not feel that their sacred ceremonies would rightfully have worked on a recording such as this.

From my own personal experiences with shamanic ceremonies and rituals, I have found that the shaman leading the ceremony will oftentimes allow outsiders to participate. However, many of these shamans believe that to record these sacred rituals is definitely wrong. It is believed that the sound energy has the ability of invoking the ancient spirits and beings through ceremonies and rituals and that this sound energy would be captured on the tape. Not only might the ritual itself be impaired, but, when played back later, the recording could have the capability of summoning these beings. Naturally, a shaman would feel that a recording that had this capability might be improper. It would damage the relationship that the shaman had with the invoked spirits, as well as being quite dangerous to those who inadvertently summoned the spirits without knowing what to do with them. Knowing this, it is understandable why many shamanic rituals and ceremonies are not recorded.

The use of vocal harmonics is practiced in a number of other regions of Outer Mongolia besides Tuva. Our next chapter, "Tantric Harmonics," focuses on a particular form of overtone chanting practiced by Tibetan monks. However, forms of producing vocal harmonics as a shamanic tool are not limited to Asia and are practiced in decidedly different cultures, from African to Alaskan Eskimo. There are undoubtedly many other traditions that also utilize this form of sonic shamanism that the uninitiated will never know about.

THE MAYA

In the introduction I related an experience I had had in the ancient Mayan center of Palenque where I had the occasion to create both harmonics and light in a totally dark room. Recently, I was talking with a man who had spent years with a people, the Lacandon Maya of the Mexican Rain Forest, who are said to be the descendants of the Mayan builders of Palenque. When I told him of my experience in Palenque, he nodded his head and said: "You are very lucky to have experienced this! It is something that the Mayan shamans teach, this creation of light through harmonics. It is the higher harmonics that do this."

This of course is information that you would not find in any historical book about the Maya, nor would it be available through an ethnomusicologist who was recording the sounds of the Lacandon Maya. Yet the experience I had had in Palenque was real, and I believe the verification that I received about the Maya and their knowledge of harmonics. It is a strong indication that vocal harmonics may be part of many other shamanic traditions, but this knowledge is hidden from the public.

Along with this creation of light through sound, it seems likely that, with the correct intent, different spirits and beings can be summoned through use of overtone chanting. The psychic Kaimora, while in trance, talked about the different planes of existence (astral, causal, etc.) being resonated by harmonics. It is possible that harmonics can actually create an opening or a gateway between different realms of existence. This would be in keeping with the belief of the Australian Aboriginal shamans.

THE ABORIGINAL PEOPLE

The Aboriginal people of Australia utilize a form of harmonics in their sacred ceremonies that is not created from the voice but from an instrument. The didjeridoo is a hollowed-out tree limb that is blown into to produce a very low fundamental tone as well as very distinct overtones. The sound is very similar to the One Voice Chord of the Tibetan monks.

The basic sounds of the didjeridoo are quite simple to achieve. One simply breathes out while vibrating the lips. However, one of the primary ingredients in the sounding of this instrument is the ability to do circular breathing. Circular breathing is a very advanced technique that requires the breather to let out a continuous flow of air, so that the sounding of the didjeridoo never stops. This naturally means that the breather must be able to take in-breaths through the nose while continuing to exhale air through the mouth. It is quite a complicated technique that, interestingly enough, has also developed in Tibet. Even without the exquisite sound of the didjeridoo, circular breathing creates a very altered state of consciousness in the person practicing the technique.

The story of the didjeridoo was related to me by Julius, a white Australian who had lived with the Aboriginal people and learned their use of the didjeridoo.

Aboriginal people believe that before the first Aboriginal people came to this planet, there was a race of supernatural beings called the Wandjina. They were a "Dreamtime" race and responsible for the creation of the various creatures and forms on the Earth. When the Aboriginal people were created, it was time for the Wandjina to depart. They left these people the didjeridoo as a gift. When the didjeridoo sounded, it created a sonic field, a sort of interdimensional window, through which the Wandjina could travel to the Aboriginals and vice versa.

It is not just any tree limb that can be used for making a didjeridoo, but the limb of a very special tree that has been hollowed out by termites. In order to find these trees, it is necessary for an Aboriginal shaman to enter the altered state of consciousness called "Dreamtime." Once they are in Dreamtime, they set out on a journey and are guided to the special trees that will supply the limb for the didjeridoo.

Julius confided to me that while living with the Aboriginal people, he had often tried to find such a tree but had been totally unsuccessful. Yet he had seen tribal elders enter Dreamtime and always come back from their search with the hollowed-out tree limbs. He also told me that besides being used in ceremonial work to invoke the Wandjina, the didjeridoo was used for healing. A person with an illness would lie on the ground and the shaman would blow the didjeridoo over the afflicted part of the person to facilitate the healing. This struck me as being very similar to some resonant healing techniques that are described elsewhere in this book, including overtoning, where one person projects their voice into the body of another person; or cymatic therapy, where specific frequencies are projected, via an instrument, into another person.

The use of vowel sounds in shamanic ceremonies is commonly reported by researchers encountering such rituals. Vowel sounds, as I have previously related in this book, contain the energy of harmonics. The use of vowel sounds may be found in different shamanic traditions though no comprehensive study of the subject has yet been undertaken. These shamanic chants are described by Jeanne Achterburg in *Imagery and Healing:* "Normally, the chants are phonemes strung together. There is no ready interpretation or translation for them available in the language of ordinary reality, only in feeling states."

NATIVE AMERICAN SHAMANS

Frequently, there are specific songs, passed down from generation to generation, that shamans of different traditions use. However, just as frequently, various spirits will direct the shamans in new and original songs. Often, these songs sound to us, as Dr. Achterburg described, like a series of meaningless phonemes. An example of this might be found in certain Native American songs that seem like the sound "Ah Hey Ya" repeated over and over again and again.

It was my privilege to attend a medicine ceremony of some Huichol shamans. The Huichols engage in peyote as a sacrament that guides them in their rituals. Many of the medicine songs sounded very much like the repetition of vowel sounds. During a break in the ceremony, I had the opportunity to ask the chanting shaman where he learned the songs.

"Some of them," he replied, "are traditional songs I have learned. But most of them come from the medicine which teaches me as I sing them."

Joseph Rael, known as "Beautiful Painted Arrow," a Native American of the Ute-Tewa tradition, works with what he calls the "Five Vibrations." In 1983, Joseph had a vision during a sun dance in which he was shown "sound chambers" placed throughout the world. In these sound chambers, sacred sounds were chanted that allowed attunement and resonance through all the created beings on the planet.

There are now eighteen of these sound chambers throughout the world. I met Joseph at one such chamber in Gold Hill, Colorado. Looking very much like a Native American kiva, this circular chamber was designed specifically for chanting the "Five Vibrations." These are sounds found in Joseph's lineage, but also in every other major lineage on the planet. They are vowel sounds. In his vision, Joseph was given these vowel sounds to utilize, working with a specific energy inherent in these sounds. They are:

AH—washing, to cleanse and purify the individual;
AYE (eh)—relativity, to understand our relationship to all things;
EEE—clarity, to get in touch with Divine Intelligence;
OH—innocence and curiosity;
OOO—that which is lifting us, God presence

We chanted these vowel sounds for about five minutes each while focusing our attention on the energy inherent in the sound. After each vowel sound, Joseph would tell us to listen in silence to the vowel sound. During these exercises I became aware of the importance of my focus upon harmonics. As I chanted each vowel sound, I noticed the specific harmonic that was created through each one. It is this harmonic, I believe, that, in conjunction with the fundamental tone, creates the attributes that Joseph works with. I also became aware during the listening in silence between the vowel sounds of how our nervous system will attune to the frequencies and energy of the vowel sound when chanted for just a brief time. The listening between the vowels proved to me as helpful as the creation of the vowel sounds themselves. Each silence was different. My nervous system was different. The inner listening I experienced was different. I had done similar exercises many times before, but never had I quite had the inner validation of the effects of vowels and their harmonics as resonating tools for our brains and complementary systems.

During a break I spoke with Joseph and shared with him my understanding of the sacredness of vowels and the harmonics inherent in them. I asked Joseph if the elder medicine people in his tribe or other tribes would be willing to validate the use of vowel sounds as sacred tools.

Joseph laughed and replied that they knew a great deal about vowel sounds but would probably say that they had no idea what anyone was talking about, professing ignorance. We both had experienced warnings from medicine people from specific traditions who felt they "owned" specific sounds and that it was incorrect to share this information with others as well. These medicine people are also unwilling to realize an interconnectedness with all the sacred sounds on the planet. We then talked of the need for openness in terms of working with sacred sounds.

Due to a lack of information, the true relationship between harmonics and shamanism can only be speculated upon. However, it seems likely that in Mongolia and many other parts of the world, vocal harmonics are an inherent part of shamanic rituals. It may be that the shamans have extraordinary knowledge about harmonics as a key for transformation. Harmonics may create interdimensional windows through which the shaman can travel or through which an invoked spirit may enter this domain. It may be that each vowel and its related harmonics have particular attributes and energy forms through which the shamans may focus their intention.

From a physiological viewpoint, vocal harmonics create changes in the heartbeat, respiration, and brain waves of the reciter, altering consciousness and allowing the shaman to be in a state where they are receptive to spirit journeys. Perhaps different portions of the brain are also resonated and activated by these sounds, releasing different hormones and neurochemicals that facilitate an altered state. For the time being, we can only speculate upon the subject and hope that such information will be revealed to us in the future.

FIVE
Tantric Harmonics

THE GYUME AND GYUTO MONKS

One night in 1433, the Tibetan lama Je Tzong Sherab Senge awoke from a startling dream. In it he had heard a voice unlike any voice that had ever sounded on the planet. It was a low voice, unbelievably deep, sounding more like the growl of a wild bull than anything human. Combined with this first voice, there was a second. This voice was high and pure, like the sound of a child singing. These two voices, so totally different, had come from the same source, and that source was Je Tzong Sherab Senge himself.

In this dream, Je Tzong Sherab Senge had been instructed to take this special voice and use it for a new chanting style that would embody both the masculine and feminine aspects of Divine energy. It was a tantric voice, a sound that could unite those chanting it in a web of universal consciousness. The next morning, Je Tzong Sherab Senge began to chant his daily prayers. The sounds that came out of him were the sounds he had heard in his dream—unearthly sounds, tantric sounds—and he gathered his fellow monks together to tell them of his dream.

That year, more than 500 years ago, the Gyume Tantric Monastery began in Lhasa, Tibet. The monks of this monastery learned to chant in the same voice that Je Tzong Sherab Senge had heard in his dream. It was a voice that enabled each monk to chant three notes at the same time, creating One Voice Chords. Within that same century, another monastery in Lhasa, the Gyuto Tantric College, was founded. The monks at this fellow tantric college also incorporated this chanting technique in their sacred rituals.

For centuries the magical sounds and rituals of Tibet lay enshrouded in the mysteries of a country refusing communication with the outside world. Stories of this unearthly chanting would filter back to the "civilized" world along with tales of seemingly superhuman abilities that the Tibetan monks were said to possess, but these seemed to be nothing more than myth.

In 1950 China invaded Tibet. Certain monks escaped to India, where they continued their tantric rituals. Their spiritual activities remained esoteric, but certain teachers of religion and ethnomusicology were finding their tantric rituals somewhat more accessible. These scientists and scholars would come back to the West with reports of a remarkable chanting technique utilized by the Gyume and Gyuto monks.

One of the most startling descriptions of Tibetan chanting came from Huston Smith, Ph.D., a Tibetan scholar, who reported in the film *Requiem for a Faith:*

> They discovered ways, we still don't know how, of shaping their vocal cavities to resonate overtones to the point where these became audible as distinct tones in their own right. So each lama thus trained could sing chords by themselves. They are singing D, F#, and A simultaneously. The religious significance of this phenomenon derives from the fact that overtones awaken numinous fields, sensed without being explicitly heard. They stand in exactly the same relationship to our hearing as the sacred stands to our ordinary mundane lives. Since the object of worship is to shift the sacred from peripheral to focal awareness, the vocal capacity to elevate overtones from subliminal to focal awareness carries symbolic power. For the object of the spiritual quest is precisely this; to experience life as replete with overtones that tell of a reality that can be sensed but not seen, sensed but not said, heard but not explicit.

The tantric chanting Smith is describing cannot adequately be described in words; it must be experienced in order to be understood. To hear the monks chant in their growling voices, with the seemingly falsetto overtones accompanying, is one of the most powerful sonic experiences imaginable.

Musicologists later determined that the bass note that the Gyuto monks chant is two octaves below middle C, vibrating at an astounding 75.5 cycles per second. The deepest range of an opera singer is closer to 150 cycles per second, nearly twice as high as the extraordinary bass of these monks. This first note seems to be a subharmonic or an undertone of a note that is an octave below the fundamental tone. The monks also create another very distinct note, a harmonic that is two octaves and a third higher than that bass note, making an E. The 5th and the 10th harmonics are also pronounced but less distinct. The Gyume monks create a different distinct "second voice" in their chanting, a harmonic that is two octaves and a fifth higher than their lowest note, making a G.

The Gyuto monks practice the *mdzo skad* or "voice of the hybrid yak-bull." This enables soloists to sing in parallel thirds. The Gyume monks practice the *gshin rje'i ngar skad* or "roaring voice of the Slayer of the Lord of Death." Solo chanters can sing by themselves in parallel fifths using this voice.

In Tibetan tantric chanting the goal of the chanting is to invoke and then unite with a particular deity or being. The monks literally become the gods and goddesses to whom they are praying. It may be that the overtones that are pronounced by the different tantric colleges are specific invocations to particular entities.

The exact reason why the monks of the Gyume and Gyuto monasteries use the voice given to Je Tzong Sherab Senge remains a mystery. But there are a number of theories. As Huston Smith suggested, the monks may use this voice to shift their awareness from the mundane to the spiritual. The abbot of the Gyuto Monastery indicated that the voice was utilized in order to represent the masculine and feminine aspects of Yama, the Slayer of Death. Another source claims that the voice was created in order to disguise the words of the sacred text being chanted. Dr. Alfred Tomatis, an otolaryngologist from France who has studied chanting throughout the world, believes that due to the high altitude of Tibet it was necessary to chant in the extremely deep voice in order to create higher overtones. Ethnomusicologist Peter Michael Hamel suggests that the voices are utilized to affect the chakras of the monks.

Terry Jay Ellingson has done extensive research into Tibetan chanting styles. In *The Mandala of Sound* he writes of the Gyume Tantric College:

> All monks are required to learn and use this special voice; perhaps somewhere over 60 percent were able to do so (it was said that those who couldn't just "sang quietly"). Several reasons are given for its use: First, it masks the words of the text from uninitiated listeners. Second, the simultaneous presence of several pitches in the sound creates the acoustic effect of transforming words into the three ritually important mantras Om Ah Hum, an explanation lent credency by Western acoustic analysis. Third, the special breathing technique, requiring conscious coordination of abdominal and diaphragm muscles and the resonating cavities of throat and head, may relate to Tantric meditation and yoga, which emphasizes coordination of "wheels" or chakras in these body areas via breath related energies. Fourth, this style of voice produced is symbolically associated with "Rdo rje' Jigs byed," the special Yi dam deity of the Lower Tantric College. Since he represents Buddhist teaching and practice in the form in which it "slays" Death and since Tantric practice aims at realizing the presence of the deity in one's own self, chanting with "his" voice helps to develop qualities that allow one to overcome death. On a more phenomenal level, since he is visualized with a bull's head (the South Asian water buffalo), the sound of the chanting is "like a bull."

THE ONE VOICE CHORD AND HOOMI SINGING

Comparisons are often made between the One Voice Chord of Tibetan chanting and the hoomi or throat-singing style found in the Tuvic region of Mongolia. This is natural since these two traditions are foremost in their use of harmonics as an integral part of their sacred sounding.

The Kargiraa style of Mongolian overtone chanting is characterized by an extremely low fundamental pitch sung with much resonance deep in the chest. Using vowel sounds, singers produce the low pitch and create harmonics two and a half to three and a half octaves above that note. The major difference between the Tibetan chanting style and Mongolian overtone singing is that the Tibetans incorporate the use of sacred text in their chanting while the Mongolians create wordless melodies with their harmonics.

There is conjecture by some researchers that the One Voice Chord may have developed from the Mongolian style of harmonic chanting. Tibetan Buddhist monks and monasteries were present in Mongolia until the late 1920s. There is also other research to suggest that the Tibetan chanting style may have developed from the Bon tradition.

Before Buddhism became the religion of Tibet, the religion of the country was an animistic shamanic practice known as "Bon" (a Tibetan word meaning "to chant"). Little information exists about the exact nature of the Bon chanting techniques, but there are indications that it was similar to chanting styles utilized by Mongolian shamans in which open vowels were used to create harmonics.

According to Terry Jay Ellingson, in *The Mandala of Sound,* the Bon chanting style "seems to have made use of sound modification based upon vowel changes in sequence of meaningless syllables—that is, it may have included tone-color elements similar to those found in modern Buddhist chants."

Padmasambhava, the Tibetan spiritual figure who initiated Buddhism into Tibet in the ninth century, wrote in one of his sacred Buddhist texts: "Vocalize with the chanting style of the earlier Holy Ones, the Bon, the clear high voice that is produced in a low place, like the black dog's barking."

This sounds like a description of a chanting style in which high overtones are created from a deep fundamental. Padmasambhava warned that chanting in the One Voice Chord without creating words invoked the voice and energies of the Bon. He gave instructions to the Tibetan followers of the Tantric tradition that the chanting style of the Bon was permissible as long as the purity of the holy words was not lost.

Without the chanting of the sacred scriptures, the sound degenerated into the wordless, melodic chant of the Bon magical tradition.

When the Gyuto monks were touring the United States in 1985, I talked with the head abbot of the Gyuto Monastery and played a recording of the Harmonic Choir for him. This New York–based group sings wordless melodies created by emphasizing the harmonics found in the vowels they chant. As he listened to the recording, the abbot seemed amused. After the recording was over, he said: "Very interesting, but where are the words?" It was later that I realized that the sounds he had heard may have seemed much like the meaningless chanting of Bon shamans to him.

Tibetan chanting employs mantric formulas that make up their sacred texts. These are mantras that are fundamental to their spiritual practices. Each sacred scripture is an invocation to a specific deity or a collection of deities. The chanters visualize these deities while creating a mandala, a circular cosmological painting that they inwardly visualize in archetypal symbols. These mandalas may involve over 150 deities and entities, all in specific placement. This combination of vocalization and visualization allows the monks to become the embodiment of the energies they are invoking.

The Tibetan Buddhist path to self-realization involves the understanding of the Three Mysteries. These are the Mysteries of Body, Speech, and Mind, whose experience has been condensed into the mantric formula OM-AH-HUM. Speech is the interconnector between the Mind and the Body. Speech is the understanding of sound as the creative force and incorporates the knowledge of using mantra as a sacred tool for summoning the appearance of gods and the forces of the universe. Through the creation of several tones at the same time, the One Voice Chord may be a further condensation of the Three Mysteries into an expression of Body, Speech, and Mind as pure tone.

CREATING THE ONE VOICE CHORD

How the Gyuto and Gyume monks create the remarkable sound of the One Voice Chord remains a mystery. As I have described, I had the opportunity to spend time with monks from both the Gyuto and Gyume Tantric Universities when they separately toured the United States in 1985 and 1986. Despite my best efforts, the monks would not divulge information about their chanting techniques. I had not been initiated into their teachings and was therefore unable to receive this information.

Sometimes when the knowledge is not known, the theories become extreme. A guide who was traveling with the Gyuto monks told an interested group of people at a performance that the monks were able to develop their technique by attaching a piece of meat to a string and swallowing it. The monks would then practice chanting with the meat in their throats. A year later someone who had heard the story asked the abbot of the Gyume Monastery about this. Hearing the question from the interpreter, the monks burst into laughter. The abbot replied that it was not a matter of swallowing meat. It was a matter of practice.

Practice was something I had tried for some time in order to gain the Tibetan One Voice Chord, but it had not seemed to work. I had been fascinated by the extraordinary sound since I had first heard it years before, but nothing I had tried seemed to be effective in allowing me to create the same sounds. I had strained my vocal cords attempting to learn the technique, but to no avail. I had even tried whistling while toning a deep sound. The One Voice Chord would not come no matter what I did.

One night, it was my privilege to record the Gyume monks in a recording studio for the first time in history. I went home that night with a cassette of these sacred chants. After listening to these tantric harmonics for some time in my meditation room, I fell asleep.

The next morning when I awoke, the sounds of the monks were reverberating within me. As I often did, I attempted to duplicate this sound. This time, however, instead of a half-hearted sound, the One Voice Chord emerged from my throat. It has been with me ever since, but though I can create it, I cannot tell you exactly how I am able to make this sound. Peter Michael Hamel, in *Through Music to the Self,* writes of the Tibetan One Voice Chord:

> It should be stressed that this remarkable sound is in no sense vocal acrobatics; rather, the chords are produced when the structural

> connection of sound, breathing and mind is transformed by the performance of the sadhana. ["Sadhana" is the recitation of a meditation during which the adepts unite with the deity they are invoking.]

In *The Mandala of Sound,* Terry Jay Ellingson writes of the Tibetan chanting technique:

> It seems to be produced by a special method of tensing some throat muscles while relaxing others to allow very low frequency, high amplitude vibrations of the vocal cords when strong breath pressure is applied by special coordination and effort of upper and lower body muscles.

While I am adept at giving instruction on other methods of harmonic chanting, the Tibetan One Voice Chord is not something I have thus far taught via technique. I create a growl-like sound at the back of my throat, as deep and as low as possible without strain. My vocal cords are very relaxed. If there is any constriction in the throat, the sound stops there. In order to properly create the Tibetan voice, I next project the sound as deeply as I can into my diaphragm and lung area. It sometimes feels like the sound is reaching all the way to my stomach. I believe this is how the subharmonic, that tone an octave below the fundamental, is created. The sound comes up from the deepest part of my diaphragm and reaches my throat again. I then tense my cheeks and purse my lips as the voice comes out of my mouth.

The voice appears to be a gift I received by being with the monks. In Tibetan Buddhism, it is said to be the result of making an offering to the Buddha on a conch shell in a past life. I do not know. In my own dreams, I recall a meeting with the monks in which I was given the voice. During this dreamtime experience, I was told never to misuse the voice for ego or attention. It is perhaps an extraordinary example of harmonic transmission, a musical power that is transferred directly to a student due to being in the vibratory presence of an expert.

Later I discovered that the way the Tibetan monks learned to create this voice was by being in the presence of other monks who already had the voice. Perhaps this is the way the voice has been passed down since Je Tzong Sherab Senge first heard it in a dream 500 years ago.

Part of the methodology in the tantric colleges for teaching the One Voice Chord is to have the younger monks chant with the older monks who have developed this voice. Through association, they are able to learn to project sound to the deepest part of the lungs and the diaphragm. Then, if their throat chakras are sufficiently opened, they can begin to establish this sound.

As Robert Thurman, professor of Indo-Tibetan studies at Columbia University, has stated:

> The young monks sing with a master, learning to imitate his sound. However, it is not considered possible to achieve the technique mechanically. They train simultaneously in all aspects of the dharma. The particular realization which makes multiphonic singing possible is the meditation on selflessness. Only those who have reached a certain stage in this meditation can become open enough to be vessels of this sound. The sound is produced by persons, who while present, are aware on a level in which they are not present. The sound is coming through them and not from them.

The Tibetan monks believe that in the creation of the One Voice Chord, the monks do not "make" the sound. Rather, they become a vehicle through which the sacred sound may manifest. This is a basic principle contained in the Tibetan Buddhist teachings of sacred sound. The chanting of the Gyuto and Gyume monks embodies this understanding of sound, and their powerful multiphonic chanting exemplifies the application of this principle. The harmonics that they create are a result of their becoming one with sacred sound.

SIX
HARMONICS AND MEDITATION
Listening as Transformation

LISTENING AND HEARING

When you first become aware of harmonics as a phenomenon of sound, your entire way of listening becomes altered. You may hear harmonics in the dripping of a tap or overtones in the wind as it rushes past your window. As you become aware of harmonics, your listening patterns change and, as this occurs, so does your consciousness.

Listening is one of the great active experiences in which we can easily learn to partake. It is one that we are quite naturally born to do, although unfortunately it is an ability that many of us lose as we grow older. Hearing is a passive experience in which sounds may or may not be received and perceived by the ear and then sent into the brain for stimulation. Listening is not passive. It is active.

Tomatis

Alfred Tomatis, M.D., is a French physician and specialist in otolaryngology who has been working with understanding the functions of the human ear and the importance of listening for forty-five years. He explains the three main functions of the ear: (1) to assume balance (equilibrium, body tone, and integration of motor and sensory information); (2) to analyze and decode movements from outside the body (cochlea) and inside the body (vestibular) so that auditory-vocal control is established; and (3) to charge the brain.

Tomatis believes that there are two kinds of sound: (1) sounds that tire and fatigue the listeners, and (2) sounds that "charge" the listener. In particular, Tomatis found that sounds that contain high-frequency harmonics, such as those found in Gregorian chants, are extremely beneficial. It is these high frequencies (around 8,000 Hz) that are capable of charging the central nervous system and the cortex of the brain.

In order to help his clients learn to listen more actively, Tomatis invented an instrument called the "Electronic Ear," which uses headphones and a filter to allow listeners to relearn to hear high-frequency sounds. By listening to recordings that are high in upper partials, such as those recordings recommended in our discography, we have found that many of the sacred chants of the different traditions are full of high-frequency overtones that offer stimulation to the brain. Part of the Tomatis Method also involves teaching clients how to utilize the high harmonic frequencies found in their own voice.

Tomatis discovered the therapeutic effects of high-frequency chanting after the leaders of a Benedictine monastery approached him for help. After the Second Vatican Council, the new abbot of the monastery felt that the six to eight hours of chanting that the monks engaged in served no useful purpose, and the chanting ceased. Within a short period of time, the monks became fatigued and depressed.

Various physicians were called in to remedy the situation, but with little effect. One well-known French doctor examined the monks and decided they were in this state because they were undernourished. This doctor decided that the almost completely vegetarian diet that the monks ate was bad for them, and he prescribed a basic meat-and-potatoes diet. This M.D. had apparently forgotten that the monks had basically eaten as vegetarians since the twelfth century and had been able to keep up their rigorous lifestyle without any previous problems. The monks ate meat and potatoes and became worse.

Finally, Dr. Tomatis was called in. Tomatis discovered that the monks had stopped their daily practice of Gregorian chanting. Without the therapeutic and charging effect of their chanting, the monks were unable to continue their rigorous schedule of work and prayer. Once Tomatis reestablished their daily chanting, the monks were soon able to return to their twenty-hour workdays.

Dr. Tomatis believes that one of the basic functions of the ear is to provide, through sound, both a charging of the cortex of the brain and 90–95 percent of the body's total charge. Gregorian chants, according to Tomatis, "contain all the frequencies of the voice spectrum, roughly 70 cycles per second up to 9,000 cycles per second." These are also the frequencies found in the One Voice Chord of the Tibetan monks, as well as in many of the hoomi or vocal harmonic techniques discussed in this book.

Dr. Tomatis stated in an interview published in *About the Tomatis Method* that, in particular,

> The most important range for this activity is between 2,000 and 4,000 cycles per second, or the upper part of the speaking range. It is this range which gives timbre to the voice, whereas the lower frequencies are used simply for the semantic system.

For Tomatis, a major aspect of the therapeutic effects of vocal harmonics lies in the conduction of the bones, which are stimulated by resonance of around 2,000 Hz. He says:

> The sound produced is not in the mouth, not in the body, but, in fact, in the bones. It is all the bones of the body which are singing and it's like a vibrator exciting the walls of the church, which also sing.

Bone conduction actually amplifies the sound through resonance of the cranium and the skull. According to Tomatis, bone conduction stimulates the stapes, a tiny bone in the ear, which he believes is a key to stimulating and charging the brain. Tomatis states that four hours per day of either listening to sounds rich in high harmonic frequencies or in creating your own correct sound is sufficient to charge the brain. Tomatis himself manages with a small amount of sleep, less than four hours a night. He attributes this to his listening to sounds that are rich in high harmonics.

Tomatis has described a phenomenon that has been called the

"Tomatis Effect." The Tomatis Effect states that the voice can only create and duplicate those sounds that the ear is able to hear. This means that until you are able to hear various overtones, you will not be able to create them in your voice. Further, as you begin to hear the various aspects of the sound spectrum, not only does your hearing change, but your voice as well. Therefore, as we begin to listen actively and open our ears up to harmonics, we are not only charging the cortex of the brain and energizing ourselves, but we are also able to actually change the quality of our voice. David Hykes, the founder of the Harmonic Choir and the person who is responsible for bringing awareness of overtones as an artform to the West, had this to say about harmonics and listening in the program notes of a Harmonic Choir concert:

> Is there a way to re-open the idea of listening in the world? What would be BETTER LISTENING? By listening better to the sound of life, rather than shutting it out, we are led to search for a harmonizing force appearing in the hollow din of our situation. That will be a second listening and there are many more; they come from silence. There are levels of listening and one leads upward toward the next. Viewed in this undivided way, Harmonic Music is the source stream of essential human and musical facts relating the laws of vibration inside and out.

Listening is undoubtedly a key, not only in obtaining the ability of creating vocal harmonics, but of understanding aspects of other levels of consciousness. In the Hindu tradition there is a great awareness of listening as a tool for enhanced consciousness, an understanding of the *Shabda,* the "sound current," which can be ridden like a flying horse to other planes of existence. This is accomplished through meditation on sound.

INNER AND OUTER SOUND

In the Vedic language of Sanskrit, there is a differentiation between inner and outer sound. There is audible sound, called "*ahata.*" This is also called struck sound and is the result of vibration on the physical plane. There is also the *"anahata,"* the inaudible, inner sounds that are not the result of some physical vibration, but rather are "unstruck." Almost everybody can hear "ahata." However, "anahata" can be perceived and experienced only by advanced meditation practitioners.

I have always wondered if harmonics might not somehow be the bridge between "ahata" and "anahata," the struck and the unstruck sound. The fundamental may be the struck sound, but the harmonics that are created do not occur from having been physically struck. Perhaps they are the bridge between the physical and the metaphysical.

Spiritual teachers have indicated that the last statement is true; overtones are the link between that which is created on the physical plane and that which is created on higher planes. Pir Vilayat Khan, head of the Sufi Order of the West, said that the overtones can be followed with the conscious mind and used as a "Jacob's Ladder" to climb to other planes of existence.

Similarly, the psychic Kaimora said in trance that harmonics were the sounds connecting the seven levels of existence: physical, astral, causal, mental, as well as three other planes. Harmonics could be utilized to connect a person to these levels through vocally creating these sounds or listening to them.

HARMONICS AND MEDITATION

Listening to harmonics is an excellent key to meditation. The sonorous bell and whistle-like tones that are created by various harmonic singers allow us the opportunity to open up to another level of consciousness. These are sounds within sounds that we can begin to perceive when we expand our listening in this manner.*

Nigel Charles Halfhide, an overtone singer from Europe, writes:

> What is perceived by the human ear as timbre turns out on closer examination to be the reflection on a universal principle. This

*In the discography, a number of excellent recordings are listed that may be useful for meditation and listening purposes. These feature, for the most part, different overtone singers creating vocal harmonics and are excellent sources of sound.

> principle, the overtone series, forms the smallest constituents from which sound is made up. It is not restricted to musical phenomena but can be found in every kind of sound.

As mentioned earlier in this book, the first time I listened to *Hearing Solar Winds* by the Harmonic Choir in that crowded hotel lobby in Washington, D.C., I either fell asleep or was transported to another realm of consciousness. Subsequent listenings produced similar experiences. There was something that happened when I listened to the vocal harmonics found on that recording that created a powerful transformative effect upon me. Many others also seem to have been affected by these sounds. Robert Palmer, writing of *Hearing Solar Winds* in the *New York Times* stated:

> The listener hears what sound like huge, ghostly orchestras of string instruments, celestial choirs, lush banks of french horns and reeds. . . . Sooner or later, one's attention wanders, and when one focuses on the music again, suddenly the voices of Mr. Hykes and his six singers have been transformed into the sighing of a huge distant orchestra, or the droning hum of a celestial choir. Startled, one begins to listen more closely. And the more one listens, the more one learns to hear.

According to Dr. Alfred Tomatis, nearly all the cranial nerves lead to the ear. In particular, the ear is understood to be neurologically involved with the optic and the oculomotor nerves, and therefore is interrelated with the process of vision and movement. The ear is also related to the vagus, or tenth cranial nerve. This nerve affects the larynx, the bronchi, the heart, and the gastrointestinal tract and thus our voice, our breathing, our heart rate, and our digestion are affected by the ear. Is it any wonder then that on a purely physiological level listening to the soothing music created by the sacred sounds of vocal harmonics can and will help create states of deep relaxation and meditation?

It is important to point out that while this chapter does not specifically focus upon "healing," the health benefits of relaxation and meditation are well known by those in both the holistic and allopathic medical professions. The relationship between the body and the mind has been explored in many remarkable books. Through meditation and relaxation, it may be possible to alleviate many different medical problems including heart disease, stroke, and imbalances of the immunological system. There is, in fact, a new field of medicine called psychoneuroimmunology, which is dedicated exclusively to this mind/body connection.

The Relaxation Response

Mark Ryder, Ph.D., of Southern Methodist University, found that people who listened to the music of the Harmonic Choir, as opposed to other types of music, showed decreased heart rate, respiration, and galvanic skin response. As we have indicated, merely by listening to music that is high in harmonic content we can:

1. Charge the cortex of the brain
2. Reduce respiration and heart rate
3. Lower brainwave activity

By actually creating vocal harmonics we can also achieve this phenomenon, called "the Relaxation Response" by Herbert Benson, M.D. He investigated the effects of mantras on physiology. What he found was that the repetition of a single word would produce a measurable effect: a decrease in the body's oxygen consumption and respiration rate, a decrease in the heartbeat by an average of three beats per minute, and a decrease in pulse rate and rate of metabolism. There was also an increase in alpha waves.

While no one has yet researched the effects of creating vocal harmonics, Mark Ryder found that people who toned elongated vowels experienced a greater relaxation response than did people who merely listened to the sound of recorded harmonic music. As has been previously discussed, different vowel sounds create different harmonics. Toning elongated vowels is a simplified method of beginning to create vocal overtones.

There seem to be two direct paths of working with harmonics as a tool for meditation. The first involves the power of pure listening. We listen to the sounds of the harmonics and travel on these sounds to other realms of consciousness. The second involves the power of sounding coupled with the power of listening. We create the harmonics and then travel on these self-created sounds to those other realms of consciousness.

LISTENING AND SILENCE

An excellent place to begin the first path is to work with the energy of silence. Honoring this energy allows us to come to a place of stillness. In silence, it is possible to perceive all sounds that can be created. Sitting in silence enables us to begin to know the inner symphony that is ourselves. If you have tried to sit in this way, you will know that there really is no silence. We are truly a celestial orchestra filled with sound; the heartbeat, respiration, circulatory system, auditory system, nervous system, and brainwaves all create myriad sounds that we can become aware of through silence. When we sit in this manner, we also become aware of externally created sounds. We notice nature sounds, such as birds chirping or the wind blowing, and perhaps electrical sounds, such as the 60-cycle hum of lights or refrigerators.

I have found that one of the fastest ways of altering consciousness is to sit silently for a few moments. As we begin to tune in to the inner and outer sounds we truly change the way our everyday perception works. We are altering the auditory system and our brainwaves as well. As we open to hearing these sounds that we may have been tuning out or ignoring, it is very easy to expand our awareness of who we are and where we are. Sitting in silence is the basis of much sound yoga meditation. Silence is the beginning of this work and also the end.

Listening is an active activity, as opposed to hearing, which may be understood as a passive activity. Listening involves really using our ears as an organ of consciousness. When we hear, we do not discriminate between the sounds around us. We may be unaware of them. This is why sitting in silence allows us to empower listening. There are many levels of listening. The first level involves this enormous step of going above the passiveness of hearing into the activeness of actually listening and becoming aware of the multitude of sounds that surround us. Through listening we can begin to open up to sound.

More than anything else, the ear is an organ that actually shields us from the myriad sounds in the universe. Our hearing range is somewhere between 16 Hz and 16,000 Hz. This is, of course, a broad range but it gives us some indication of the limited range of normal hearing. While we may not be aware of them, there are hundreds, perhaps thousands of sounds above and below that range that may be bombarding us every second of the day. Yet, while they exist, we don't hear them. Most animals have hearing that far surpasses ours. They seem to be aware of sounds that we can't perceive. Bats, for example, use a sophisticated method of sonar to hunt and locate prey. Dolphins can send and perceive sounds up to nearly 200,000 Hz. Elephants seem to utilize an extremely low frequency, far below our level of hearing, for forms of communication and mating rituals.

What would happen if we could open our ears to the incredible levels of vibrations that exist? It is quite possible that they would be too much for us to endure. This is why the ears may be shielding and protecting us.

Listening to Audible Sounds

This first level of listening involves our opening up to the levels of sound that are within the audible range. By becoming aware of sounds that we may not have heard before, we allow ourselves to become greater vehicles for the sound current. A common example of this is a psychoacoustic phenomenon called "the Cocktail Party" effect.

You may be in a crowded party with everyone talking at about the same sound level, yet you can communicate with one person, although there may be three or four conversations occurring at the same time. The ear has the unique ability of focusing on sounds in this manner. Another example of this takes place at the same party. Have you ever been engaged in an intense conversation at a party and suddenly you hear your name? You turn and find out that someone next to you has mentioned you in their conversation. They were not speaking any more loudly, but for some reason you were able to hear your name. Our attentiveness to our name caused us to unconsciously go from the passive act of hearing to the activity of listening.

Listening to Harmonics

A second level of listening involves the perception of harmonics in the sounds we are hearing. This began to occur quite frequently with me when I first became aware of harmonics. I would be sitting somewhere and become aware of a sound I had not initially heard—perhaps water dripping in a sink or the hum of an electrical appliance. Then I would become aware of the sounds of the harmonics being created. This altered my consciousness as I began to tune into these sounds within sounds.

Since harmonics exist as a phenomenon whenever sounds are being created, it is quite likely that there is a world full of harmonics that you have been missing. Once you become aware of harmonics, you really do have the ability of perceiving the sounds in the universe differently. They will be the same sounds as before and yet they will be different; they will be full of overtones. The sound spectrum may be changed forever once you begin to perceive in this manner. It will seem like you can go deeper into the sound and understand more about it.

Harmonics and the Imagination

A third level of listening involves the use of imagination. We often do this naturally when we listen to certain pieces of music that seem to take us places. Helen Bonny, Ph.D., has created an entire genre of therapy based upon this ability. She calls this therapy "Guided Imagery in Music." It is based upon the premise that certain pieces of music will elicit certain responses that enable listeners to travel deeply into their own consciousness. Bonny believes that such traveling can be as powerful a mind-altering experience as a psychotropic drug, with none of the dangers that are attached to drug-induced altered states.

When working with harmonics, it becomes very easy to use our imagination, for harmonics will quite naturally elicit such responses, especially when listening to harmonic singers. Ethereal sounds such as bells or the voices of angels are commonly heard and experienced by listeners.

Transforming Reality through Sound

A fourth level of listening involves transforming the physical plane reality of the sound to an alternative reality, traveling to other planes of existence on the sound. Each level of listening involves utilizing the other levels and, of course, this level cannot be achieved without use of our imagination. In his book *Music and Sound in the Healing Arts,* John Beaulieu, N.D., Ph.D., gives a wonderful example of this:

> I was walking down a New York street with two friends. The trucks were idling, and the workers were unloading crates. Something about the sound of the trucks caught my attention. I asked my friends if they would be willing to watch out for my safety while I sat down and listened more deeply to the sounds of the trucks.
>
> I sat in a safe spot and allowed my body and mind to relax. The sounds of the trucks formed a distinct rhythm: da-da-daa—boom, da-da da-da-daa—boom, etc. I let myself go with the sound. At first I imagined being a teenager in Indiana and going to the drag races and listening to the sound of the engines idle. I remembered how these sounds fascinated me, and I imagined driving a race car.
>
> Listening even deeper to the sound I felt myself "move inside" its pulse. My imagination and memories were still present, now accompanied by a new sensation. A profound quietness or stillness came and, for a moment, I experienced myself just being the sound.
>
> Then there was a shift in my awareness, and I found myself with a group of Aborigine chanters. They were communicating a message about "dream time." I was just as clearly with them as I had been with the truck just a few minutes ago. I allowed myself to absorb their message. An old man signaled that they must move on into the desert. I understood.
>
> At that moment, a friend tapped me on the shoulder, I came back to the reality of a New York City street. The truck was driving away.

John's experience is an excellent example of these different levels of listening. In this fourth level, he became the sound and was able to travel on it. Most interesting, as well, is his experience with the Australian Aboriginal people. As mentioned on page 59, when the didjeridoo was sounded, it would create an interdimensional sonic window that would allow the Wandjina to come through and let those who heard the sound travel to the Wandjina. John's journey with the sound of the truck parallels this use of the didjeridoo, for he was able to use the deeper levels of listening as a means of traveling on the sound current.

Becoming one with the sound is a key to meditation with sound. It allows the Tibetan monks to create their One Voice Chord. Sound is not viewed as a physical phenomenon created by the vocal cords, but rather as a living energy that may manifest through those attuned to become vehicles for it. It involves use of the imagination as well as a total letting go of control and surrendering to trust. If we try to control the sound as opposed to becoming the sound, we can never achieve this next level.

Another example of this level of listening could involve something as mundane as the sound of your refrigerator. First you might become aware that the refrigerator is creating sound. Then, as you listen to the sounds you might become aware of the harmonics being created by the refrigerator. Then you might use your imagination to hear these sounds, not as a refrigerator, but as a group of monks chanting a "rolling om." Finally, you could actually become this sound and travel with it to another plane or dimension.

When listening to harmonics on this fourth level, it is appropriate to say that one actually becomes one with the harmonics and travels to the source of the harmonics. This is easier said than done. Such a level of listening is a highly advanced form of meditation and not easily experienced. My own personal experiences on this fourth level have been rarer than I would like them to be. In these experiences, I have traveled interdimensionally and met with all sorts of celestial beings that seemed to have been the source of the sound: gods, goddesses, deities, spirits, etc. These certainly have been subjective encounters, but they have also been extremely transcendent and highly enjoyable experiences.

When I have listened on this level, without making sounds, I have usually traveled out of my body, as was the case when I first heard the Harmonic Choir. When I have sounded on this level, it is even more unique. In order to continue the sound, it is necessary to become the sound, travel on it and yet at the same time, still be the physical source of the sound. In other words, I cannot completely leave my body or else the physical sound would cease. Therefore, I am both in my body and out of it when sounding on this level. It is a unique experience and perhaps an example of bilocation, if not tri-location.

One thing that frequently occurs is the sensation that I am not creating the sound at all. Often, the sound seems to change and become impossible for a human being to create. At best I become aware that I am being sounded by some other energy or consciousness.

Silence and Meditation

A fifth level to meditate upon is silence. As we began in silence, so we end in silence. For all sound comes from silence and returns back to silence.

It is said that the creation of the universe occurred through sound. The creator moved/stirred/yawned/toned, and the various planes of existence were created. But before there was sound, there was silence. Through silence we can travel to the first source and back to the end of creation.

SUMMARY

In review, these are the levels that apply both for listening and creating harmonics:

1. Start in silence. Become aware of the inner sounds and the outer sounds.
2. Listen to a recording or sound on the first level, being purely aware of the physical aspects of sound.
3. Listen or sound on the second level, really becoming aware of the harmonics that you are hearing or creating.
4. Listen or sound on the third level, using your imagination with the harmonics you are hearing either from a recording or yourself.
5. Listen to or sound the harmonics on the fourth level, becoming one with the harmonics you are hearing and traveling to other realities.
6. End in silence, becoming aware of the inner and outer harmonics that are always there.

Meditation is a wonderful tool for enhanced relaxation and reduction of stress. Used in this fashion, it is an extraordinary means of maintaining health and balance. By reducing our heart rate, brain waves, and blood pressure we will be able to find balance with many of the stresses that modern-day living creates. Making sounds, particularly those that focus upon harmonics, is a very simple and easy way of achieving those results. By producing long, drawn-out sounds, we are breathing more slowly and reducing our heart rate and brain waves as well. Creating vocal harmonics by itself becomes a form of meditation.

Coupled with the intention of experiencing the different levels of sound, listening to or creating vocal harmonics elevates the meditational practice from the therapeutic to the transformational. David Hykes of the Harmonic Choir has written in the notes of their program:

> Harmonic Music, which on the whole seems to have been lost in our culture, might help us hear the state of things, were it to come to life. That is, music—the active understanding of the cosmic laws of harmony—may have a role to play in the effort needed globally to harmonize the current situation; not through proselytizing, but through calling for better listening, and thus, perhaps, helping to create conditions where people might hear an important message calling to them . . . within them.

When we listen or sound in this manner, our entire scope of consciousness changes. We begin to understand the interrelationship of ourselves and the cosmos, and we may find answers to previously unthought of questions. Barriers within ourselves disappear, as do those between ourselves and others. We begin to experience a "oneness" that helps us realize our interconnectedness with all things. This is an awareness that the spiritual masters from different paths have spoken of throughout time. It can be achieved through harmonics and sound.

SEVEN
HARMONICS AND HEALING
The Medicine of the Future

INTRODUCTION

The psychic Edgar Cayce predicted that sound would be the medicine of the future. As we examine some of these uses of sound for healing, we may find that the future is fast approaching us. Healing means to become whole or sound in body and mind. In this chapter, we will take a look at some sound therapies that specifically utilize harmonics in their work. Most of the different sound therapies utilize resonant harmonic frequencies.

While the use of sound for healing is extremely ancient, it has, for the most part, been restricted to spiritual and esoteric traditions. Within the past several decades,* however, the use of sound as a healing modality is coming more into focus in both the scientific and the medical communities. There now exist organizations such as the International Society for Music in Medicine and the Arts Medicine Association, which draw together doctors, scientists, and others working with sound as a therapeutic tool.

*Originally this read "Within the past decade . . ." but time frames have been updated to reflect the time that has passed since the earlier editions of this book.

HEALING AND RESONANCE

As we have discovered, there is a basic principle of using sound as a healing modality and this is the concept of resonance. Resonance is the basis of every sound therapy that I have examined. As you may recall, resonance is the basic vibratory rate of an object. Everything in the universe is in a state of vibration. This includes the human body. Every organ, bone, tissue, and other part of the body has a healthy resonant frequency. When that frequency alters, that part of the body vibrates out of harmony, and this is what is termed disease. If it were possible to determine the correct resonant frequency for a healthy organ and then project it into that part that is diseased, the organ should return to its normal frequency and a healing should occur.

CYMATIC THERAPY

One of the pioneers in using sound to heal is Peter Guy Manners, D.O. An English osteopath, Dr. Manners became aware of Dr. Jenny's cymatic experiments discussed in chapter 2 and learned of the extraordinary ability of sound to affect form. Since 1961 he has been engaged in research into the effects of sound upon the structure and chemistry of the human body.

Dr. Manners is the creator of cymatic therapy, which utilizes the Cymatic Instrument. For over twenty years, he has been treating various illnesses with sound. Working under the premise that disease is an "out of tuneness" of some aspect of the body, Dr. Manners has correlated different harmonic frequencies to the healthy resonant frequencies of different parts of the body. He states:

> A healthy organ will have its molecules working together in a harmonious relationship with each other and will all be of the same pattern. If different sound patterns enter into the organ, the harmonious relationship could be upset. If these frequencies are weak in their vibration, they will be overcome by the stronger vibrations of the native ones. If the foreign ones prove to be the stronger, on the

> other hand, they may establish their disharmonious pattern in the organ, bone, tissue, etc., and this is what we call disease.
>
> If, therefore, a treatment contains a harmonic frequency pattern that will reinforce the organs, the vibrations of the intruder will be neutralized and the correct pattern for that organ reestablished. This should constitute a curative reaction.

The Cymatic Instrument is composed of a portable computer, which is about the size of a briefcase, and a sound generator that resembles a hammer-like vibrator.

The harmonics of the Cymatic Instrument are tabulated and reconstructed by computer, and the corrected frequency is then projected directly into the affected area. The harmonics from the Cymatic Instrument are a composite of five different frequencies that Dr. Manners has found most effective for creating sounds that heal the human body. These sounds from the Cymatic Instrument are very different from the vocal harmonics we have been discussing in this book. They are electronically created and are really single tones. Yet they are harmonics of the calibrated frequency of the human body. They are usually octaves of this frequency, brought up many, many times in order to put the sound into the audible level, or brought down many, many times. Nevertheless, as tones that are octaves of a tone (whether this fundamental is in the ELF range or ultrasonic), these tones can technically be called "harmonics."

The Cymatic Instrument contains calculations for literally thousands of different composite harmonics designed to place the body back into alignment and health. There are the frequencies for every organ in the body and for specific diseases. There are also frequencies for emotional and mental problems. Some imbalances treated with cymatic therapy include: anemia, asthma, colitis, constipation, diabetes, eczema, glaucoma, heart disease, hernias, kidney disease, multiple sclerosis, sciatica, sleeping sickness, syphilis, and tonsillitis. If the theory of resonant frequency healing is correct, there would be few, if any, illnesses that could not be effectively treated with sound.

Cymatic therapy is but one of the new sound-related therapies that are being utilized for healing. While there are many testimonials of people who have had extraordinary healings through this and other therapies, the hard scientific data needed for verification of these therapies is often lacking. A reason for this is that the proper research needed to collect data that is suitable for the traditional scientific and medical communities requires a lengthy and costly process. Many times grants and funding are needed, and sadly most organizations that give grants will not extend their finances to unproven methods—which is an example of a Catch-22, for how can one prove a method if the funding is not available?

Nevertheless, though adequate research is not presently available, this does not mean the various sound therapies do not work. I have talked with people who have experienced extraordinary transformations and healings through the use of different sound therapies. I have also witnessed amazing healings with sound therapies, particularly using vocal harmonics for healing, as described in chapter 10, "Overtoning."

Unfortunately, the video cameras are never running when these healings occur. It is hoped that in the near future, the necessary research for the validation of these sound healing modalities will take place. It is my belief that the emphasis of these studies should be on *why* they work, rather than if they work. This research would no doubt indicate the importance of resonance as a phenomenon in this process.

On first meeting Dr. Manners, I asked how the frequencies for the Cymatic Instrument were determined. He replied that many of the frequencies were scientifically determined but that others were the result of radionics, or radiesthesia. Radionics works with the premise that all matter radiates energy. This energy, which is not simply "magnetic" or "electric," operates at very subtle and refined levels of vibration. Using devices such as pendulums, which seem to swing back and forth in response to this energy, radionic practitioners have been able to determine frequencies for various parts of the body.

Dr. Manners stated that in actual laboratory tests the frequencies found for the liver, for example, match the frequencies given by radionic devices. The laboratory tests take several hours, while the use of a radionic device may take a few minutes.

THE LAMBDOMA AND HEALING

Another frequency-based healing modality that utilizes harmonics is Barbara Hero's Lambdoma frequencies. In our chapter on the science of harmonics, we briefly discussed the Lambdoma diagram. The Lambdoma is a mathematical table that is said to have been discovered by the master Pythagoras and saved from destruction by his disciple Iamblichus.

Barbara Hero was a mathematician and artist who worked with the Lambdoma for over forty years. She believed that the Lambdoma is actually a formula for healing with sound, and she created a series of recordings designed to balance and resonate the chakras based upon these frequencies. The chakras are subtle centers of energy located along the center of the body. They align with the spinal column. Different esoteric traditions believe that the energy that affects the physical body comes from the chakras. Scientists are now attempting to validate the existence of the chakras, as well as another subtle energy system, the meridians, which are the basis of acupuncture. Imbalances in chakras are said to affect the physical body. Balancing the chakras may therefore balance and heal problems in the physical body.

When I first listened to and experienced Barbara's Lambdoma sounds, I thought they were quite interesting, though I don't know if I was attuned enough to feel any effect from them. I was impressed by their synthesized sounds, which were single tones moving up and down the scale. I was also intrigued by how these frequencies might have been calculated. My former wife, Karen, is much more sensitive than I am. During her experience listening to the Lambdoma frequencies, she actually felt her chakras being affected and balanced by the specific sounds. Many others who have worked with Barbara Hero's Lambdoma frequencies also report beneficial results.

When I investigated the Lambdoma frequencies, I found that they were all harmonically related. In fact, the Lambdoma diagram is nothing more or less than a table of ratios based upon the overtones. The sounds that Barbara had recorded were simply harmonically related frequencies. It seems quite possible that the chakras are harmonically related and that they do respond to harmonically related frequencies.

Many scientists, including Izthak Bentov, author of *Stalking the Wild Pendulum,* believe that the etheric fields of the body, such as the astral and mental, are all harmonically related to each other. The chakras and the physical body are also understood to have this harmonic relationship.

THE HUMAN VOICE AND HEALING

Thus far, the harmonics we have been discussing in this chapter have all been electronically created sounds either recorded or projected out of the end of an instrument. But what of the harmonics that we can produce with our voice?

During my first meeting with Dr. Manners, I told him about a technique called "overtoning." In this process, described in chapter 10, the voice can be used to scan the physical or etheric body of a person and then project vocal harmonics into that person. I had seen many remarkable healings from this technique and asked Dr. Manners if this was not similar to the use of the Cymatic Instrument. He replied that indeed it was. He felt, however, that the medical community would be more interested in an instrument that projected sound rather than having a person making strange sounds to another person.

In theory, anything that can be done with a machine can be done with the human voice, and probably better. This is especially true when you contemplate the importance of "Frequency + Intention = Healing." When using your voice, it is quite easy to focus upon the intention that you are sending. It sometimes becomes more difficult to remember to do this when you are pressing keys on a synthesizer or programming a numerical sequence into a computer.

BALANCING THE CHAKRAS WITH THE VOICE

The use of the voice to balance and align chakras has been part of Hindu Ayurvedic medicine for thousands of years. This application of sound is usually practiced through recitation of mantras. However, there are harmonically related vocal sounds that also work on the chakras. The use of vowel sounds, for example, is discussed at length in chapter 8 and elsewhere in this book. There are also other applications for using harmonically related sounds to affect the chakras.

McClellan's System

Randall McClellan, Ph.D., author of *The Healing Forces of Music,* created a system for balancing the chakras using the human voice. He suggested that a person sing notes that are harmonically related to each other. (This is not actually overtone chanting, but the principles are the same.) Thus a series of fundamental tones are being sung. McClellan suggested, "The use of the harmonic series does require at least a two octave vocal range. . . . The fundamental or first harmonic of the series, lying a full octave below our 2nd harmonic, is below our vocal range. We might consider this to be our fundamental."

In Randall McClellan's system the root chakra resonated by the fundamental of a note an octave higher than the first note (in the key of C, this would be a C); the second chakra resonated by a note (a G) a fifth higher than the previous note; the navel chakra resonated by another octave fundamental (a C); the heart chakra resonated by a note (an E) that is a major third above the last note; the throat chakra resonated by a note (a G) that is a fifth above the previous octave C note; the third eye chakra resonated by a note (B♭) that is a flattened seventh above the last octave C note; and the crown chakra resonated by a final octave note (a C). Thus the notes created from the first seven overtones are used to resonate the chakras.

Drawing upon the pitch relationship from the harmonic series, specifically the second, third, fourth, fifth, sixth, seventh, and eighth harmonic, we find that the natural relationship of the base of the spine, solar plexus and of the crown is reflected in the corresponding octave relationships of the second, fourth, and eighth harmonics of the overtone series (remember that the rate for the octave is 2:1) that are assigned to them. The relationship of the second chakra and the sixth chakra is reflected in the octave relationship that occurs between the third and sixth harmonics of the overtone series assigned to them. The heart chakra receives the fifth harmonic and the stabilizing effect of the major triad. The third eye receives the seventh harmonic.

When I first came upon McClellan's system, I had already done some experimentation myself in terms of chakra resonance and tones. Using a fundamental tone as the frequency to resonate my physical body, I found that the first overtone created could resonate my root chakra, the second overtone resonated the next chakra, the third overtone resonated the navel area, the fourth overtone resonated the heart chakra, the fifth overtone resonated the throat chakra, the sixth overtone resonated the third eye and the crown chakra was resonated by the third octave harmonic. This is an exercise that those who become proficient in the creation of vocal harmonics could practice and validate for themselves.

Gardner's System

Musician Kay Gardner, author of *Sounding the Inner Landscape,* has a system of harmonically related notes for chakra resonances that is relevant to this topic. Citing Peter Michael Hamel, author of *Through Music to the Self,* Kay states that Raga Saraswati is composed of (in the key of C) C, D, E, F#, G, A, and B♭. She further explains that these are the notes that would be created from the overtones within the first four octaves of a fundamental. Kay then relates the note C to the root chakra, the D to the second chakra, the E to the navel chakra, the F# to the heart chakra, the G to the throat chakra, the A to the third eye and the B♭ to the crown chakra.

When working with these tones to resonate chakras, Kay actually uses the fundamental and not the harmonics. Nevertheless, since they are composed of the notes found in the first four octaves of the harmonic series, we include them in this portion.

Stockhausen and Resonation of the Brain

Another potential healing use of harmonics involves the resonation of the brain with these sounds. Many people report being aware of vibrations in their heads when they create vocal harmonics. Sometimes they see light when their eyes are closed. Others indicate they can actually feel different parts of their brain being resonated by the harmonics. I too have experienced these sensations and more. I have always been intrigued by the possibility that the creation of vocal harmonics may be used to resonate and stimulate portions of the brain. This intrigue can be traced back to a recorded lecture I heard in 1984 on "Healing with Sound" by Pir Vilayat Khan, head of the Sufi Order in the West. In this lecture, Pir Vilayat related:

> I visited some time ago Stockhausen, who is a German composer . . . and he demonstrated at a meal his extraordinary skill in producing overtones. And he was able to produce something like twenty-eight overtones as clear as a bell. He said that he concentrates on a particular point in the brain above the palate for each overtone and that each overtone is placed higher up in an area within the brain.
>
> It occurred to me that you should be able to produce an overtone that is resonant with the specific resonance of the pituitary for example. You set the pituitary into action, which would immediately start secreting hormones which would have various effects. But you would have to know exactly what you are doing. It would be quite dangerous just to simply stir up the pituitary without specifically knowing which hormone. Is it going to be the growth hormone? Or is it going to be the gonad hormone or what is it going to be? So it's much more complex than that. But I'm just giving you an indication of the lines of research that will hopefully be followed up in the next decade.

Karlheinz Stockhausen is an avant-garde composer. He is also considered a mystic and visionary. Stockhausen was the first to compose music which he titled *Stimmung* (meaning "tuning"), created entirely for overtone singers. His influence in the growth of vocal harmonics has been great. Among his students were British overtone singer Jill Purce and German overtone singer Michael Vetter.

Stockhausen had these comments to make about his 1969 recording *Stimmung:*

> You will hear my work *Stimmung,* which is nothing for seventy-five minutes but one chord—it never changes—with the partials of natural harmonics on a fundamental, the fundamental itself isn't there, the second, the third, fourth, fifth, seventh, and ninth harmonics and nothing but that. . . . The singers needed six months just in order to learn precisely how to hit the ninth harmonic, or the tenth, eleventh, thirteenth, up to the twenty-fourth. . . . It's a wonderful technique to learn because you become so conscious of the different parts of the skull which are vibrating. If you met the singers, you'd see how as human beings, they've changed. They're completely transformed now that they've sung it more than a hundred times since the World's Fair in Osaka.

Stockhausen was able to observe physiological changes in the skulls of the singers he had trained to create vocal harmonics. The question remains: What exactly are these physiological changes? Are these changes restricted to the bones of the cranium or are there actual changes in the brain as well? If it is possible to resonate different portions of the brain through self-created sounds such as vocal harmonics, this seems a great deal safer than drilling a hole through the cranium and then attaching electrodes to the brain. This latter method is currently the only available way modern science can stimulate and directly affect the brain.

OTHER RESEARCH INTO OVERTONE CHANTING AND HEALING

Don Campbell, in *The Roar of Silence,* writes of the power of harmonic tones. His words apply both to sounds projected to the body and to the brain:

> The vowel sound that carries the vibration to the body determines the effect of the sonic charge. The pitch of the vowel sound determines the location of the epicenter. There is no other way to localize oxygenation, energy flow, and pulsation as noninvasively within such a short period of time.

In interviews, overtone singer Jill Purce has stated:

> Overtone chanting is extremely healing. . . . When you're doing overtone chanting you're beginning to differentiate mental and physiological processes that are not normally differentiated. This requires incredible concentration—you use parts of the brain that you don't normally use—and when you do that something else happens and you enter into the world of spirit.

Harmonics and Cranial/Brain Resonation

In presentations to various medical doctors and scientists I have often suggested the possibility of resonating different portions of the brain with vocal harmonics and the important need for research in this area. Thus far, there has been virtually no work regarding this. However, I have personally had some interesting experiences that seem to validate this use of harmonics to resonate the cranium and brain.

The Sound Healers Association is a nonprofit organization I founded that held meetings once a month featuring guest speakers who talked on their area of expertise about using sound and music as healing modalities. During October 1986 at a Sound Healers Association (SHA) meeting in Boston, our visiting guest was Dr. Harlan Sparer, a chiropractor from New York. Dr. Sparer talked of the uses of sound to affect the body and the brain. As part of his presentation, we conducted an experiment in which I began to tone other people harmonically while Harlan checked out their bones, in particular, those of the cranium. He found that the bones of the cranium were able to move when a subject was chanting vocal harmonics. This also occurred when someone else was toning the harmonics into the head of another person. While we experimented using only live sound, it seems quite likely that listening to recorded music of vocal harmonics would also have this effect.

According to Dr. Sparer, and later validated by Dr. John Beaulieu, harmonic toning seems to affect not only the cranium and the entire brain, but also the primary respiratory rate and the flow of cerebral spinal fluid through the cranium. The flow of cerebral spinal fluid may be the physical counterpart to the kundalini energy of the Eastern mystical traditions, discussed in chapter 8, "Vowels as Mantras." Cerebral spinal fluid seems to have an overall effect upon the health and wellness of an individual. A blockage in this flow can create imbalances in the physical body. The use of vocal harmonics may alleviate these imbalances and help restore energy and health to individuals.

Helga Rich

In 1985 I was a lecturer at the Fourth International Symposium on Music: Rehabilitation and Human Well-Being, being held at Goldwater Hospital in New York City. I had completed my lecture and was preparing to leave for a Medicine Wheel gathering being held in New England.

Before I caught a taxi to the airport, I decided to have lunch at the cafeteria where the symposium was being held. I bought a sandwich and a drink and sat down at a table. A woman was sitting opposite me and although I had not seen her before, I thought she might also be here for the symposium. I asked her about this and she replied, "Yes!" Her name was Helga Rich. She was a vocal instructor and a yoga teacher who had just arrived from Denmark to give a presentation that afternoon.

I asked Ms. Rich what she did and she told me that she worked with sound to help patients suffering from aphasia, muscular disorder, Down syndrome, and other problems. When I asked her more specifically how she did this she replied, "I teach them to sing vowel sounds and project them here," and she pointed to her forehead.

My mouth dropped open in amazement and I excitedly said, "You have them project harmonics to the third eye!"

"Yes," she replied, "but I cannot call it that!"

I asked if she had had any success with this technique and with a knowing smile, she said, "Come to my presentation this afternoon and find out."

I told Ms. Rich I had to catch a plane, but that I would be in further contact with her. That was the last I saw or heard from her. A student of mine from Denmark recently told me of her death in 1990.

Here is an extract from the symposium about Ms. Rich's presentation, called "Theoretical Aspects of Vocal Teaching":

> The first phase in teaching vocal production to a handicapped student is instruction in slow and relaxed breathing. The second phase involves teaching the student to breathe so that the airstream passes through the vocal cords and up to the central part of the forehead. The importance in tongue placement in relaxing the throat muscles is stressed. After a period of exercise and training of the tongue and lips, the patient follows a program using two different groups of vowels. The speaking and singing functions are generally restored after several weeks of intense training.

Though it was extremely brief, my meeting with Ms. Rich greatly affected me, for I am positive that there was great validity in her work. Contained in the vowel sounds are different harmonics and Ms. Rich's work indicates that, through teaching people with neurological disorders the ability to create vowel sounds, it may be possible to restore imbalances in the brain. It seems likely that through resonating the brain with harmonics new connections may be made, connections that bypass damaged areas that no longer function properly.

Susan Gallagher Borg

At the First International Symposium on the Study of Subtle Energy Medicine in Boulder, Colorado in 1991, I met Susan Gallagher Borg, a singer, bodyworker, and movement therapist who utilized a process called Resonant Kinesiology. She gave a presentation on "Singing in the Brain: Using Vocal Sounds to Evoke a Healing Response" that focused upon using vocal harmonics to resonate the brain. We shared similar thoughts on the effects of vocal harmonics to stimulate the various epicenters of the brain.

Susan had come upon vocal harmonics on her own and had spent much time investigating the mechanism of the body and the brain. In particular, Susan had studied the effects of sound upon the fascia. The fascia, a gelatinous substance, is the connective tissue of the body. Sound makes extremely fast physiological changes in this tissue as it is easily affected by sounds. The fascia also plays an important part in the connection of the synapses of the brain.

Susan believed that it was possible to resonate different portions of the brain with sound. She also felt it was possible to create new neural synaptic connections in the brain using vocal harmonics. In a conversation, she told me:

> By stimulating the neurons of the brain, you cause them to pay attention. When they pay attention over a period of time, the portion of the brain in which this occurs will habituate and will grow a synapse. The synapse perpetuates that particular attention. This will cause brain cells to connect.

Susan's statement indicated that, by stimulating the brain with sound, it was possible to create new neural synaptic connections. This came very close to my own understanding of the potential power of harmonics to affect and activate the brain. At her presentation, Susan suggested to those scientists and doctors present the need to investigate whether the brain can be resonated by sound and, if so, which portions of it are resonated by which harmonics. This is a most important area of investigation that may produce extraordinary information about new ways of helping people suffering from head injury and other neurological disorders.

There is research to indicate that sounds that are discordant and disharmonic may have damaging effects upon the brain. In 1990 Schreckenberg and Bird, a neurobiologist and a physicist, experimented with exposing rats to different sounds. One group of rats listened to Strauss waltzes while another group listened to disharmonic sounds in the form of incessant drumbeats. The group that heard the discordant sounds developed difficulties in learning and memory and also incurred structural changes in their brain cells. The neurons showed signs of wear and tear from stress. The researchers believed that what they were observing was the effect of disharmonic sounds on mammalian brains.

There is also research that indicates that it is possible to grow new brain cells. Ten years ago, Fernando Nottebohm and colleagues at Rockefeller University discovered that songbirds have the ability to grow new cells in the brain—a phenomenon previously considered impossible in adult animals. Songbirds, which are capable of singing two notes simultaneously, can grow new nerve cells and increase the size of the HVC, the area of the avian brain involved with singing. This study of "neurogenesis" has excited many scientists with the prospect of someday stimulating a damaged human nervous system to repair itself. These researchers are attempting to find the gene that controls the process of nerve regeneration. Perhaps the key to neurogenesis in songbirds lies not in the gene itself, but in the sounds that the songbirds make.

Judith Hitt

Judith Hitt, a registered nurse from Vermont specializing in rehabilitation, has worked with patients suffering from strokes and other neurological disorders using vocal harmonics. A schooled musician, she also studied sound and bodywork with Susan Borg.

Judith says of her work:

> Sound seems to be a very powerful and direct way to "touch" the brain and nerves. I find that I can vibrate specific areas of the brain by using certain harmonic frequencies. These frequencies vary from person to person, even from day to day on the same person. The same is true for each of the cranial nerves as well as the spinal cord and spinal nerves. The flow and pulse of the cerebral spinal fluid, very much affected by a stroke, for example, can be altered with sound, helping to clear up blockages.

Judith applies visualization and vocalization in her work, using both guided imagery and harmonics with her clients to enhance the intention of the sounding.

> If, for example, we are focusing on hand movement, I will ask the person to visualize making a fist with that hand, imagining what it would feel like to squeeze the hand into a fist. When that intention is fully placed, I will sound into the corresponding area of the brain

> and travel down the appropriate nerves. I will ask the person to be aware of the connection between their brain and their hand, and to feel the nerve impulses traveling from their brain to their fist and back again as they visualize this. So, I sound into the appropriate areas of the nervous system while the intended movement is being visualized. I believe that this creates an environment for new learning in the nervous system; for new synapses to be created, making new connections to relearn a movement.

Judith finds that the harmonics from "the vowels AYE and EEE resonate brain tissue the best and that the first octave and the fifth harmonics resonate the larger areas of the brain. The highest harmonics that I can create seem to be the most effective on the smaller, more specific neural areas such as the caudate nucleus or a cranial nerve junction." While Judith has not yet tried teaching clients techniques of self-created vocal harmonics, this is an area of therapy she plans to explore. In her work, Judith utilizes many of the concepts and techniques found in chapter 10, "Overtoning."

Tomatis and Brain Resonation

The work of Alfred Tomatis, M.D., on the ear and listening has been discussed in chapter 6, "Meditation and Harmonics," though it could easily apply here as well. Dr. Tomatis's research into sound seems to validate the use of harmonics to resonate the brain. While he believes that the actual charging of the cortex of the brain occurs through sound stimulating the auditory nerve, it is quite possible that mechanical resonance of the brain through sonic stimulation may also occur.

Dr. Tomatis, through his Tomatis Method, utilizes both the Electronic Ear and the human voice, rich in high-frequency harmonics to dramatically correct many problems related to speech, language, motor control, and motivation. Tomatis has enjoyed success with those who are dyslexic, autistic, stutterers, adopted, or depressed. Enhanced learning, improved music ability, and increased attunement in acquiring a second language are also possible outcomes for those without specific problems.

Heat Thermography to Measure Effect of Vocal Harmonics

In February 1989 I was a guest speaker at the First International New Age Music Conference. One of those in attendance was Elizabeth Phillips, Ph.D., who was conducting some tests with heat thermography equipment. She was attempting to correlate the relationship of music and relaxation via this process. Heat thermography measures changes in skin temperature. When subjects are relaxed, their skin temperature is raised.

Phillips was just about to disassemble her equipment when I wandered by her booth and asked her about her work. When she told me about her project, I asked her if it was still possible for her to take pictures using her equipment. She replied affirmatively. A few minutes later, Phillips was photographing my chest and head with her equipment while I sang Tibetan and Mongolian overtones. I left the conference before Phillips had a chance to look at the resulting photographs. Several months later I received a phone call from her. She had forgotten about the photographs she had taken until that afternoon when she had developed them and then telephoned me. She had never seen such rapid changes in skin temperature. She wanted to know what I had been doing.

I explained to Phillips about vocal harmonics. Then I asked her what the changes meant. Heat thermography, she explained, showed changes in skin temperature. There seemed to be a major relationship between these changes in skin temperature and the organs behind or below the skin. In my case, it was the organ behind the skin of my forehead—the brain. The photographs showed incredibly rapid changes in color on my forehead and the top portion of my skull. There were changes in the activation of skin temperature that matched the portion of my head where I had been projecting the vocal harmonics.

Phillips consulted a neurologist with the photographs to see his response. The doctor was baffled by the changes in the skin temperature and, believing I was somehow able to affect the autonomic nervous system, he wanted to know if I had been doing any visualization while making these sounds. I had not, but I had been consciously projecting the sound to different portions of my brain.

Phillips asked if I thought there was a possible use for treatment of headaches using this technique. I replied that I thought this would be just the tip of the iceberg. I told her that I felt there were extraordinary healing possibilities with the use of vocal harmonics as a means of stimulating the brain. While heat thermography shows only changes in skin temperature, it gives an indication of activity in the organs below the skin—in this case, the brain. This is another example of the potential validation of the brain being resonated by harmonics.

THE PINEAL GLAND

In the introduction, I related the story of my journey to Palenque in Mexico and having the darkened room become illuminated as I sang vocal harmonics. This experience was one of the more dramatic episodes in my life. It was only later that I began to process the experience and try to understand what had gone on.

As often happens after I have a fairly unexplainable event occur in my life, I meditate. After I returned from Palenque, I began to meditate on what had actually occurred during that experience. What I received in my meditation was interesting. It was this: through the use of vocally created harmonics, it is possible to resonate and stimulate the pineal gland.

The pineal gland is a small, pine-cone-shaped gland located in the middle of the head. Esoterically, the pineal is often associated with the "third eye" and was believed by Descartes to be the "seat of the soul." It was once thought to be a vestigial organ and is now known to be a light-sensitive clock affecting sleep and the sex glands. Research by scientists such as Robert Beck suggest that the pineal is an organic device that is tuned toward magnetic north to give both humans and animals their sense of direction. Other scientists believe that the pineal is a bioluminescent organ that has the ability to create light.

The pineal is rich in neuromelanin, which, according to scientist Frank Barr, is a phase-timing, information-processing interface molecule that is a phototransducer. This is a substance that has the ability, among other traits, of absorbing and converting light energy to sound. It also has the ability to turn sound energy into light. Barr believes that melanin and its brain counterpart, neuromelanin, may be the key link between the mind and the brain.

Through stimulation of the pineal gland, neuromelanin is produced. Neuromelanin, a light-sensitive compound, triggers the release of a substance that contains phosphorus, a light-producing chemical. By stimulating the pineal gland through vocal harmonics, it may be possible that actual fields of light around the body are enhanced. In other words, the auric field becomes more luminescent. I hypothesize that through this luminescence, I was actually able to produce light in the room in Palenque.

While this phenomenon is not too widely known, there does seem to be some reference to it in certain texts. Dhyani Ywahoo, a Native American medicine woman, writes in *Voices of Our Ancestors* that in the ancient Mystery Schools the initiations were held in total darkness. The initiates had to be able to produce their own light. I believe that this was done through the creation of vocal harmonics.

Spiritual scientist J. J. Hurtak writes of the phenomenon of creating light through the pineal gland in *The Keys of Enoch:*

> The "light" which activates the pineal gland is not the conventional light of the sun . . . the brain produces its own light field on a molecular level . . . our neurocircuitry can produce its own light field.

I discussed with Dr. Tomatis my experience of producing light through sound and suggested my hypothesis of the pineal creating this light. Dr. Tomatis knew of this phenomenon of creating light through sound but believed that this light was created not through the pineal (the third eye) but through the heart. It is interesting to note that the heart is an organ that is also extremely rich in melanin.

What would be the healing benefits of creating light in this manner? The possibilities seem limitless. We would be enhancing and adding energy to the fields around our bodies, creating or restoring health and balance to areas of imbalance and disease. These possibilities of resonating the pineal through sound are yet another example of the potential use of harmonics to influence and affect the brain for health and wellness.

RECENT RESEARCH

In October 1986, I presented a workshop called "Awakening for Lost Chord" for the Third International Symposium of the International Society for Music in Medicine in Ludenscheid, Germany. It was truly a groundbreaking gathering that was full of scientists and medical professionals who were investigating the uses of sound and music for healing. These included Peter Guy Manners, D.O., founder of cymatic therapy, Charles Eagle, Ph.D., professor of music therapy at Southern Methodist University in Texas, and Olav Skille, pioneer in the field of vibroacoustics. It was a great honor to be among these extraordinary people and a thrill to share with them some of my work with the therapeutic effects of vocal harmonics.

My workshop focused on vocal harmonics and included listening to recorded examples as well as describing the fundamentals of creating these remarkable sounds. One of the sounds I taught at the workshop was the "NURR" sound. When I prefaced the teaching of this sound, I said something like, "We call this sound Sonic Dristan"—a humorous attempt at suggesting that the sound was useful if someone had a blocked nose. No one laughed, and I supposed that there was some sort of language barrier. Dristan is a nasal decongestant—an antihistamine useful for opening stuffy noses, but perhaps a similar substance went under a different name in Germany. Or perhaps no one understood the true implications. This information about the therapeutic effects of such sounds was not to manifest until decades later.

Within the last fifteen years, clinical data has emerged to indicate that nasalized sounds such as the NURR or the hum are good at assisting sinus infections such as sinusitis. This seems to be due to the release of nitric oxide (NO), a powerful molecule that is a vasodilator, which relaxes blood vessels and increases circulation. Nitric oxide, when generated in the nasal cavity, initiates a gas that has antibacterial and antiviral properties, reduces inflammation, and opens up the sinus pathways.

This information has basically laid dormant until recently when a number of medical doctors and sound therapists (including myself and my wife, Andi) have brought the antiviral properties of nasalized sounds to the general public. Nitric oxide was named "Molecule of the Year" by *Science* magazine. It has many extraordinary properties. The discovery of the relationship between self-created sounds and the generation of NO is recent. The importance of this continues to reveal future aspects of the healing nature of sound.

In addition to the production of nitric oxide, within these last two decades there has been important research showing that our voice does indeed have amazing abilities to create positive shifts and changes in our body. Some of the scientific data on the beneficial physiological effect of the self-created sounds of vocal toning includes:

- Increased oxygen in the cells. Oxygen in our cells is vital for most life functions. With increased oxygen levels, our red blood cells can become fully saturated. Oxygen helps replace cells that wear out, provides energy for our bodies, supports the way our immune systems function, improves wound healing, vision, mental clarity, and intelligence, reduces stress levels, improves the heart and respiration, removes waste, reduces tissue swelling, and more.
- Lowered blood pressure and heart rate. Research has shown that the simple act of taking a deep breath and then releasing it with an extended audible tone such as a hum or a vowel sound such as AH can bring immediate reduction of blood pressure and heart rate—sometimes to levels that equal those of pharmaceuticals. The next time you're feeling tense, just make a simple sound for a few minutes. It's that simple and that profound.
- Increased lymphatic circulation. The lymphatic system is a crucial part of your immune system. It removes metabolic waste and toxins from our body. Increasing lymphatic circulation improves immune functions by carrying white blood cells that help prevent infection, reduce swelling, improve relaxation, and reduces stress.
- Increased levels of melatonin. Melatonin is a hormone that is associated with the circadian rhythms of several biological functions. Melatonin is a hormone with antioxidant properties. Melatonin has many different attributes, including its ability to enhance sleep. Data indicates that melatonin works with our immune sys-

tem and has anti-inflammatory effects. Some studies also suggest that melatonin has antiviral ability and might be useful in fighting infectious disease.

- Reduced levels of stress-related hormones including cortisol. Stress is one of the great causes of illness. Making our own self-created sounds is a wonderful way of reducing stress-related hormones such as cortisol that amplify anxiety and reduce our immune functions. Simply toning a vowel or making a hum for a minute or two can be a profound method of reducing stress and is, unto itself, a great healing technique simply because of this.
- Release of endorphins. Endorphins are the self-created opiates that work as natural pain relievers. We naturally make sound when we are in pain. Whether it's a moan or a tone or some other sound, making elongated sounds seems to accompany our discomfort and help ease our pain. There are a number of theories as to why this occurs, but most certainly, the fact that we produce endorphins when we make such sounds is one reason.
- Boosted production of interleukin-1. Interleukin-1 is a protein that is associated with blood platelet production. It has the ability to reduce inflammation and boost production of T-cells, which are vital for fighting infection.
- Release of oxytocin. Oxytocin is a hormone produced by the hypothalamus and stored and secreted by the pituitary gland. Known as the "trust" or "love" hormone it facilitates bonding—an empathic feeling between people. Production of oxytocin makes us feel good and allows the boundaries between people to dissipate.
- Increased stimulation of the vagus nerve. The vagus nerve is the largest nerve in our body. It is responsible for the regulation of several bodily functions including heart rate; constriction of blood vessels; regulation of the heart, lungs, digestive tract, liver, and immune system, as well as control of gastrointestinal sensitivity, motility, and inflammation. When the vagus nerve is relaxed, vagal tone is increased, which assists in lowering blood pressure, stress, and depression. Research has shown that vocal toning is effective in creating higher vagal tone.

- Increased heart rate variability. When we have stimulation of the vagus nerve, higher vagal tone occurs. We are more relaxed, have less inflammation, and our immunity is enhanced. Heart rate variability (HRV) occurs when vagal tone is high. HRV is simply a measure of the variation in time between each heartbeat. People who have high HRV have greater cardiovascular fitness and are more resilient to stress. Toning has been shown to be an effective way of creating high vagal tone and HRV.

SUMMARY

In this chapter we have focused upon the potential use of harmonics for healing the body and the mind, from instruments and recordings that use harmonically related frequencies to the use of the voice to create vocal harmonics.

In forthcoming chapters we will focus upon learning to use vocal harmonics to balance the chakras and to resonate the physical and etheric bodies. Harmonics are an extremely accessible and easy tool for helping us become sound in both body and mind. Tomorrow's scientific research may validate the mysterious healing abilities of harmonics and their use in the fields of health and wellness. Until then, we can still experience for ourselves the extraordinary benefits that can be derived from the therapeutic application of vocal harmonics.

EIGHT
Vowels as Mantras

MANTRAS

Mantra is a Sanskrit word meaning "the thought that liberates and protects." Mantras are sounds or words that when recited have the ability of changing the consciousness of the reciter. In the Hindu tradition, there are literally thousands of mantras, each with a different purpose and intention. Some mantras are designed to unite the reciter with a particular deity or energy form. Other mantras are designed to empower the reciter with specific *siddhas* or "powers." Still other mantras are utilized to resonate and activate the chakras of the reciter. In this chapter, we will examine the use of vowels as mantras for the third use—the resonation of the chakras.

CHAKRAS

Chakras are energy centers located along the center of the body. Clairvoyants and others with the ability to see these subtle energy centers are able to view them as vortices of shifting colors, sounds, and densities. Indeed, the meaning of *chakra* (a Sanskrit word) is "wheel," and they are seen as spinning wheels of energy.

Knowledge of chakras is by no means limited to Eastern traditions, though it is from the Hindu and Tibetan systems that the greatest information about chakras has come. Many esoteric and occult traditions talk of energy centers along the body and it seems that anyone with real sensitivity can sense them. A friend of mine who was born with the ability of actually viewing subtle energy always wondered what the spinning disks of light he saw on people were, until he found out about chakras.

While chakras have been incorporated into the spiritual beliefs of Hindus and Tibetans, their existence seems not to be based upon religion, but sensitivity to energy. The concept of subtle energy is becoming more recognized in the West. There is, in fact, an International Society for the Study of Subtle Energy Medicine whose membership is composed largely of medical doctors, scientists, and alternative healers who work with subtle energy. These modalities of healing include acupuncture and homeopathy.

SUBTLE ENERGY

Subtle energy is energy that seems to bypass the normal measurable aspects of energy, such as heat, which can easily be measured by a thermometer. Subtle energy may be electromagnetic in nature or it may be something else. It is, for the most part, energy that cannot be easily seen, felt, or perceived either by normal people or instrumentation. However, individuals with heightened sensitivity can perceive this energy and new scientific instrumentation is being invented that can now measure this energy.

In Russia, Semyon and Valentina Kirlian experimented with photographic plates that were exposed to high-frequency electrical fields. They observed that when a subject placed a finger or hand on the plate, there appeared some unknown substance surrounding the physical organ. This substance often varied in brightness, depth, and size, depending upon the health and vitality of the subject. The Kirlians speculated that they had found a way of measuring the "aura" of the body, long claimed to be visible by psychics, seers, and sages.

In the 1980s, Hiroshi Motoyama, a Japanese scientist, invented instrumentation for measuring aspects of the subtle body, including acupuncture points and chakras. Using highly sensitive photoelectric equipment, Dr. Motoyama measured advanced masters of yoga as they activated their chakras. He was able to detect light being emitted from the chakras of his subjects. With other instrumentation designed to measure minute changes in electric current, Motoyama was able to show changes in skin current at acupuncture points. As more and more instrumentation becomes available, other scientists are making rapid progress in the ability to measure subtle energy and the existence of the subtle energy centers known as chakras.

The concept of subtle energy is nothing new to those of us working with sound. If we perceive that all is in a state of vibration, the varying degrees of this vibration would cause things to have different densities. Working with sound, and particularly harmonics, enhances the ability to affect many of these subtle energies. The chakras may be influenced by sound, and in this chapter we will work with a very simple way of doing this. Before looking at how this may be done, let us first gain a preliminary understanding of the chakras.

LOCATION OF CHAKRAS

Chakras seem to be the focal point of manifestation for energy that makes up the subtle body. From the chakras, the energy is thought to become more dense, first appearing as the points utilized in acupuncture and then, as they become even denser, this energy actually makes up the physical body. In most esoteric traditions, there are seven major chakras that are centrally located along the front of the body. Figure 8.1 on page 112 illustrates the locations of these chakras.

The chakras are said to be related to the endocrine system, the ductless glands of the physical body. The chakras also influence and affect the area of the physical body where they are located. Many physical imbalances may be perceived as being the result of imbalanced chakras. A short summary of the chakras follows on the next page.

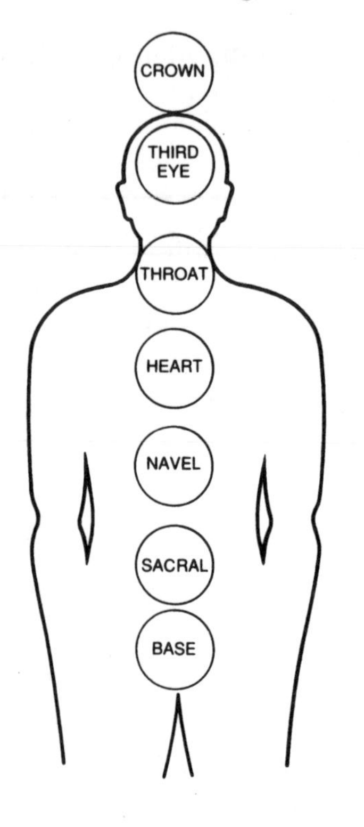

Figure 8.1. The chakras and their positions

1. The base chakra (in Sanskrit, *Muladhara*) is located at the base of the spine and is also associated with the anus. This chakra is related to the adrenal glands and associated with survival.
2. The sacral chakra (*Svadhishthana*) is located three to five centimeters below the navel. This chakra is related to the sexual organs and reproductive problems.
3. The navel chakra (*Manipura*) is located around the navel and is associated with the digestive organs. It is often thought of as the chakra from which our power and mastery of self originates.
4. The heart chakra (*Anahata*) is located in the center of the chest between the nipples. It is associated with the organs of the heart and respiration as well as the thymus gland. This is the chakra of love and compassion. As noted previously, the term *anahata* also means "inner" or "unstruck sound."
5. The throat chakra (*Vishuddi*) is located in the throat. It is associated with speech and hearing and with the thyroid gland. It is the chakra of communication and creativity.

6. The brow chakra (*Ajna*) is located between the eyebrows. This is the energy center known esoterically as the third eye. This chakra is primarily concerned with imagination, psychic abilities, and the seeking of God. There seems to be much debate about the gland associated with it. Many traditional systems believe the pineal gland is controlled by the third eye. Other traditions, however, place the secretory functions of pituitary, the master gland of the endocrine system, under the influence of the third eye.
7. The crown chakra (*Sahasrara*) is located at the top of the head. It is said to control every aspect of the body and mind and is associated with full enlightenment and union with God. In many religious pictures, the halo that surrounds the heads of saintly beings is the representation of an activated crown chakra. There is some confusion as to whether this energy center controls the pituitary or the pineal gland. Like the third eye, both of these glands have been associated with the crown chakra. This chakra is rarely fully opened, except in cases of very high spiritual beings.

This summary of the chakras is merely that—a summary. There are many books written about the chakras that should be consulted if more information is desired. Not all information about the chakras is consistent. Different systems place different emphasis on specific ones, associating these chakras with different sets of glands and organs. This is particularly true with the first and second chakras and the sixth and seventh chakras. For example, some systems place the first chakra as being responsible for sexual activity while other systems place this energy in the second chakra. As noted, there is a discrepancy regarding whether the pineal or the pituitary is the gland for the sixth or the seventh chakra. Indeed, some systems have only five chakras in them, with the first and second chakra considered as one and the sixth and seventh considered another.

There are, however, many more specific similarities about knowledge of the chakras than differences. The heart and throat chakra, for example, are generally perceived by all as being related to the thymus and thyroid, respectively. Despite the development of numerous instruments that are believed to measure the chakras and other aspects of the energy field, the data from these instruments is not consistent, and there is no overall agreement about the validity of these findings. Since there is no instrumentation that can accurately measure chakras, knowledge of chakras remains based upon the ability of different individuals to perceive these energy centers. One thought as to the differences in perceptions about the chakras may be due to the fact that the individuals who are able to perceive them may be attuned to different aspects of the electromagnetic spectrum and therefore may disagree in their description of the chakras.

SOUND AND THE CHAKRAS

Each of the chakras is said to resonate with different sounds. Many years ago, I did a study of different systems that utilized sound to resonate the chakras. Currently, it is common and popular to use the C major scale—C, D, E, F, G, A, B, which are the white keys on a piano—as being the optimum resonance of the chakras. However, the popularity of this may be simply due to the simplicity of such a system and not necessarily anything else. There are other chakra tonal systems that continue to exist. There are many of these systems, and they all seemed to work. This was for me a time of great confusion since I could not understand how different sounds and frequencies could seemingly have the same effect. It was then that I began to become aware of the importance of intention in this work with sound and the fact that the intention coupled with the frequency would be the reason why these different systems should all be effective.

One of the important points of awareness about chakras is that there seems to be a direct relationship between the chakra and the portion of the body it is associated with. Imbalances in chakras seem to lead to imbalances in the physical body and vice versa. Often, by aligning and balancing a chakra associated with an organ that is experiencing discomfort, the organ can become healthy and the problem may disappear.

Another important aspect of chakras is that, as they are activated, the individual opening these chakras seems to become more highly conscious and spiritually transformed. In some Eastern philosophies, there is an energy called "kundalini" that sleeps in the base chakra. As this energy becomes awakened, the kundalini moves up the spine to the next chakra and then the next until, finally, as an individual becomes fully awakened and conscious, it reaches the crown chakra. With the rising of the kundalini and the activation of succeeding chakras, different powers and abilities seem to manifest. By the time the energy reaches the crown, an individual has been truly transformed. The subject of kundalini has been itself the focus of a number of books. It seems to be a very powerful energy, and in many of these texts warnings are given not to awaken the kundalini before an individual is ready. I concur. This is one of the reasons for working with our own sound. Sound seems to have the ability of being a tool that will allow an individual to go only as far as he or she is vibrationally ready to go in terms of activation of this energy. It is therefore safe. You cannot force open a chakra with your own sound and do damage. Sound is safe and gentle and works with the natural resonance of the individual.

Vowel Sounds and the Chakras

In particular, working with the vowel sounds has been particularly effective. One reason for this is that many of the people in groups I have worked with have had problems with the different mantric formulas, using foreign words such as Sanskrit or Tibetan. A devout Christian, for example, might feel strange chanting a Bija mantra but he or she may have no difficulty working with vowel sounds. The second reason I prefer to work with vowel sounds is that they truly do create a resonance in the physical body. We can actually feel different portions of our body vibrate with sound. For those who have had no experience working with the subtle body, this physical resonance makes it easier for them to accept the possibility of resonating subtle energy as well, for if the stomach area is being activated by sound, it seems entirely possible to them that the etheric fields may also be affected.

The third reason I work with vowels has to do with harmonics. As we have stated before, there are particular harmonics (called formants) that seem to be associated with specific vowels. While each vowel has the potential of creating every harmonic, each vowel also has particular harmonics that are stressed. Often by working with vowels as mantras and focusing upon the vowels, individuals will begin to hear and create the harmonics without any further training.

While there are many varying schools of thought about the relationship between sound and the chakras, one relationship that seems to be fairly consistent is that of pitch and the chakras. It seems that the lower chakras are influenced by lower sounds and the upper chakras are influenced by higher sounds. This is also true about our body cavities. For example, the lowest sound that we can make seems to resonate the very deepest part of our trunk and also influences the base chakra. Mid-range sounds seem to resonate the middle part of our trunk and, depending upon the pitch, can influence the navel, heart, or throat chakra. The upper ranges, and in particular, the highest sound we can make seems to vibrate the top of the head and the crown chakra.

There also appears to be a direct relationship between specific vowels and different portions of the body. These vowel sounds also seem to work by themselves to resonate the chakras. Such resonation techniques are said to be very old. Edgar Cayce talked of the priests of ancient Egypt learning to resonate their energy centers with vowel sounds. When these vowel sounds are combined with pitch, we have a very powerful sonic formula for resonating both the physical body and the subtle energy centers.

There are actually a number of different systems that utilize the vowel sounds to resonate the chakras. While all these systems are inherently similar, there seem to be subtle differences. A reason for this may lie in the fact that pronunciation of different vowel sounds from written text is quite difficult. "EH" and "AYE" for example, may be meant to be the same sound, or they may be meant to be different.

VOWEL SOUNDS TO RESONATE CHAKRAS

Goldman's System

This particular system of using vowel sounds and pitch to resonate chakras is one I have worked with for several years by myself and in the teaching of groups. It is the most effective system I have encountered. This does not mean it is the only method for working with the vowels and the chakras. It is, however, the most universally accepted system.*

When working with self-created sounds, the intention behind the sound is of extreme importance. It may, in fact, be as important as the actual sounds that are created. I have made this point in other chapters and will continue to do so throughout this book. In the following exercise, focus your intention on projecting the sound to the particular part of the body where you would like the sound to resonate. With continued experience in sounding, you may learn that it is possible to resonate virtually any portion of your body (and chakra as well) with any sound. However, for this exercise, please direct your attention to the portion of the body and the corresponding chakra as instructed.

Before we begin this exercise, find a comfortable position sitting either on the floor or in a chair. You may put your hands in any position that is comfortable—on your knees or in your lap, or you may put them over the part of your body where you are resonating the sound. This sometimes amplifies the effect of the sounding and helps focus intention. When you tone these vowel sounds, use one complete breath with each vowel. When working with this and other exercises in which you make sounds, it is recommended that you be aware of your posture and keep your spine as straight as possible.

It is important when working with self-created sound to take a deep breath, doing diaphragmatic breathing, so that as you breathe in, the stomach expands. More explicit details about this are given in chapter 10, "Overtoning." Figure 8.2 on the following page illustrates the vowel chakra system we will be using for this exercise. You may find it helpful to refer to this chart during the exercise.

Begin with an "UH" sound (as in the word *huh*) that is the very deepest sound you can make. Focus your attention on the base chakra, located at the base of the spine. If you would like to add a color visualization to this exercise, use the color red.

*The exercise "Vowels as Mantras" is available in the appendix and in the downloads that accompany this book.

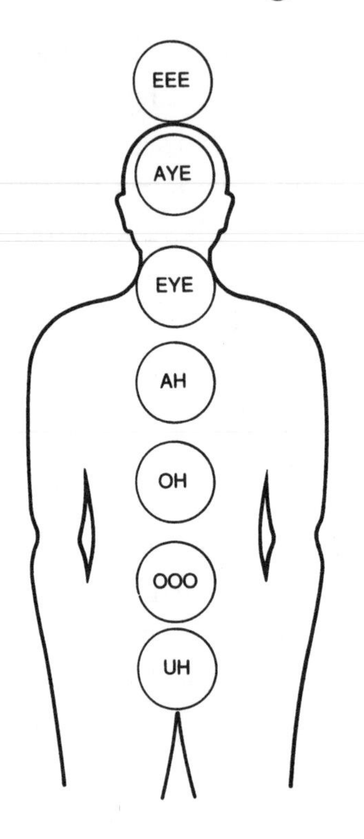

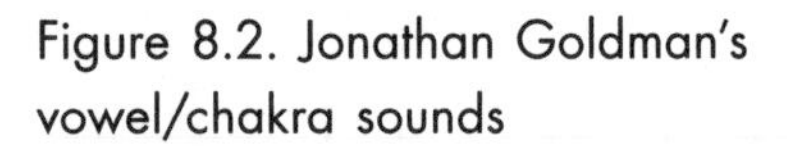
Figure 8.2. Jonathan Goldman's vowel/chakra sounds

Now begin to tone the very deepest "UH" sound that you can make. This sound can be very soft and gentle. It does not have to be loud. Close your eyes while you are making this sound. Become aware of where the sound is resonating in your body. The sound will always resonate in your throat, but become aware of where else that sound is resonating. Now focus your attention on the lowest part of your trunk and project your intention so that you visualize the sound resonating at the base of your spine and in your reproductive area. Feel the sound vibrating that area and, as it does, become aware that the energy center associated with that area is also resonating, becoming balanced and aligned. Make this "UH" sound for a minute or two, or for however long you feel comfortable. We suggest doing this for no more than five minutes.

Now focus your attention on the second chakra located about three inches below the navel. The vowel sound for this is an "OOO" sound (as in the word *you*). A color that will complement a visualization for this sound is orange.

Begin to tone an "OOO" sound, making it a little less deep and a bit higher in pitch than the last sound. This sound should be soft and gentle, as should all the sounds we will be making for this exercise. Close your eyes and become aware of where the sound is resonating in your body. Now focus your attention on the area of the second chakra and project the sound there. As the sound resonates the second chakra, experience this energy center balancing and aligning with the other chakras. Make this "OOO" sound for a minute or two. As with the base chakra and the other vowel sounds for the chakras, we recommend that you do this sounding for no more than five minutes. As you become more experienced at sounding and resonating your physical and subtle self, the time can expand.

The sound for the navel chakra, located at the navel area and several inches above is "OH" (as in the word *go*). Yellow will complement your visualization. Begin to tone a very gentle and soft "OH" sound, which is beginning to fall within the midrange of your voice. This sound should be higher than the last sound. Become aware of where that sound is resonating in your body. Now focus your attention on the navel and solar plexus area and focus the sound there. As the sound resonates this area, experience this energy center balancing and aligning with the other chakras. Make this "OH" sound for a minute or two.

The vowel sound for the heart chakra, located in the middle of the chest, to the right of our physical heart, is "AH" (as in the word *father*). "AH" is often a sound we make when we are in love, and the heart chakra is the center associated with love. If you wish to add a color to complement this sound, use green. Begin to tone a soft and gentle mid-range "AH" sound, higher in pitch than the last sound. Become aware of where the sound is resonating in your body. Now focus your attention on the heart chakra and project the sound there. As you resonate the heart center with sound, experience this energy center balancing and aligning with the other chakras. Make this sound for one or two minutes.

The vowel sound for the throat chakra, located at the throat, is "EYE" (as in the word *I*). A color to complement this sound is blue. Begin to tone a soft and gentle "EYE" sound that is still higher in pitch than the last sound. Become aware of where the sound is resonating in your body. Now focus your attention on the throat chakra and project sound there.

As the sound resonates the throat chakra, experience this energy center balancing and aligning with the other chakras. Make this "EYE" sound for a minute or two.

The vowel sound for the third eye, located in the forehead between the two eyes and slightly above them, is "AYE" (as in the word *say*). A color that works well with this sound is indigo. Begin to tone a soft and gentle "AYE" sound, higher in pitch than the last sound. Close your eyes while making this sound and become aware of where that sound is resonating in your body. Now focus your attention on this chakra and project the sound to that area. As the sound resonates the third eye, experience this energy center aligning and balancing with your other chakras. Make this "AYE" sound for a minute or two.

The vowel sound for the crown chakra, located at the top of the head, is the very highest "EEE" (as in the word *me*) sound that you can create. A color that is used here is purple. Begin to tone the highest "EEE" sound that it is possible for you to make. For men, it is often useful to use a falsetto voice to achieve this. Make this sound soft and gentle. Close your eyes and become aware of where that sound is resonating in your body. Now focus your attention on your crown center and begin to project sound there. As the sound resonates the crown chakra, experience this energy center balancing and aligning with the other chakras. Make this "EEE" sound for a minute or two.

At the completion of this exercise, which should take between ten and twenty minutes to experience properly, you may feel very lightheaded. I suggest that you sit in a state of meditation and enjoy this experience. Are there any images or thoughts that are coming to you in this state? Take adequate time when you have completed the exercise for processing the experience you have had with sounding the chakras in this manner. What did you feel like before you began the exercise? What do you feel like now that you have completed it? Log and note any changes you may have experienced during this exercise in your journal.

With this exercise, we are moving energy up the body from the root chakra to the crown chakra. It is powerful. If at the end of this exercise, you wish to bring the energy back down into your body, tone the deepest "UH" sound you can make. This was the first chakra vowel sound we experienced. If you tone this sound it will immediately bring the energy back into your physical body and help ground you.

OTHER VOWEL/CHAKRA SYSTEMS

As mentioned earlier, there are slight variations in the vowel/chakra relationships. Randall McClellan, in his book *The Healing Forces of Music,* uses the relationship between the chakras and the vowels, shown in table 8.1 and figure 8.3.

Table 8.1 Randall McClellan Vowel/Chakra Sounds

Chakra	Vowel
1st (base)	OOO
2nd	OOO
3rd	OH
4th	AH
5th	AYE
6th	EEE
7th (crown)	MMM

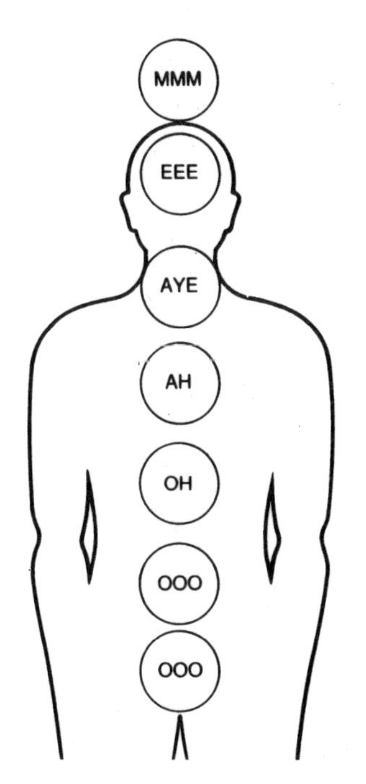

Figure 8.3. Randall McClellan's vowel/chakra sounds

Kay Gardner, in her book, *Sounding the Inner Landscape,* finds the vowel/chakra relationship shown in table 8.2 and figure 8.4 useful; Peter Michael Hamel, in *Through Music to the Self,* uses the relationship between the vowels and the chakras shown in table 8.3 and figure 8.5.

Table 8.2. Kay Gardner's Vowel/Chakra Sounds

Chakra	Vowel
1st (base)	OOO
2nd	OH
3rd	AW
4th	AH
5th	EH
6th	IH
7th	EEE

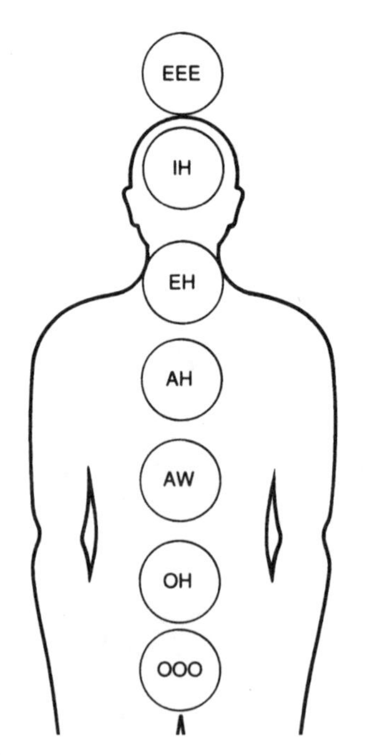

Figure 8.4. Kay Gardner's vowel/chakra sounds

When experimenting with these other systems, it is suggested that the relationship between pitches will still apply. That is, to go from the lowest possible pitch you can produce for resonance with the base chakra to the highest possible pitch you can produce for resonance with the crown chakra. These other systems are very close to the one I have focused upon in this chapter. They are offered as an alternative. You might experiment with one of these different systems and find if they work more successfully for you. You may end up creating a combination of all these systems that will work best for yourself.

Table 8.3. Peter Michael Hamel's Vowel/Chakra Sounds

Chakra	Vowel
1st (base)	UH
2nd	UH
3rd	OH
4th	AH
5th	EH
6th	EEE
7th (crown)	EEE

Figure 8.5. Peter Michael Hamel's vowel/chakra sounds

Remember, we are all unique vibratory beings and what works best for one person may not work as well for another. As you practice sounding these vowel sounds for extended periods of time, you may become aware of sounds within the sounds you are creating. These are harmonics. In our next chapter, we will focus upon the conscious creation of harmonics. However, it is quite possible that they are already beginning to come to you through sounding the vowel sounds as you work to resonate the chakras. Continue with this work. The material in the next chapter can only enhance the resonance of the physical body and subtle energy centers.

NINE
The Fundamentals of Vocal Harmonics

INTRODUCTION

In the ancient shamanic traditions of Mongolia, Africa, Arabia, and Mexico, in the arcane Kabbalistic traditions of Judaism and Christianity, and in the sacred spiritual traditions of Tibet, vowel sounds and harmonics, also known as overtones, have been utilized to heal and transform. They have been used to communicate with and invoke deities, to balance the energy centers of the body, and to affect the resonances of the brain.

Throughout my years of research and study in the field of therapeutic and transformational sound, there is no single technique I have found that so truly embodies the power of sacred sound as does harmonics. The ability to create two or more tones at the same time is nothing less than magical. The fact that these sounds may be used to affect our physical, emotional, mental, and spiritual bodies makes them even more extraordinary.

Until recently, knowledge of the creation of vocal harmonics has been enshrouded in the esoteric mystery of traditions that would not allow the uninitiated access to this remarkable aspect of sound. Within the past several decades, all this has changed. The Gyume and Gyuto Tibetan monks have given public performances throughout the world. Field recordings of

Mongolian hoomi singers are commercially available. Western musicians, meditators, and teachers of sound such as David Hykes, Jill Purce, and Michael Vetter are bringing harmonic abilities to light.

In this chapter we will learn to explore the mysterious and sacred ability of harmonic toning. This powerful and mystical ability enables us to create two or more notes simultaneously. It is one of the more extraordinary phenomena of sound. Creating vocal harmonics is an advanced form of self-transformation and healing where you will be able to sing harmony with yourself. Once you have achieved even the most rudimentary skill in harmonic toning, the very way that you hear and make sounds will be altered forever. It will open up the untold possibilities to be found in the vast spectrum of sound that resonates and reverberates throughout the universe.

We will learn some of the techniques utilized by shamans and others for the creation of vocal harmonics. While these are simple exercises that anyone can try, they are powerful tools. These exercises require no previous musical knowledge or singing ability. If you follow these step-by-step instructions you will find that, with practice, you will begin to hear other tones, those mysterious sonic particles we call overtones, along with the normal sounds that you are used to hearing.

CREATING VOCAL HARMONICS

Preparations

Complete reading this chapter before beginning the exercises found within it.* If possible, try to listen to recordings of harmonic singers (as listed in the discography) while you are reading and practicing. Before trying these exercises, find a comfortable space where you can make sounds and not be disturbed. When practicing these exercises, sit up straight, either on the floor or on a chair. While these techniques can eventually be done standing up or lying down, in the beginning sitting is best. You might want to keep a journal or a notebook to record any

*The "Fundamentals of Vocal Harmonics" exercise is available in the appendix and as part of the downloads that accompany this book.

changes you observe in your physical, emotional, or mental states that you may experience from your practice.

Toning the Vowel Sounds

The first step in the creation of vocal harmonics involves toning the different vowel sounds. The ability to create vocal harmonics is interrelated with the formants that are found in these sounds. As we discussed, formants are those clusters of harmonics where the energy of the sound spectrum is concentrated. They are the harmonics in various instruments, for example, that give these instruments their timbre or tone color. Different vowel sounds emphasize different harmonics. When we tone an "AH" sound (as in the word *father*), different harmonics are created than when we tone an "EEE" sound (as in the word *me*) or when we tone an "OOO" sound (as in the word *you*).

All harmonics are found within every vowel. However, the formants found within each vowel stress particular overtones. Because each voice is unique and we all pronounce vowels slightly differently, the exact harmonics that are created by the different vowel sounds will differ slightly depending upon the individual. If you have been practicing the exercises in the preceding chapter, you may have already begun to hear sounds within the vowels sounds. These were overtones.

Michael Vetter, an accomplished overtone singer from Switzerland, learned his ability in this manner from Karlheinz Stockhausen:

> To sing overtones and to deal with them musically requires, as with any other musical instrument, a long and arduous training. But the voice as a tool for acoustical communication is innate in man. If one actually listens, one requires no further teacher for the development of the voice. One need only sing slow, continuous tones for half an hour each day in the comfortable register of quiet speech making all the vowel form movements of normal speaking. Everything else follows.

As you may have already discovered, all the vowel sounds we make have naturally occurring harmonics within them. If you sing the vowel sounds "UH," "OOO," "OH," "AH," "EYE," "AYE," "EEE," linking them together in one breath, you will begin to hear different harmonics naturally being created by your own voice. Since each vowel sound has its own set of formants associated with it, singing the vowel sounds will create different harmonics. This phenomenon is the basis of harmonic toning.

The "OOO" vowel sound, for example, will help create the overtones of the octave and the fifth of the fundamental. The "OH" vowel sound will produce the overtones of the major third and the fifth of the next octave. The vowel sound "AH" will help create the overtone of the seventh. These may vary, of course, depending upon your pronunciation. You will also find that as you change from one vowel to another, specific harmonics will be created. As you proceed from "OOO" to "EEE," you will hear the overtones following the harmonic series becoming higher with each vowel sound that you create.

As in the previous exercise, sit in a comfortable sitting position with your hands on your knees or in your lap. Now find a comfortable note to tone, making sure it is not too deep or too high for your voice. Begin to tone the vowels going from "UH" to "OOO" to "OH" to "AH" to "EYE" to "AYE" to "EEE" in one breath.

The less you vocally enunciate the different vowel sounds, the more focused the harmonics will become. Instead of actually singing the vowel sounds from "UH" to "EEE," consciously keep the vowel sound in the throat and project the sound energy out as harmonics. It is as though you are shaping your mouth to form the vowels, but not actually pronouncing them. By changing the structure of the jaw, tongue, and cheeks, you will be altering the way the sound comes out.

Experiment with this now. Try toning the vowel sounds while adjusting the shape of your mouth, cheeks, and tongue. Many of us used to do this when we were children, experimenting and enjoying the different sounds we could create. Move your mouth, opening it all the way and then closing it, while toning the vowel sounds. Play with this exercise and have fun with it.

In order to hear your own harmonics, especially in the beginning, take one hand and cup it around an ear in the same way as you would do if you were trying to hear someone talking in a crowded room. This amplifies the shell of the ear and allows us to hear the sound more clearly. At the same time, take your other hand and place it, with the palm toward you, about two or three inches away from your mouth. This allows the sound to reflect off your hand and bounce back toward your ear so that you can hear the harmonics more clearly.

It is helpful to understand that a loudly created fundamental will not create a loud harmonic. The two seem to have an inverse relationship at the beginning of learning to create vocal harmonics. With a loudly sounded fundamental, you are focusing the majority of the sound energy outside your mouth. This is ideal for certain styles of singing, but not for the creation of vocal harmonics. In Central Asia, the style of creating vocal harmonics is known as "throat singing." Keep the sound energy inside your mouth, forming the fundamental tone deep in your throat. Then use your mouth and other vocal resonators such as the nasal cavity, cheeks, and lips for the creation and amplification of the harmonics. This will create a stronger, louder series of harmonics. It is often helpful at first to make sounds that are not much louder than your normal speaking voice. As you gain the ability to create vocal harmonics consciously, you may increase the volume of the sounds that you are making.

Experimenting with Harmonic Toning

After having experimented with toning the different vowel sounds and trying different positions with your mouth, many of you will already have begun to hear other, high-pitched sounds that you may not have noticed before. These may sound like whistling or buzzing noises, or perhaps like another note being created. Sometimes they are very high, almost seeming to be ultrasonic, or they may be very close to the fundamental sound of which you are normally aware. These may even be sounds that you hear when you sing. These are the overtones. They are already present whenever we make sound. You are merely focusing on them and becoming more aware of them.

There are a number of different phonemes, or basic sounds, that are helpful to use in the creation of some basic harmonics. We will now experiment with them as we expand our ability in harmonic toning.

First, begin to hum an "MMMM" sound, using a note that feels comfortable to you. As you make this sound, project the sound energy of the "MMMM" sound so that your lips are vibrating strongly. Take one of your fingers and put it to your lips in order to feel them vibrating.

Try this "MMMM" sound using the different vowels, going from "MMMUUU" (as in *moo*) to "MMMOOO" (rhythms with *go*) to "MMMAAA" (as in *ma*) to "MMMIII" (as in *my*) to "MMMAYE" (as in *may*) to "MMMEEE" (as in *me*). Make these sounds softly, vibrating your lips and then opening them just wide enough for each particular vowel to be audible with the "MMMM." You will hear and experience different harmonics that seem to almost pop up out of your lips as you make these sounds.

Now put your lips together as though you were about to whistle and slowly begin to open your mouth, keeping your lips rounded. It is helpful to imagine that you are making a face like a fish or a rabbit when you do this.

As the sound energy is vibrating on your lips with the "MMMM" sound, begin to open your mouth, still keeping your lips puckered and make a "MMMMOOOOORRRR" sound (as in the word *more*). Use one complete breath to make this sound, drawing it out and making it elongated.

With vocal harmonics, it is important to understand that each of the different vocal resonators, such as the lips, the cheeks, and the tongue, plays a role in the creation of vocal harmonics. The nasal cavity is particularly important in this. Many of us in the West are not accustomed to projecting sound into the nasal cavity. Yet the use of the nasal cavity as a vocal resonator is necessary in order to create certain vocal harmonics. As your toning becomes more nasal, higher harmonics will be created. In order to experience this, let us first make a "NNNNEEEE" sound (as in the word *knee*). Put two of your fingers on either side of your nose and see if you can vibrate your fingers while you are making this "NNNNEEEE" sound.

It may seem a little strange at first, especially to those who are not used to resonating this area with sound. As this area begins to vibrate, your sinuses may start to clear and you may find it helpful to have a tissue handy. Now that you have worked with the "NNNNEEEE" sound and have allowed your nasal cavity to resonate, let us tone another phoneme that is extremely useful in the creation of harmonics.

The "NNNNUUUU-RRRR" sound (rhyming with the word *her*) is a wonderful phoneme to practice. First begin by getting the nasal cavity to vibrate with a "NNNN" sound. After this has happened, begin to add in the "UUUU-RRRR" sound. What occurs is that the "NNNN" sound will still be vibrating in the nasal cavity while the "UUUU" sound will be vibrating in the back of the throat.

As you make this "NNNNUUUU-RRRR" sound, become aware that the "RRRR" is created by the tongue's moving forward against the roof of the mouth. There is a particular placement of the tongue with this and other sounds that is extremely helpful in controlling the creation of higher harmonics. If you place your tongue just about a quarter of an inch behind the front teeth, barely touching the roof of the mouth, the tongue will vibrate like a reed. Be aware that the tongue actually vibrates on a layer of saliva and is not firmly touching the roof. If the tongue were firmly touching the roof of the mouth, it would block and muffle the sound.

An interesting side note to this is that in many yogic traditions there is said to be a little "button" on the roof of the mouth, which adepts will touch with their tongue in order to stimulate the pineal gland. This is about the same place where the tongue slightly touches for the "NNNNUUUURRRR" sound.

Experiment with toning the "NNNNUUUU-RRRR" sound while slowly moving your tongue from the back of your mouth to the front. You will find that there is one particular spot where a high, whistle-like tone will become noticeably louder. Once you have found this spot, work with changing the shape of your mouth; for example, try making a face like a fish. As you do this, you will begin to create different harmonics.

Another phoneme that is very effective is an "NNNNGONG" sound. This opens and closes the glottis, the muscle at the back of the throat, another place where harmonics can be created. To do this, first nasalize that "NNNN" sound and then say the word "GUNG" (rhymes with *tongue*). Now nasalize the "NNNN" sound and say the word "GONG." Then nasalize the "NNNN" sound and say the word "GANG." Finally, nasalize the "NNNN" sound and say the word "GING" (rhymes with *sing*).

Now, with one breath, go from "NNNNGUNG" to "NNNNGONG" to "NNNNGANG" to "NNNNGING." Essentially, you are keeping the "NNNN" sound going while you chant "GUNG," "GONG," "GANG," and "GING," toning different vowel sounds while you open and close the glottis. When you do this, you will notice different harmonics seemingly popping out from the back of your throat.

Now that you have individually experimented with the "MMMMOOOORRRR," the "NNNNUUUU-RRRR" and the "NNNNGONG" sound, see what happens when you combine these different phonemes. Begin with the "MMMMOOOORRRR" sound and then shift into the "NNNNUUUU-RRRR" sound, ending with the "NNNNGONG" technique. Do this all on one breath, experiencing the different harmonics that are created by these different phonemes.

Now try beginning with the "NNNNGONG" sound and shift into the "NNNNUUUU-RRRR" sound, ending with the "MMMMOOOORRRR" sound.

Now try beginning with the "MMMMOOOORRRR" sound, going into the "NNNNUUUU-RRRR" sound and ending with the "NNNNGONG" sound.

These three phonemes are the easiest and most effective sounds for creating vocal harmonics. They are, by no means, the only ones. Here are others that you might also try:

- "WWWWOOOOWWWW" Tone this slowly, sounding the word *wow,* in one breath. As you open and close your mouth making this sound you will hear different harmonics. If you nasalize the sound, you will hear even more overtones.
- "HHHHUUUURRRR-EEEE" Very much like the "NNNNUUUU-RRRR" sound, this brings the tone and the harmonics from the back of the throat to the front. With one

breath, tone it in two distinct parts: "HHHHUURRRR" (as in *her*) and "REEEE" (rhymes with *me*).

- "OOOOEEEE" This works best in a high-pitched voice or in a falsetto. The "OOOO" (rhymes with *you*) creates the lower harmonics, while the "EEEE" (rhymes with *me*) creates the upper harmonics. Some people find it particularly easy to hear harmonics while making this sound.

These different phonemes are the beginning of learning to create vocal harmonics. The next step in developing the ability to do harmonic toning is to gain control over the harmonics that are created.

Working with the different vowel sounds enables you to create different harmonics. Going from "UH" to "EEE" and then back, you will be sounding vowels with formants that go up and down the harmonic series, creating overtones that are vibrating many times the speed of the fundamental of your voice. With a little practice, you will probably be able to create and hear eight or more different overtones.

Practicing Toning Specific Harmonics

After you have learned to produce different harmonics you will want to pick out one particular harmonic that you are creating. Then focus your attention on this harmonic, holding it and making it louder. It does not matter which phoneme you have used in order to create it. Once you have done this with one harmonic, focus on another harmonic and do the same.

As we all have different singing ranges, it appears that we all have different harmonic ranges. If you have tried the various exercises in this chapter and are still having difficulty hearing your harmonics, try going up a little bit higher in pitch with your voice, or perhaps down a little deeper. You might find that a slight change in the fundamental you are toning makes all the difference in the world.

Along with listening to recorded examples of vocal harmonics from other singers, recording yourself is an excellent aid. Record these exercises and then listen to the sounds you have made. Often we are so concerned about creating vocal harmonics that we cannot hear them, or do not believe we actually have made them when they occur. By recording these exercises and then listening to them, we can hear the changes in our tone and pay attention to the naturally occurring harmonics in our voice. This is helpful in reinforcing the knowledge that everyone can consciously create vocal harmonics.

Remember that practice is the key. The more you practice, the better you will be able to acquire the ability of creating vocal harmonics. It is an ability that you can acquire. Sometimes you will begin to hear your own harmonics immediately after trying one of the exercises in this chapter for the first time. Sometimes it takes days before you can hear them.

As you practice these techniques for creating vocal harmonics, you will be exercising muscles of the vocal mechanism in a manner in which they may not have been previously used. It may also take some time to develop the ability to project sound to places in the throat, mouth, and nose that you may not have consciously resonated with sound before.

Allow yourself adequate time for these exercises. A minimum of fifteen minutes per day is recommended. Allow time to assimilate the experience in sound that you have had. You will be resonating your physical body with these tones and affecting your heart rate, respiration rate, flow of blood, skin temperature, brain waves, and more. As I have suggested, keeping a journal during this time is particularly useful.

In many traditions, harmonics are viewed as sacred sounds. You are awakening these sounds in yourself when you begin this process of learning to create vocal harmonics. These sounds should be made with reverence and respect. Yet, in the creation of these sounds, you will also enjoy yourself immensely. In Psalm 66 of the Old Testament it is written: "Make a joyful noise unto God. . . ." Work with the joyful energies of sound. A whole new world is awaiting you!

TEN
OVERTONING

INTRODUCTION

Of all the sound-making devices and instruments found on this planet, the human voice is believed by many to have the most healing qualities. No other instrument is capable of such a wide variety of different sounds and textures and, in fact, many other instruments were created in order to emulate the various qualities of the human voice. The range of sonics found in the human voice can go from the growl-like depths of the Tibetan monks to the birdlike qualities found in South American Indigenous tribes. We can sound like musical instruments, including percussions, nature sounds, and other sounds not found anywhere else in nature. We can create an extraordinary spectrum of frequency and timbre using only our own voices.

TONING

"Toning" is the use of the voice as an instrument for healing. It is a term first used by Laurel Elizabeth Keyes in her book *Toning,* which has now become something of a classic in this field of sound healing. While toning has no doubt been used since the first cave person stubbed their toe and made a sound to release the pain, Keyes is credited with using this term in the early 1960s to describe the use of vocally created sound as a therapeutic tool. As she described in her book, "Toning is an ancient method of healing . . . the idea is simply to restore people to their harmonic patterns."

Since the time Keyes first reintroduced toning as a term to our culture, the use of the human voice as an instrument for healing has become more well known and has been described in a number of other books.

Laeh Maggie Garfield, in *Sound Medicine,* writes: "Toning is a system of healing that utilizes vowel sounds to alter vibrations in every molecule and cell in the body."

Don Campbell, in *The Roar of Silence,* comments thus on this use of the voice: "Tone is simply an audible sound, prolonged long enough to be identified. 'Toning' is the conscious elongation of a sound using the breath and voice."

John Beaulieu writes in *Music and Sound in the Healing Arts:* "Toning is the process of making vocal sounds for the purpose of balance. . . . Toning sounds are sounds of expression and do not have a precise meaning."

Randall McClellan, in *The Healing Forces of Music,* describes toning as "the sustained vocalization of individual pitches for the purpose of resonating specific body areas to which the voice is directed."

Steven Halpern writes in *Tuning the Human Instrument:* "Toning is an activity that releases and allows the natural flow of energy to move through one's body."

An additional definition of toning that I would like to use is that toning is the use of the voice to express sounds for the purpose of release and relief, or to resonate the physical body and the etheric fields. It is nonverbal sound, relying primarily on vowels, though it may incorporate the use of consonants to create syllables as long as they are not utilized to create coherent meaning. Sighing, moaning, and humming may also be recognized as forms of toning.

Toning is not chanting as we normally perceive it, although toning may sound like chanting. Chanting uses words as either liturgical texts or incantations for a specific purpose with meaning. Mantras that use predetermined sounds are also a form of chanting such as "Om Na Ma Shiva Ya" or "Om Mani Padme Hum," though the single elongation of a seed syllable such as "Om" or "Ra" can be considered a form of toning. However, as soon as words are utilized to create meaning and are repeated in recitation, they become chant.

TONING AND HEALING

There are a number of reasons why toning may be the most effective use of sound as a healing instrument. First, we can learn to use our voice to resonate different areas of our body and bring them into balance. This is based upon the principle of resonance. Every organ, bone, and tissue in the body has a healthy frequency at which it normally vibrates. When disease sets in, the vibrations in that portion of the body become different. By creating sounds that are harmonious with the resonant frequency of the healthy organ, it is possible to change the vibrational rate of the diseased portion of the body back to its natural frequency.

There are a number of scientists, including Dr. Peter Guy Manners, who are working with specific frequencies that are applied through instrumentation to the body for just this purpose. It seems, however, that we have this ability to project the correct vibrations to imbalanced portions of our own bodies using our voices. What is particularly appealing about using our own voices is that the resonant frequencies of each organ, for example, may differ slightly from person to person. While an instrument may have a frequency that can resonate the liver, for example, it will be an overall frequency that can be thought of as being generic for all livers. We can become much more specific with the use of our own voices.

Second, the importance of "intention" has been stressed in various chapters throughout this book. Intention is the energy behind the sound being created. It is the consciousness we have when we are making a sound. While intention seems to be a very ethereal concept and certainly difficult to quantify, I have little doubt that as we become more aware of the power of sound to heal and transform, intention will become an aspect of sound that receives much more attention.

The human voice is able to focus and project energy of intention during sound-making better than any other instrument. Some scientific machinery may be geared toward projecting the specific frequencies of an organ to that organ. However, it is easy enough for the applier of these sounds to be using such instruments on someone while daydreaming of a time at the beach or something else. When we use our voice on ourselves or on someone else, we immediately focus on the present moment in order to create a healing situation. We become in the now, and our intention is similarly focused.

We can easily understand this concept of intention in relationship to the human voice by thinking of the ability of singers to affect us. We can listen to a vocalist with an extraordinarily excellent voice (a voice whose frequencies are correct) and yet be perfectly bored. We may hear this excellent voice, but something is missing, and the sound does not affect us. Yet, we can listen to a singer whose voice is craggy and perhaps critically defined as poor and be moved to tears.

The difference in the ability of these two singers to affect us is certainly not in the frequencies they are projecting. It must lie, therefore, in the intention they have in creating their sounds. We may find as we continue this investigation into the therapeutic effects of sound that intention is of equal, if not greater, importance than the actual sound being created.

Where is intention created? It is created in our minds and our hearts before we make a sound. It can be an imaging or a visualization that we focus upon, which we project upon the sound when we make it. When is the intention created? It is usually created during the breath we take before we make the sound. In particular, it seems to be most effective at the stillpoint that occurs when the breath is already in our lungs waiting to be released.

BREATHING

This stillpoint between the in-breath and the out-breath (in our case, the sound) is believed by many to be the time during the cycle of the breath when the human body is locked in resonance with itself. Scientist Itzhak Bentov, among others, believes that during this time, the body creates a wave form that operates at about 7.8 cycles per second. This is a frequency that is believed to be the resonant frequency of the Earth.

In that time, we are, however briefly, also locked in resonance with the energy of the Earth.

For a moment, take a breath, hold it, and then release it. See if you feel this stillpoint. The breath is the key to all sounds that we create using our own voice. Without our breath, there is no sound. Breath is the essence of life, for without our breath, we would have no life. In many different traditions, the life energy inherent in breath is considered sacred. This energy is called *prana* in the Hindu traditions. In East Asia, it is called *chi* or *ki.* The Hebrew word for breath is *ruach,* which is the same as the Hebrew word for "spirit."

The science of breath is a subject that truly demands its own book and, in fact, a number have been written on the subject. There are many different thoughts on the proper way to breathe. Some believe that breathing should be done through the nose in a certain way. Others believe proper breathing occurs only when done through the mouth. We suggest doing whatever feels comfortable to you. However, it is recommended when working with toning that you initially try to be aware of your posture and keep your spine as straight as possible. The reason for this is that the energy inherent in the breath seems to work best in conjunction with the other systems of the physical and etheric body when the spine is upright. It is also much easier to take a deep breath when the spine is straight.

While there is a question of whether to use the nose or the mouth to take an in-breath, especially when working with sound, there seems to be universal agreement that the breath should go down to the diaphragm. The diaphragm is located at the bottom of the lungs above the stomach. This has always been a very natural way for me to breathe, but I have been surprised to find that many people do not do this. I believe many have been taught improper breathing techniques during school or some other time when we were told that taking a deep breath meant bringing up our shoulders.

Take a deep breath now and observe what happens to your body. If your lower rib cage and stomach are expanding when you take this breath, you are doing diaphragmatic breathing. Usually this is a very relaxed breath. However, if you notice that your shoulders are rising and the stomach and lower ribs are not moving, you are not breathing from the diaphragm. You are also probably tense.

Diaphragmatic breathing allows us to breathe much deeper and take much more air into our lungs. It is also much easier to do than the other type of deep breathing that really only uses our upper lungs. Diaphragmatic breathing expands our lung capacity and enhances the life energy we take into ourselves.

Breathing from the diaphragm is natural, but sometimes it takes a bit of concentration to unlearn breathing techniques we may have learned when we were young. To learn to use your diaphragm when you breathe, simply focus your attention (your intention) on bringing the air down to the bottom of your lungs. At first, you may consciously have to expand your rib cage and your stomach area when you take a deep breath in. Sometimes it helps to lie on your back and put your hands on your belly. When you take a breath in, feel the area above your stomach expand and the air fill the diaphragm. Hold that breath for a few seconds and feel that area contract as the air is expelled out of your lungs. Be aware of your shoulders and pay attention not to have them rise or fall with the breath. Many people who have learned incorrect breathing techniques will first consciously raise their shoulders in anticipation of using their upper lungs for breath. You can easily unlearn this habit. You will find that taking a deep diaphragmatic breath is a relaxed and easy thing to do. It will expand the breath you take and the energy you put into it.

TONING AND OVERTONING

This chapter is called "Overtoning" and not "Toning" because it will focus upon the relationship between vocal harmonics and self-created healing sounds. I created the word "overtoning" some years ago to define those who practiced toning with knowledge and use of overtones. Before I learned about overtoning, I had been practicing toning, which I had learned from my friend and teacher, Sarah Benson. Sarah taught me a particular technique, which we will learn later in this chapter, that enables an individual to use his or her voice to scan a person's body and energy field and then project sound into specific portions of the person's body and this field. It was and still is an extraordinary and powerful technique.

Some time after I had learned this manner of toning, I was introduced to harmonic singing through hearing the Harmonic Choir, and, as I have related elsewhere, I learned how to create vocal harmonics. It was not long after this that I began to hear a very mysterious phenomenon. I first became aware of it during a toning workshop I was giving at the Maine Healing Arts Festival.

I was teaching the participants of this workshop how to scan another person with their voice and then project sound into them. I began to notice that when the person doing the toning had found the right sound and the right place, the sound would change. While I had noticed this before, I had never been aware of exactly what these changes in the sound were. There, at the festival, I suddenly realized that when my students were attuned with the sound and projecting their voices into another person, harmonics would come out! I could close my eyes or have my back to those doing this work and know exactly when the sound was right. Suddenly the sounds I heard would change. I would be aware of vocal harmonics being created by people who had never heard these audible overtones before.

Time and time again, I observed this phenomenon occurring. I had at first noticed this during my own toning work, where specific harmonic frequencies would be present. However, I had thought that these were my own unique sounds, the result of my previous experience learning vocal harmonics. Once I started teaching others this toning technique, it became apparent to me that vocal harmonics would become stronger and more enforced in the sounds of anyone doing this toning technique.

It was at this point that I consciously began teaching vocal harmonics in conjunction with toning. My reason for doing this was that if vocal harmonics were being created anyway in my students, perhaps consciously teaching them some techniques to create overtones might strengthen and enhance their sound-healing capabilities. I like to use the simile that when toning without using specific harmonics, the voice can be likened to a shotgun aiming for a target. You hit the target with some of the shot, but there is a lot of wasted energy and pellets. When consciously using vocal harmonics during overtoning, the voice becomes much more like a sonic laser able to hit the bullseye. We are able to focus and project specific frequencies into another person, making these sounds much more powerful and accurate.

QUARTZ CRYSTALS AND TONING

Among my greatest teachers in this aspect of toning were quartz crystals. As I have mentioned earlier, during my initial work with sound healing, I was also fascinated with the ability of quartz crystals to be transducers of energy. One day, I picked up a crystal and began to tone into it. I found, much to my surprise, that specific harmonics were resonated and enforced by that crystal. I picked up another crystal and heard different harmonics being resonated and enforced. A friend to whom I taught vocal harmonics verified this when he began toning into quartz crystals.

One night a woman who had worked with the Harmonic Choir was visiting. She was not particularly interested in sound healing nor had she ever worked with quartz crystals. She was into vocal harmonics as an art form and that was all. As an experiment, I asked her if she would sing into a quartz crystal. She already thought I was a bit unusual, so the request did not strike her as being particularly bizarre. Being an accommodating guest, she complied with my request.

"I can't believe it!" she said, after singing into that first crystal. "It's amplifying the fifth harmonic."

I gave her another crystal. "Oh no!" she exclaimed. "This one is amplifying the third harmonic. Give me another."

And so on and so on throughout most of the night. My guest sang into different quartz crystals, finding that they would resonate and amplify different and specific harmonics. I think she went away that night feeling rather mystified and a bit shaken by the whole experience. It was soon after this that I contacted for the first time Marcel Vogel, the IBM research scientist who had been researching the therapeutic uses of quartz crystals.

"I do this form of singing where you are able to create harmonics with the voice," I told him. "I have found that different quartz crystals will resonate and amplify different harmonics. Is this crazy?"

"Congratulations!" he began. "You have come upon a very ancient and powerful technique for working with quartz crystals. Yes, different crystals will oscillate to different harmonic frequencies and no, it is not crazy. You may be the first person to actually have rediscovered this."

Quartz crystals have the ability of turning sound into light, a phenomenon we discuss in regard to vocal harmonics in chapter 3. To quote another phone conversation with Marcel Vogel:

> The quartz crystal is an oscillator. You can tune it with pressure. You can cut it to a specific configuration so that when you tune it, it produces a sound which is subsonic. That sound induces a luminescence in the body of an individual. It is cold light produced by an electronic vibration change. To convert sound into light, you are moving from a lower energy level into a higher level. The energy must be compressed and pulsed in order to convert it into light. Crystalloluminescence is the term for the conversion of sound vibrations into light in crystals.

While this chapter is not on the relationship of quartz crystals to toning or vocal harmonics, I mention this most interesting relationship simply because I believe it was through my initial experience of toning into a quartz crystal that I became aware that different harmonics may be created when resonating different crystalline substances. Since the human body is composed of many crystalline substances, from our bones to the liquid crystal colloidal structure of the brain, it is not unreasonable to suppose that this may be an explanation for why the sound changes when we are toning.

There are a number of different explanations for what may occur during the toning process, some of which I have created myself in order to explain a fairly simple but mystical phenomenon regarding the changing of the sound once it finds the correct area. One explanation is that the voice somehow creates the proper resonance with an organ or portion of the body that is out of alignment and through this resonance changes the tone of the voice. Another explanation is that there is some sort of hole in the auric field that somehow amplifies and resonates various aspects of the harmonic spectrum.

Kay Gardner, in her book, *Sounding the Inner Landscape,* describes this phenomenon of toning:

> The howling of wolves is similar to the siren sounds taught by Sarah Benson and Jonathan Goldman of the Sound Healers Association. Using a technique described by Laurel Elizabeth Keyes, the sound healer stands in front of the person he or she is working with and, directing the beginning sound at the person's feet, creates a siren sound, slowly rising to the person's head. Within this siren is a tone felt by the toner to be "sticky" or "thick." It is at this area of the person's body that the sound healer repeats the sticky sound in short, gentle pulses in order to resonate and thus release the stress, tension, or pain.

While I tend to describe the technique a bit differently (and I would not use the image of howling wolves!), Kay's description gives a succinct view of the Siren technique, which is discussed in greater detail later on in this chapter.

PROJECTING SOUNDS INTO OURSELVES

Before we begin learning the Siren and projecting sound into someone else, let us work with some exercises for learning to project sounds into different parts of ourselves. This form of toning is a very natural aspect of the use of the voice that most of us have forgotten. A key to this may lie in our intention. We can project any sound into any portion of our body if we practice, and specifically if we focus our intention on doing this. We can use almost any sound to resonate almost any area, from our big toe to the top of our head, if this is our intention.

Most of us practice some form of toning, though we are probably unaware of it. Remember that sighing, groaning, moaning, and other sounds we make for release are all part of toning. Toning can be an extraordinary tool for relief of pain. What happens when you stub your toe? You usually make some sound. Have you ever stubbed your toe and not made a sound? What happens? It hurts more!

We make sounds when we are in pain and these sounds help ease the pain. I know of people who have been able to completely eliminate chronic pain through use of toning. One explanation may be that toning helps create endorphins, those pain-killing neurochemicals that are a hundred times more powerful than morphine. Regardless of the reason, toning during a painful experience is extremely effective. This includes, of course, emotional pain. Many of us are able to weep and moan during some extraordinary emotional trauma, which helps release psychic pain.

Toning to Release Pain

One note on the use of toning to release pain. When you make the initial sound, do not constrict yourself. Relax and release. These sounds can be loud and powerful, but they should not be restricted. They should be sounds of release, with the sound going out of the body. Here is a story that may help illustrate what I mean.

One day, for reasons that escape me now, I was really angry. I wanted to use sound to release this anger. I did not want to make these sounds in my house for it was summer and the windows were open. Knowing the power of my voice, I thought that if I got too carried away with sounding, my neighbors might call the police. In order to remedy the situation, I went with my wife and a friend into the woods that were nearby with the intention of releasing this anger with sound. I took one deep breath in, constricted my body and screamed! My shoulders were tight. My entire body was tense. And this bloodcurdling yell was inwardly directed, though it certainly came out of my mouth loud enough. Immediately, I felt worse because I could no longer move my head. No, I wasn't paralyzed. But I had popped three vertebrae out in my neck from making the sound!

"Get me to a chiropractor," I moaned. After a session with Dr. Steven Brown, my vertebrae were back in place and I had learned a serious lesson about toning that I pass on to you. It is the only warning I give about toning. When making sounds for release, be as relaxed as possible, even if you are in serious physical or emotional pain. This does not mean that the sound cannot be one of pain, but your body should not be tight when making the sound.

You will find that if you groan or moan, it will be more effective for release than if you scream. Constricted sounds can keep the pain in the body and reinforce the damage. Released sounds will release the pain.

Exercises to Resonate Different Parts of Your Body

We will next work with some exercises to learn to resonate different portions of our body. In order to do any of these exercises, it is recommended that you sit or stand with the spine straight. And find a place where you can make sounds without disturbing others or have them disturbing you. To learn to resonate different portions of your body with sound, a good place to start is with the vowel sounds described in chapter 8. By working with these sounds, you will have already learned to resonate the different cavities of your body with specific sounds.

The best way to learn to project sound to different parts of yourself is to experiment with the vowel sounds. Spend fifteen minutes a day working with a different vowel sound, such as "OH" or "AH," making that vowel sound in different pitches. Experiment around, going from a very low sound to a very high sound or from a very high sound to a very low sound. Try doing this low-to-high or high-to-low range with just one breath.

Become aware of where the sound is vibrating in your body. Is a high "OOO" resonating your neck and a low "AH" resonating your belly, or are you experiencing the reverse? Remember that since we are all unique vibratory beings, there are no "right" and no "wrong" sounds in terms of personal resonance. This is why I am not suggesting that you try to resonate your big toe with an "AYE" sound and your left ear with an "OH" sound. While we can learn to resonate any sound to any portion of the body, it is much easier initially to use sounds that work for us. What works for one person may not work for another.

Becoming in tune with the way the different vowel sounds and pitches resonate may happen immediately, but for most it takes some time. Some teachers suggest working with the vowel sounds in this manner for many weeks or months. Do what feels comfortable to you. After you have experimented with each of the different vowel sounds and their associated harmonics in this manner, try projecting specific sounds to specific portions of your body. Now try sending an "AYE" to your big toe and an "OH" to your left ear and vice versa. See what happens. The more proficient you become at knowing your own sounds, the easier it will be to do this. Some sounds will resonate more easily than others, and you may not want to try projecting a sound that does not feel natural to a particular portion of your body.

Remember that your intention to project a sound is of equal importance to the sound you make. If you want to project an "AYE" to your big toe, with time and practice you can do it. If, however, your big toe prefers an "OH" sound, this will work much more easily in conjunction with your intention. It is not necessary to learn to tone yourself in this manner in order to learn to scan and do the Siren. However, it is helpful. It is also extremely useful in the event that you are in pain and there is no one around who can tone you.

One of the main reasons for learning to project sound to different portions of your body is as a healing tool. If you have a stomachache, for example, and have learned to project sound to your belly, you can resonate that area with sound and feel much better. I know of many people who have learned to use sound in this manner and have been able to help release pain. Sometimes they have been able to take care of chronic conditions they have had for many years by toning imbalanced areas with their own sound. Headaches, sore throats, hurt knees—all may be helped by toning the area with your own sound.

THE SIREN TECHNIQUE

The Siren is the technique that I mentioned earlier. You can use your voice to scan the auric field and physical body of another person, in much the same way that people who practice therapeutic touch can do this with their hands. After you have done this scan, the voice is then used to project sound to the imbalanced area to resonate and align it.

How does this work? As I speculated previously in this chapter, it probably works off some aspect of the phenomenon of resonance. Your voice entrains an imbalanced organ or part of the auric field back into resonance. These sounds may also break up crystallized structures that are creating blockages in the body or energy field. However, there is at present no specific explanation for the effectiveness of this technique.

I have taught thousands of people how to do overtoning and nearly every one of them has been able to learn it. Yet I cannot explain exactly how we are able to do it. In fact, when I teach this technique, I usually tell people in workshops to turn off the left, logical portion of the brain because the exercise we are about to do makes no sense. Frequently, the questioning aspect of our brain gets in the way, and if we think too much about what we are doing, we won't be able to do it. It is not logical. It does not make sense. Yet it works.

When I do this technique, I will often do it with my eyes closed. My reasons for doing this are twofold. First, I find that by keeping my eyes closed, I will not consciously be aware of where I am projecting the sound. Second, I will also not interfere with the sound that wants to be projected.

Vickie Dodd, a bodyworker who does wonderful work with toning in her practices, says that we should not project our own sounds into another person. I agree. By this Vickie means that we should not send what we think are the correct sounds into someone else. The most important aspect of doing the Siren properly is that we become vehicles for creating sacred sound. We simply become instruments for the Sound Current, allowing whatever sounds that wish to be present for the healing to occur.

If someone comes to me with a sore throat, for example, and I am about to do some overtoning with them, my logical mind might think, "A sore throat? This calls for an "AYE" sound directed at their throat." With that situation, I would be projecting what I thought would be the correct sound, my own sound, into them. By closing my eyes and not knowing where the sound is being projected, I can usually get out of the way of my own ego, which thinks it knows best, and let the sound do its work.

Over the years, I have learned to trust sacred sound to do what it needs to do, in spite of myself. In the example above, I might find that the left knee needs the sound (perhaps because of an imbalanced meridian there) and not the throat at all. Usually, of course, it would be the throat that I find myself projecting the sound to. But not always.

Researcher Tom Kenyon, director of Acoustic Brain Research, did some preliminary study of toning. He found that when a person had an imbalanced acupuncture meridian, the sound would go to that meridian and balance it regardless of where the sound was being directed. The sound would go where it was needed, and the body would take in these sounds and use them for balance in spite of any expectations of what should occur on the part of the person doing the toning. Yet, to be most effective in the toning process, I repeat my belief that it is best for the person doing the toning to get out of the way and just become an instrument for the creation of the sound.

To learn to do the Siren, it is necessary to have a partner with whom to work. Have this person stand in front of you. If there is a third person around, he or she should stand behind the person you are toning. If there is not another person, have the person you are working on stand against a wall. The reason for this is that the effects of this exercise are so powerful that the person receiving the sound may become lightheaded and unsteady. The wall provides something to brace against, ensuring the person does not fall over during the experience.

Begin by breathing in a slow, steady fashion with the breath going down to the diaphragm. During this time, I always say a little prayer asking that I become a vehicle for sacred sound and that all healing and transformation be for the good of the individual. I make sure that I am grounded, feeling my connection to both the earth and the sky. I also understand that I am protected during this experience. The sacred sound is coming through me and not from me and there is nothing that I may pick up from the other person I am working on. This is my intention before I actually begin to sound. I suggest it is a good intention for anyone doing this work.

Next, begin with the very highest sound that you can make, starting at the top of the head and working down with the sound going lower and lower as you project the sound down the person's body until you end up at their feet. The sound goes from a high sound to a low sound, like a siren. Then, do the reverse, going from their feet to their head, using a low to high sound as you do this.

Laurel Elizabeth Keyes, in *Toning,* suggests starting with the lowest possible sound that can be made and then moving upward in pitch. This works very well, too. The importance of the Siren is to create the fullest range of sounds possible so that those tones that are necessary for healing may be created. If you feel more comfortable starting with a low sound, please do so.

After you have scanned the person with the Siren, you will find yourself being drawn to a particular area of the person's body. You may need to do the Siren several times before this occurs, but it will. As I have mentioned before, this is a totally intuitive experience, and I sometimes feel as though I am in a trance or some other altered state. I am not thinking of what sounds I should be making or where I should be making them. My intention is merely to be a vehicle for sacred sound.

Allow the sound coming through you to go where it chooses. Go into that area where you perceived that the sound was needed and project whatever sounds wish to be made there. You may find that after a minute or two at one spot, the sound wants to move again. Allow the sound to go where it wants to go. When the sound has achieved its purpose, it will end. Usually the first toning exercises last for five to ten minutes. To complete this exercise, place your hands on the shoulders of the person you have been toning and gently squeeze them as a tool for grounding.

After the exercise is completed, talk and share with the person you have been toning. Find out what was experienced. How does the person feel now? What did the person feel? Did your sound affect the areas the person thought needed work? If the person is interested, switch places and have the person tone you. Remember that the more you do this, the more trust you will have in it as a technique for healing.

You may find, as you are scanning the body with these tones, that harmonics seem to come out at particular areas. This is often an indication of areas where the sound wishes to be projected. Allow the overtones to emerge from your voice and to be focused as healing energy into the other person. Do not consciously create specific overtones but let them come out of you if they wish.

I sometimes conceive of the overtones, when utilized in this manner, as being sonic laser beams breaking up thought forms and blocked energy and allowing balance and alignment to return to wherever the sound was being projected. The ability to create harmonics enhances this toning technique. It seems to amplify and make even more effective the use of vocally created sounds for healing. As I stated before, I observed that harmonics seem to come out naturally, even when the person doing the toning was unaware of their existence. They become even more present when the person doing the toning knows how to create them. They seem to be a part of this sacred sound work that is active in the process of healing. By working with harmonics in toning you have one of the most powerful sacred sound healing experiences.

Please remember that harmonics are only one aspect of this work with sacred sound. The intention of being a vehicle for the sacred sound is essential. A particular overtone may come out when you are sounding a specific area, and if you can enhance the projection of that harmonic, then you are aiding the sound that wants to occur. However, if you think, "I'm going to create a specific harmonic and then project it into this person because that is what they need to heal them!" then the point is lost. You would then be projecting your own sound, and this is not the same.

GROUP OVERTONING

Overtoning in a group setting is similar to individual overtoning. It is very simple to learn and quite powerful. Have the person receiving the sound work lie in the center of a circle created by the people in the group. Be sure that everyone in the circle has a similar intention. Then begin to have the group make sounds directed with this intention at the person in the center.

A good way to begin overtoning in a group situation is to begin with the sound "OM." This ancient mantra is an excellent sound that will immediately create a resonance among members of the group. Harmonics will naturally occur during a group "OM," for this sound has within it a majority of vowels. When creating the "OM" sound, start by humming an "MMMMM" sound. Then, slowly begin to open your mouth making the "OOO" sound, widening it to create an "OH" and an "AH" sound until your mouth is completely open. Then slowly close your mouth until you are back to humming the "MMMMM" sound. This will allow for a full range of vowels and their harmonics to be created. After experimenting with the "OM" sound, try toning specific vowel sounds, such as "AH" or "EEE." These are good sounds to use to begin group overtoning. The person in the center of the group may have a particular vowel, mantra, or name that they would like to have sounded. This will also work well.

You may also add a color desired by the person in the center, as well as an affirmation. Ask the person who is in the center what color he or she would like projected on the sound, or what affirmation. Since sound is a carrier wave of consciousness, any number of different energies may travel on the sound. The person may want the color green and the thought "love," or the color gold and the thought "healing." With group overtoning, having a combined group consciousness and intention in this sonic process is very helpful.

As with overtoning with just one other person, group overtoning must allow for the sound to do what it wants to do. You may start with a particular sound, but it is important to let the sound change. Sometimes when doing this exercise, the sound will be very discordant and then suddenly harmonize. At other times, it will remain discordant or it can be very harmonized from the beginning. It all depends upon what the person in the center needs, and this means allowing the sound to have a life of its own.

VISUALIZATION FOR OVERTONING

There is one addition to these exercises that I would like to suggest when you are doing overtoning, either in an individual or a group setting. When making the sounds, imagine that there is a beam of energy coming from your heart, your throat, and your third eye. Imagine this energy coming out of your centers and meeting at the point of a triangle that is the beam of sacred sound. From your heart is coming Divine Love, from your throat is coming Divine Sound, and from your third eye is coming Divine Wisdom as you make the sound. This visualization will enhance the sacred sound and make this work with overtoning even more effective.

Conclusion

One Final Fact

In this book we have explored the mysterious world of harmonics, seeing how harmonics and the physical world are interrelated. We have learned of the mathematics of harmonics and found that the vibrations of a string are in essence the same as the pulsations of the universe. We have examined the physics of harmonics and discovered that sound creates form. Such an understanding makes the journey from the scientific to the spiritual quite natural, for this is a rediscovery of the knowledge of the ancients.

In the magical and occult traditions we have learned of harmonics as tools for self-transformation. In these spiritual and shamanic cultures, the mysteries of harmonics continue to intrigue us. We have explored the outer realms of Tibetan mysticism and looked at the potentials that are inherent in the Kabbalistic toning of vowel sounds.

We have learned exercises for resonating our inner and outer selves with sound and for the creation of vocal harmonics. We have traced the many possibilities of harmonics, from using them as guideposts for the universe as we listen to them, to learning to create sonic fields of healing energy when we make them. Yet this is only the beginning.

Hans Kayser, who called himself a "harmonicist," believed that "one of the primary tasks of harmonics must be that of activating the capacity for experience within each of the spheres of human knowledge." I do not know if I am a harmonicist, but Kayser was correct. Harmonics can teach us an extraordinary amount about the universe and our relationship to it. We are still learning new secrets about ourselves and the world we live in, on both a scientific and a spiritual level.

We are beginning to see a reemergence of the awareness of harmonics in the arts and sciences. As this continues, we may see radical changes in the way we utilize sound and in the concepts of how we perceive sound as an energy. There are frontiers in the fields of music and medicine that we have not yet begun to cross.

Healing Sounds is only the beginning of a journey that involves traveling through the sacred science of sound. It is hoped that you will continue this journey to enhance your own life on this planet.

Try to find others to sound with. They are out there. You just have to look (or listen) for them. Creating vocal harmonics by oneself is remarkable but sounding together becomes divine.

What has not been mentioned until now is the remarkable fact that when two tones sound together, a third and fourth tone are also created. No, these additional tones are not strictly harmonics. This phenomenon occurs whenever any two tones vibrate together, and they are called combination tones. They are composed of the difference between, and the summation of, the two tones that sound. If, for example, one tone is vibrating at 300 Hz and another tone is vibrating at 400 Hz, of the two combination tones that are created one is vibrating at 100 Hz (the difference between the two tones) and the other is vibrating at 700 Hz (the sum of these two tones).

When two people are creating vocal harmonics together, other tones begin to emerge. These are not tones that have been specifically created by either of the two people. These are tones that suddenly seem to appear out of thin air. When this occurs, I am always reminded of Christ's statement in Matthew: "For where two or three are gathered together in my name, there am I in the midst of them." For when two or more people gather to create sacred sounds, there are other sacred sounds that are heard. It is one of the most mystical experiences imaginable and one that you must experience for yourself.

I hope I have intrigued you with one more possibility of harmonics and that this will help guide you to seek out others. There are many fine teachers of harmonics and other aspects of sound if you wish to find further information and instructions. There are also many people who are interested in sounding together to experience the sacredness and joyfulness of doing so. If you look, you will find them.

For those of you who are interested in furthering your search into the mysteries of sound, the Sound Healers Association offers membership, discourses, seminars, workshops, and the School of Sound. Currently, the Sound Healers Association presents monthly online meetings for members. For information contact:

Sound Healers Association
Website: soundhealersassociation.org
P.O. Box 2240
Boulder, CO 80306, USA
303-443-8181

In addition, I invite you to visit my award-winning Healing Sounds website at healingsounds.com. There you'll find a great deal of useful information and materials related to this book including articles, discourses, online seminars, workshops, and the School of Sound, as well as many sonic tools for transformation: tuning forks, recordings, books, and much more.

It is said that a picture is worth a thousand words. When dealing with harmonics, it is true that one sound is worth a thousand pictures. For this reason, I have created recordings to accompany this book. The *Healing Sounds Instructional* recordings were designed to help facilitate your knowledge and techniques of creating vocal harmonics. First available as a cassette, this resource is now available as a download to accompany this book. Also included are other recorded examples that I trust will truly enhance your ability to understand and work with harmonics.

You'll find out more information about these audio downloads in the appendix.

Harmonics have been an important and stimulating area of interest in my life and continue to be. It has been a pleasure to share my research, thoughts, and experiences with you in this book. This is only the beginning of the journey. I wish you much joy!

AFTERWORD TO THE THIRD EDITION
(2002)

I trust you've enjoyed your journey through sound with *Healing Sounds*. It is my hope that you've found the information and exercises to be helpful. Perhaps both have inspired you to explore even greater depths of the healing and transformational power of sound.

Many of the ideas and suggestions in this book that a decade ago had not yet been systematically proved have now begun to see the light of science through the hard work and inspired research of many individuals.

Scientist Ranjie Singh, Ph.D., was intrigued by chapter 7 in which I suggest that the hormone melatonin is released through the toning of specific harmonically related sounds. He has researched this assertion and proved that indeed certain self-created sounds do produce melatonin. In 1997, he published his findings in *Self-Healing: Powerful Techniques*. In 2000, Japanese scientist Masaru Emoto published a book called *The Message from Water*, which documents the transformative power of sound and intention using photographs of frozen water molecules. The clean-water molecules look like snowflakes, displaying incredible geometric forms, while those of polluted water look like mud. A before and after photograph is shown for molecules of the same water: the first when the water is extremely polluted, and the second after a holy man has chanted and prayed over it for an hour. This second photo shows the water has returned to its natural, pristine molecular structure, illustrating the extraordinary power of sound coupled with intent.

I'm honored that *Healing Sounds* has inspired such research and am extremely pleased that the concepts and mechanisms upon which I've speculated have actually borne fruit. No doubt in the near future more extraordinary discoveries will be made.

On a personal level, it's been my good fortune to continue my work in the field of sound healing. My relationships with the various musicians, chant masters, researchers, and sound healers described in this book have continued to flourish and grow. A young Tibetan monk, Lama Tashi, whom I met and sponsored during the 1991 Drepung Loseling Tour, has now become the principal chant master of the monastery. We are good friends and occasionally have the opportunity to teach and record together. The musician Kitaro won a Grammy award in 2001 for his album *Thinking of You,* and I am honored to have recorded on it and on many of his other albums.

As of this writing, two of my other books have been published, *Shifting Frequencies* and *The Lost Chord;* I have created a number of very well received, award-winning meditation/healing recordings, including *Chakra Chants, The Lost Chord,* and *Ultimate Om;* and I have been featured in national and international press and on radio and television. The interest in sound continues to grow.

For those of you interested in direct participation in this work, since 1996 I have been facilitating the Healing Sounds Intensive, a unique, nine-day training offering individual and group activities to create frequency shifts that inspire transformation. We cover all the areas shared in this book and much, much more. Participants from throughout the world join us for these nine days of toning, teaching, and discovery. If this program resonates with you, please visit our website for more information: www.healingsounds.com

The world of sound is infinite. All that's needed to enter it is your voice; all that you must do to explore and experience this extraordinary world is simply to begin making sound. Experiment and practice and have fun! May joyous sounds resonate with you!

Coda to the 30th Anniversary Edition

This section is entitled "Coda" in keeping with the musical theme: a coda is defined as "the concluding passage of a piece or movement or a concluding event, remark, or section."

Harmonics continue to be an extraordinary vehicle for healing and transformation for me. May this journey into the world of sacred sound continue to be one of unfoldment and delight for you. I trust that, after experiencing this, you will experience great benefits.

As noted throughout this book, harmonics can truly be both a life-changing and reality-shifting phenomenon. To understand and to be able to perceive harmonics is profound, for harmonics are inherent in the universal principles that make up the structure of our reality. You may not become a harmonicist like scientist Hans Kayser, who perceived and understood the world in terms of harmonics, but perhaps you will have an inkling of how many things, including the sounds we create and hear, really do display harmonic order. And perhaps, by reading this book, you've become consciously aware of the harmonics that manifest throughout the different tones of our life.

During the past thirty years, I have observed the exponential growth of interest in sound for healing and transformation. More and more people are becoming aware of the power of vibration and frequency when used in this manner. More and more people are sharing their experiences and the knowledge they receive from working with sound as a therapeutic modality. I give thanks. I do implore those interested in this area to get back to their roots and explore the very fundamental aspect of sound itself, which is found in the resonance of harmonics.

The information about sound found within the pages of this book continues to be relevant and important. It is, from my perspective, fundamental for anyone exploring the power of sound to heal and transform. In chapter 7, I included some updates on the physiological benefits of self-created sounds that have recently been researched. I trust this may assist your understanding of the power of harmonics. In addition, the bibliography of this edition has been greatly expanded to include many fantastic resources that have been created since the first edition of this book. There you will find even more information for your journey with sound.

Through your power of listening and through the power of your own voice, you can explore the realm of harmonics and the world of healing sounds. Just opening your ears to deep listening can shift the very way that you perceive reality. Through intoning simple vowels, you can begin to shift and change the very sound that you create. Then, via focusing your intention upon these sounds, you can actually enhance and amplify their healing power.

It is not necessary to become a master of vocal harmonics in order to open up to this new and extraordinary aspect of sound. It is only necessary that you take a brief amount of time and begin to practice some of the simple exercises and techniques in this book. Daily practice in this manner will only increase your ability to open to the universe of sound—what many perceive as the very fundamental creational aspect of reality.

Remember—the more experiences you personally have with the healing power of sound, the more readily available these experiences will be for you to share with others. Once you understand and embody the power of sound in this manner, then it is real for you. And once this occurs, you can assist others with expanding their awareness of sound as an extraordinary means of shifting and transforming consciousness. Harmonics are a key to understanding and experiencing sound. I trust

Healing Sounds has helped bring the power of harmonics into your life.

Thank you so much for being part of this journey into sacred and healing sounds. It has been my life's work. I realize that after thirty years, it has only just begun.

Blessings of Light and Love through Sound.

JONATHAN GOLDMAN
BOULDER, COLORADO, 2022

APPENDIX

A Celebration of Sound

Musical Downloads

In this 30th anniversary edition of *Healing Sounds,* I am honored to present a number of musical examples that are designed to enhance and assist your resonance with the material in this book. Many of these examples have never been made public before. I trust that with regard to these sounds, if a picture is worth a thousand words, when dealing with a book on sound, an audible download is worth many times more. And I trust that the addition of the audio downloads to this book will deepen your ability to understand and experience the power of harmonics. The nine audio tracks can be downloaded at

audio.innertraditions.com/heasou

The following is information about the different tracks—what they are and how they relate to this anniversary edition. You also will find additional detail and relevant information about each of these nine tracks following the list.

1. "Harmonic Tuning Forks" by Andi and Jonathan Goldman (4:45)
2. "Always Do Your Homework" (3:02)
3. "Vowels as Mantras" from the *Healing Sounds Instructional* by Jonathan Goldman (30:23)

4. "Fundamentals of Vocal Harmonics" from the *Healing Sounds Instructional* by Jonathan Goldman (26:36)
5. "Vocal Harmonic Demonstration" by Alec Sims (5:58)
6. "Amazing Grace" by Christian Bollmann (2:02)
7. "Om Ah Hum" by Jonathan Goldman and Lama Tashi (6:17)
8. "Harmonic Meditation" (8:12)
9. "AH Global Guided Experience for Planetary Healing" by Jonathan Goldman (13:02)

Please read the information before you listen to these offerings.

1. "HARMONIC TUNING FORKS" BY ANDI AND JONATHAN GOLDMAN

Since *Healing Sounds* first appeared in print back in 1992, I have continued to teach material and techniques from it. Many of my teachings naturally involve the importance of understanding harmonics. In order to do this more effectively, I created a set of tuning forks based upon the first eight harmonics (essentially the same frequencies as found on page 26 of this book).

The recording entitled "Harmonic Tuning Forks" features these first eight harmonics, first individually struck and sounded, and then collectively sounded all together. What I found so important about this as a teaching tool was simply that when individually struck, you can hear the unique sound of each tuning fork. When they are sounded in a series you can easily differentiate the first, second, third (and so on) harmonic. They are distinct, and they are all different.

These are the first eight harmonics that occur from using the note C as the fundamental. These notes are found on page 26. As noted, when played individually, you can hear them. However, when played together, the sounds merge into one tone. This composite sound created by the multiple harmonics of the tuning forks simultaneously blending is not particularly pleasant sounding—it sounds like an inexpensive keyboard and creates a very different sound. Once you hear how the harmonics blend together in the instance of these tuning forks, it becomes much clearer how harmonics are intrinsically related to each other.

As noted in this book, harmonics are responsible for the "timbre" or tone color of an instrument. Harmonics determine how an instrument sounds. Harmonics are responsible for a violin sounding like a violin or a flute sounding like a flute. The specific harmonics vary from instrument to instrument. Specific harmonics, known as formants, are also responsible for the uniqueness of each person's voice. Which harmonics are most prominent in our voice is a quality that is as distinctive as our fingerprints.

The Harmonic Tuning Forks are available in a set of eight forks. They have different and wonderful intervals that can be used for healing. For those interested, please visit healingsounds.com.

Copyright ℗ 2002 by Spirit Music, Inc. Used by permission of Spirit Music, Inc.

2. "ALWAYS DO YOUR HOMEWORK"

John Galm, a dear friend and colleague, and head of ethnomusicology at the University of Colorado (CU) in Boulder invited me to present information on the healing nature of sound to an auditorium full of his students.

John gave me a recording one of his students made and thought it might be a useful tool for teaching harmonics. The recording was made in the CU sound laboratory where a student had slowed down someone speaking a sentence. Normally when this occurs, all we hear is a very slow voice. But this student had somehow figured out how to make the harmonics that naturally occur whenever we speak literally stand out.

Yes, harmonics are found in our speech; however, because of their speed, they are not really noticeable when we hear someone talking. With this slowed down recording, you can hear all sorts of artifacts in the person's speech. The slower the sound becomes, the more the harmonics become consciously audible. This is a wonderful demonstration of how harmonics occur whenever sound is created. With our speech, we simply can't make them out due to the speed with which they manifest. But with this recording, you can hear all sorts of different sounds. It's quite amazing.

Incidentally, as you'll note as soon as you hear this recording, the statement being made seems quite suited for an educational environment. It is: "Always do your homework."

Copyright ℗ 2002 by Spirit Music, Inc. Used by permission of Spirit Music, Inc.

3. "VOWELS AS MANTRAS" AND 4. "FUNDAMENTALS OF VOCAL HARMONICS" FROM THE HEALING SOUNDS INSTRUCTIONAL BY JONATHAN GOLDMAN

Shortly after the original release of *Healing Sounds* in 1992, my former publisher, Element Books, called me to inform me that *Healing Sounds* had been chosen as one of Doubleday's "Books of the Month" for their Health Book Club.

I was truly happy that such an event had occurred. This was a great honor. I wondered if perhaps an instructional recording could be offered by my recording company, Spirit Music, Inc. to accompany *Healing Sounds* and facilitate teaching of some of the subjects. This project manifested to much success.

Since then, the cassette has become the CD *The Healing Sounds Instructional*. It is now a part of the celebratory 30th anniversary edition of *Healing Sounds*. It is my pleasure to offer it to you as an adjunct to the written material in the book.

There are two individual tracks on this recording:

1. "Vowels as Mantras" from chapter 8 of *Healing Sounds* (30:23)
2. "Fundamentals of Vocal Harmonics" from chapter 9 of *Healing Sounds* (26:36)

Here are the original liner notes from the CD:

The *Healing Sounds Instructional* CD is designed as an accompaniment to my book *Healing Sounds.* While the exercises, techniques and information on this CD will be effective by themselves, I highly recommend that they be utilized in conjunction with the book in order to understand and receive full and complete harmonic transmission ofthis recording.

Please do not listen to this CD or attempt the exercises on it while doing any activity that requires your attention. Use it only in a place where you can achieve a deep state of meditation.

The first exercise on this CD is a sonic meditation using a relationship between vowels,pitch, and the chakras. There are many different systems of frequencies (keynotes) that work effectively with the sounds of the vowels to resonate the chakras. Some of these different systems have been utilized on my other recordings, including *Chakra Chants* and *The Lost Chord.*

For this particular recording, I utilized a system in which the chakra resonance was based upon the first seven harmonics of the frequency of 256 Hz—the note C. I would like to suggest that once you have the basic concept of toning the chakras with vowels that you do this exercise on your own, choosing pitches for the different portions of your body and your chakras which work well for you.

On the following page is an illustration showing the chakras, the vowels, the frequencies, and the pitches used for this exercise. Enjoy this exercise, as well as the powerful harmonics that you will create with the second exercise, "Fundamentals of Vocal Harmonics."

Please note that this system of notes utilized for the chakras is different than most that have been utilized since this recording was first created. A common system that has been used involves a diatonic C major scale—the notes C, D, E, F, G, A, B. This is certainly a popular and effective system. The system I've created in this recording is similar to one by Dr. Randall McClellan, who was one of the first to speculate on the harmonic relationship of the vowel sounds. His system is found on page 121 of this book.

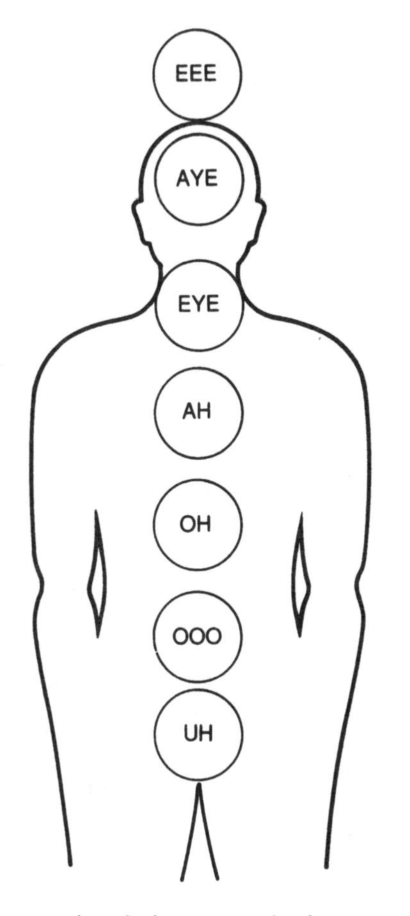

7th CHAKRA—Crown—Sahasrara
Frequency: 1,792 Hz.
Note: B♭-
Vowel: Eee

6th CHAKRA—3rd Eye—Ajna
Frequency: 1,536 Hz.
Note: G
Vowel: Aye

5th CHAKRA—Throat—Vishuddhi
Frequency: 1,280 Hz.
Note: E
Vowel: Eye

4th CHAKRA—Heart—Anahata
Frequency: 1,024 Hz.
Note: C
Vowel: Ah

3rd CHAKRA—Navel—Manipura
Frequency: 768 Hz.
Note: G
Vowel: Oh

2nd CHAKRA—Sacral—Svadisthana
Frequency: 512 Hz.
Note: C
Vowel: Ooo

1st CHAKRA—Root—Muladhara
Frequency: 256 Hz.
Note: C
Vowel: Uh

The chakras, vowels, frequencies, and pitches used for the "Vowels as Mantra" exercise as well as the exercise "Fundamentals of Vocal Harmonics"

I believe that because of the use of the specific vowel sounds and their dominant formants, these different systems all seem to be quite effective, whether the scale is major, a harmonically related system as utilized in this recording, or even a monotone (sounding the chakras with just one note—the same note).

Track four, "Fundamentals of Vocal Harmonics," is an excellent tool for helping train your ear, your brain, and your vocal cords to be able to resonate with some of the very powerful and effective sounds that are offered in this chapter. Many thousands have found this recorded exercise to be extremely useful. Some have become quite adept at creating vocal harmonics simply through reading chapter 9 of *Healing Sounds* and then listening to and following the sonic instructions given on this recording. Sometimes, as in the case of this recording, an audio example is worth more than a thousand words.

These two recordings are copyright ℗ 1992 by Spirit Music, Inc. Used by permission of Spirit Music, Inc.

5. "VOCAL HARMONIC DEMONSTRATION" BY ALEC SIMS

Listening to the sound of someone adept at creating vocal harmonics can be a very powerful and meditative experience. This recording is very different from *The Healing Sounds Instructional* that presents different techniques for creating rudimentary vocal harmonics. These vocal harmonics are performed by Alec Sims, who has been working with us at healingsounds.com for more than twenty years.

I first met Alec at a Healing Sounds workshop in Boulder where he experienced many of the different techniques that were taught (and are on the instructional recording). He had initially learned many of the techniques he uses through first reading *Healing Sounds*. Since then, he has co-authored *Sound Healing for Beginners* with my son Joshua Goldman, taught vocal harmonics at the Healing Sounds Intensive, and is the Healing Sounds correspondence course facilitator.

In this six-minute excerpt, Alec demonstrates sounding vocal harmonics. He's just sounding one note and changing the shape of his mouth and other vocal cavities in order to create harmonics. This recording is a great way to listen to someone combining different techniques to create vocal harmonics. It will help train your ear and perhaps inspire some of you to realize what is possible through the techniques provided in this book.

And as always, listening is a wonderful gateway to opening to the world of harmonics. As the Tomatis Effect states: "The voice can only duplicate what the ear can hear." So, give a listen to these excellent vocal harmonics of Alec Sims. This may have a profound effect on you.

Thank you, Alec.

Alec may be contacted at healingsounds.com

This recording is copyright ℗ 2021 Spirit Music, Inc. Used by permission of Spirit Music, Inc.

6. "AMAZING GRACE" BY CHRISTIAN BOLLMANN

Christian Bollmann is an expert overtone singer from Germany. This recording, called "Gelobtes Land (Teil 2)," is from his album titled *Drehmomente.* It was recorded live in a cathedral (if you listen carefully you can hear a door slam and an airplane flying overhead). There are no overdubs or studio effects. It is amazing on many levels.

This recording is an example of how it is possible to expertly generate very specific overtones when they are sounded. It was always the *pièce de résistance* in a workshop. I would humorously say, "this next track is amazing on many levels. As soon as you recognize the tune, raise your hand." Then I would play the track. Within thirty seconds, most people would signify that they knew the song. It is most recognizable as what we call "Amazing Grace."

This track is amazing, not only because it demonstrates Christian's extraordinary ability, but it also shows us that some songs and melodies specifically use the harmonic series.

Note once again that Christian is singing one note and generating harmonics from that fundamental frequency. He is able to sound "Amazing Grace" through vocal harmonics. Amazing!

Christian has many different recordings that feature his sacred music and are available on YouTube, Spotify and many other platforms. Besides conducting workshops on sacred sound, he is the director of the Overtone Choir.

Thank you, Christian, for your contribution of this recording.

Christian's website is lichthaus-musik.de

This recording is copyright ℗ 1991 Lichthaus-Music. Used by permission of Lichthaus-Music.

7. "OM AH HUM" BY JONATHAN GOLDMAN AND LAMA TASHI

One of my dearest colleagues is Geshe Ngawang Tashi Bapu, known as Lama Tashi. He is president of the Siddartha Foundation, has been principal chant master of the Dalai Lama's Drepung Loseling Monastery, and served as director of the Central Institute of Himalayan Cultural Studies in India.

He is a renowned scholar and speaker on subjects including compassion, wisdom, and other intricate areas of Tibetan Buddhist philosophy, yoga, and meditation. His Tibetan "Deep Voice" is world-renowned.

Chant Masters was released in 1997. Within a few years, it was out of print and never reissued. I have included a five-minute excerpt from *Chant Masters* for your listening. This excerpt is from the beginning of that recording—it is of our chanting "Om Ah Hum," a purification mantra from the Tibetan Buddhist tradition. Also known as the Vajra Mantra, this mantra is to purify negativity and amplify positive energy, increasing it into an infinite quantity.

"HUM" purifies all negativity energies. "AH" further transforms these energies into the nectar of positive energy. "OM" increases the abundance of this transformed energy into infinite quantities. The "OM" resonates the crown chakra, the "AH" resonates the throat chakra and the "HUM" resonates the heart chakra. "Om Ah Hum" corresponds to the three principles of "body," "speech," and "mind."

It is my great honor to present this excerpt, which remains, to my knowledge, the first example of a Tibetan lama and a Westerner chanting together. I trust listening to this recording will be interesting and useful for readers to experience and hear this fine example of the "Deep Voice" style. It is a unique and powerful sound. This recording may enhance the understanding and the experience of the sound described in the "Tantric Harmonics" chapter of this book.

I first meet Lama Tashi thirty years ago, and our relationship has continued to be one of mutual respect and support. Here are some of the liner notes from the *Chant Masters* cassette recording, first created in 1997:

From March 13 to March 16, 1997, the Hon. Ngawang Tashi Bapu, a Chant Master of the Tibetan Buddhist tradition, came to visit me in Boulder, Colorado. I had sponsored Tashi for several years, ever since he and monks from his monastery came to perform in Boulder in December of 1991. While we had communicated via mail when he was in India, and then on the telephone when he came back to the United States in 1996 to again perform sacred chants and rituals, this was the first actual visit we had had.

During his visit, it was my pleasure to conduct a Shifting Frequencies workshop. This was on Saturday, March 15th, at the Multi-Sensory Sound Laboratory in the Fiske Planetarium in Boulder. The Laboratory is a room designed for deaf and hearing-impaired people.

The floors and walls vibrate with sound. It is a very special place. And this was a very special experience, for Tashi facilitated the workshop with me. As one of the few Westerners adept at creating the Tibetan "Deep Voice," I was able to chant with Tashi, reverberating the floors and walls of the Sound Laboratory.

The day before, Friday, March 14th, Tashi and I were at my home, which at the time was in the mountains outside of Boulder, Colorado. I suggested to Tashi that it might be fun to go into my home recording studio and chant together. He agreed.

What emerged is *Chant Masters*. It is, to my knowledge, the first time that a Westerner, such as myself, and a Tibetan Chant Master such as Tashi ever sounded together.

We begin with the chant "Om Ah Hum," a purification mantra from Tibet. Things emerged from there.

This historic recording is the record of a powerful sonic experience between two sound beings from East and West. We trust you will enjoy it.

Since this recording was initially created, Lama Tashi and I have worked on several projects, including opening a large outdoor stadium concert with the well-known musician Kitaro together in Denver,

Colorado. It was quite an honor. Lama Tashi would often come to our Healing Sounds Intensive and give a presentation on "Sound and Compassion" as well as taking part in the some of the chanting experiences that would unfold. This was quite thrilling and enlightening for all involved. Lama Tashi and I continue to work on various creations and have recently completed an online teaching called "Tibetan Secrets of Happiness" that features teachings of meditations, visualizations, and mantra chanting.

Perhaps our greatest project together was the creation of a recording called *Tibetan Master Chants* that was released in 2006 and was nominated for a Grammy. We both went out to Hollywood and met there to attend the Grammys. On the day of the ceremony, the newspaper *USA Today* had a feature-length section on the 48th Grammy Awards. On the front page of this was a nearly half-page-long article entitled "Give Peace A Chant," which was about Lama Tashi and *Tibetan Master Chants*. It was indeed the focus of much international attention. *Tibetan Master Chants* remains the only recording by a solo Tibetan monk ever to be nominated for a Grammy.

Lama Tashi's website is: lamatashi.com

This recording is copyright ℗ 1997 Spirit Music, Inc. Used by permission of Spirit Music, Inc.

8. "HARMONIC MEDITATION"

Soon after the first edition of *Healing Sounds* was published and became available in the United States, I taught a workshop in Santa Fe, New Mexico. This workshop has a very specific memory for me—sometime during one of the breaks, a woman walked up to me and asked if I'd read a particular book. I shook my head and answered "No." I was handed a number of photocopied pages stapled together. "Here," she said. "It's channeled teaching from the Pleiades." I thanked her and she walked away.

I put the pages in my leather carryall. Perhaps I would see what I had been given later. And indeed, when I returned to the hotel room, I pulled out various knickknacks that participants had been kind enough to give me—recordings of themselves and assorted other material. I looked at these copied pages. The title on it was "Symphonies of Consciousness." I started to read them. Thirty years later, I still have these pages—many sections are highlighted in yellow marker to emphasize them. And they are also yellowed with age.

As I read the pages of text that had been given to me, I was astounded. The information focused on sound and, in particular, the power of harmonics. My mouth dropped open. I could not believe it. The information was, at least to me, perfectly accurate. It was also material that I had not specifically included in *Healing Sounds,* though it had deeply resonated with me. I'd had my own communications with aspects of consciousness (call them angels, spirit guides, extraterrestrials, or my higher self) that had given me all sorts of information on the importance of sound and harmonics—I had simply not stated this information in *Healing Sounds.*

From those same copied pages, next I read chapter 18 of *Bringers of the Dawn* by Barbara Marciniak, which talked about the power of harmonics to create new realities and change the available planetary frequencies. From my knowledge, it was all entirely correct. It was almost as though this chapter was an addendum to *Healing Sounds.* How had this information been written? Had the author taken a workshop from me, or had (dare I speculate) the Pleiadeans somehow been aware of my work? I had to get a copy of the book these pages had been copied from.

Immediately upon my return to Boulder, I went to Light House Books, which was the mainstay of high consciousness (dare I say "New Age") awareness at the time. It still is. I remember walking in and asking: "Do you have *Bringers of the Dawn*?" I had gotten the name of the book from the woman who had given me the handouts that had so deeply resonated with me.

The saleswoman pointed to her left. There against the wall was a shelf of numerous copies of *Bringers of the Dawn.* "It's our most popular book," she said.

"Thanks," I replied. I smiled, walked over to the shelf and selected a copy of the book. Then I came back to the sales counter. "You know," I began, "someone gave me a chapter of this book and it was just amazing.

Either Barbara Marciniak has taken a workshop from me or else the Pleiadeans really like my work." And at that point, all the copies of the book on the shelf literally flew several feet across the bookstore.

Really.

I was so shocked that I laughed. The saleswoman's eyes had become wide with disbelief. I shrugged my shoulder casually and said: "I guess the Pleiadeans really like my work."

During workshops, I began reading excerpts from chapter 18, "Symphonies of Consciousness," while playing soothing music in the background. Somehow, the words I read seemed to emphasize much of what I had been teaching. For about ten minutes during almost each weekend workshop, I would have the group begin to sound a sound—often an "OM" or a vowel sound, or simply hum. Then, as their sound dimmed, I would play some gentle music and read selected words from "Symphonies of Consciousness."

At the end of this reading, I would pause and, in the powerful silence, simply say: "Did you get it?" For many people, it helped provide an epiphany of the power of harmonics. They got it. They understood that ultimately the purpose for working with consciously created harmonics was simply this: to change the available frequencies of our planet and raise the consciousness of all beings.

The music used on this particular recording is a track from *Spirit Come*, a recording by Christian Bollmann, a renowned overtone singer from Germany whose version of "Amazing Grace" is part of these audio tracks. Christian and I have been friends from a long time ago, and *Spirit Come* is one of the recordings mentioned in the original discography of *Healing Sounds*. Christian is, as noted, a remarkable man. And unlike many who have become proficient at the technique of creating vocal harmonics, he is totally in resonance with the sacred and healing aspects of these sounds.

This recording, "Harmonic Meditation," is from an exercise at one of our Healing Sounds Intensives. From my perspective, it is encoded with wonderful energy. I trust you will enjoy the sounds and the message.

No version of this recording has ever been made available to the public.

I trust you will enjoy listening to "Harmonic Meditation." I'd like to suggest that when you listen to it, first sit quietly and take a few breaths. Then listen to the recording, knowing that there is indeed a message meant for you in it.

Bringers of the Dawn is copyright © 1992 by Barbara Marciniak. Used with permission.

Spirit Come ℗ 1991 by Christian Bollmann. Used with permission.

The "Harmonic Meditation" is copyright ℗ 2021 by Spirit Music, Inc. Used by permission of Spirit Music, Inc.

9. "AH GLOBAL GUIDED EXPERIENCE FOR PLANETARY HEALING" BY JONATHAN GOLDMAN

This recording is a wonderful example of utilizing the formula I created "Frequency + Intention = Healing." In this case, the intention is to bring healing to our planet earth. My inner guidance tells me I would be remiss if I did not include this in these audio files.

The AH Global Guided Experience for Planetary Healing was created ten years ago as a tool to enhance a global event that has been held on February 14—Valentine's Day—called World Sound Healing Day. It is an event in which tens of thousands of people throughout our planet send a sonic valentine encoded with the energies of love and compassion to the Gaia Matrix—our mother Earth.

I was guided to expand my focus of attention on using sound to include both personal and planetary healing. Thus, I create an event called World Sound Healing Day that first manifested in 2002 and has flourished and grown exponentially since then.

The initial World Sound Healing Day used the sound "AH," which was to be toned during that day. Since then, the tones we use have become more expansive to include all sorts of mantras, chants, and other sounds. However, the "AH" is frequently the sound that many people use.

As discussed in chapter 8, "Vowels as Mantras," the "AH" seems to be the predominant sound that is used for the heart chakra, the center of love and compassion. Indeed, besides this exercise, the "AH" sound is almost consistently found throughout our planet in the names of many of the various gods and goddesses. Whether it's Tara, Buddha, Krishna, Yeshua (the Hebrew name of Jesus), Yahweh, Apollo, Allah, or any of a hundred other names, the "AH" sound is found there.

This recording has been used for the past decade as a way of enhancing our ability to make a sound and encode it with an intention. It begins with a guided meditation designed to help create a state of heart/brain coherence. This is a phenomenon in which our heart and our brain lock in synchrony together, and the electromagnetic fields produced by both organs are amplified immensely.

As noted, there is an electromagnetic field produced by our brain. We've been measuring parts of this for years through examining brain waves. As noted in *Healing Sounds* (and the section on the creation of light), the heart produces chemicals like the brain. In fact, the heart also produces an electromagnetic field. When the heart and brain are in coherence, this field expands enormously.

The personal therapeutic resonance created by this locking in step is extraordinary—it is excellent for reducing stress and enhancing personal power. In addition, it seems that the electromagnetic field of our heart and brain—our biofield—is amplified by 50 to 500 to perhaps 5,000 times greater than normal.

First manifested and made popular by Heart Math Institute, the technique for creating heart/brain coherence is relatively easy. It involves some deep breathing and focused positive visualization that can be experienced in the first part of the guided meditation. The technique works so wonderfully with helping to encode positive intentions such as appreciation and gratitude onto sound. I always suggest encoding something similar for the intention of any exercises involving using sound for healing. As my good friend Sarah Benson said, "The true sound of healing is love." In order to project positive energy, we need first and foremost to be in a proper state of consciousness. Heart/brain coherence seems to truly assist this.

If our electromagnetic field is increased many times through this simple technique of focus and feeling, I have always suggested that we can amplify our field even more through working with the power of sound.

Think about it—if you examine the different prayers on our planet, you find that a majority of these prayers are vocalized—chanted, whispered, spoken, or sung. That is because sound amplifies the power of our prayers and meditations. Thus, when we manifest heart/brain coherence and then make a sound, such as the "AH" on the guided meditation, it may be possible that the field we create, individually and as groups across the planet, has far-reaching consequences.

There is even data to show that when people gather together in deep meditation or sacred toning such as World Sound Healing Day, incidences of violence lessen where this is happening. There is conjecture that if such meditations and soundings occur throughout the planet, it might be possible to literally affect the field of consciousness for our planet, called the "noosphere" by some and the "Gaia Matrix" by others.

The "AH Global Guided Experience" is a wonderful tool for anyone who wishes to learn how to use sound for planetary healing. The "AH" sound is composed of hundreds of people making that sound while being filled with the energy of love and compassion. Listen to the guided meditation and sound along with this recording. It is a wonderful way of projecting healing sounds for both personal and planetary healing.

Remember: we heal our planet, we heal ourselves. We heal ourselves and we heal our planet. And please be aware that it is not necessary to wait until February 14 to utilize sound in this manner. You can use this recording every day, and it only creates positive results for yourself and for those around you.

Please visit worldsoundhealingday.org for more information. And check out templeofsacredsound.com to experience the world's first online toning chambers.

The "AH Global Guided Experience for Planetary Healing" is copyright ℗ 2012 Spirit Music, Inc. Used by permission of Spirit Music, Inc.

BIBLIOGRAPHY

This bibliography has been updated since the original edition to provide readers with an expanded list of resources. Happy reading!

Abraham, Ralph. "Mechanics of Resonance." *Revision 10,* no. 1. Summer 1987.

Achterberg, Jeanne. *Imagery in Healing.* Boston: New Science Library, 1985.

Addey, John M. *Harmonics in Astrology.* Romford, U.K.: L. N. Fowler, 1976.

Adolphe, Bruce, *The Mind's Ear.* Oxford, 2013.

Alper, Frank. *Exploring Atlantis, Vols. I-III.* Irvine, Calif.: Quantum, 1986.

Alper, Harvey P. *Mantra.* Albany: State University of New York Press, 1989.

Anderson, Carolyn P. I., and Katharine Roske. *Co-Creators Handbook 2.0.* Penn Valley, Calif.: Global Family, 2016.

Andrews, Ted. *Crystal Balls & Crystal Bowls.* Woodbury, Minn.: Llewellyn, 2012.

———. *Sacred Sounds.* Woodbury, Minn.: Llewellyn, 1998.

———. *Music Therapy for Non-Musicians.* Jackson, Tenn.: Dragonhawk, 1997.

Arman, Miriam Jaskierowicz. *The Voice: A Spiritual Approach.* N.P.: Lightning Source, 1999.

Arya, Pandit Usharbudh. *Mantras & Meditation.* Honesdale, Penn.: Himalayan Institute, 1981.

Ashley-Farrand, Thomas. *Chakra Mantras.* San Francisco, Calif.: Red Wheel/Weiser, 2006.

———. *Shakti Mantras.* New York: Ballantine, 2003.

Ashton, Anthony. *Harmonograph.* New York: Walker & Co, 2003.

Assagioli, Robert. *Psychosynthesis.* New York: Penguin, 1976.

Atkinson, William Walker. *The Kybalion*. New York: J. P. Tarcher, 2008.

Baer, Randall and Vicki Randall. *The Crystal Connection*. New York: Harper & Row, 1986.

———. *Windows of Light*. New York: Harper & Row, 1984.

Bamford, Christopher. *Homage to Pythagoras*. Hudson, N.Y.: Lindisfarne, 1994.

Banek, Reinhold and Jon Scoville. *Sound Designs*. Berkeley, Calif.: Ten Speed Press, 1995.

Barret, Sondra. *Secrets of Your Cells*. Louisville, Colo.: Sounds True, 2013.

Beasley, Victor, R. *Your Electro-Vibratory Body*. Boulder Creek, Calif.: University of the Trees, 1978.

Beaulieu, John. *Human Tuning*. New York: BioSonics, 2010.

———. *Music and Sound in the Healing Arts*. Barrytown, N.Y.: Station Hill, 1987.

———. *Sound Healing and Values Visualization*. New York: BioSonics, 2018.

Beck, Guy L. *Sonic Theology*. Delhi: Motilal Vanarsidas, 1993.

Becker, Judith. *Deep Listeners*. Bloomington: Indiana University Press, 2004

Becker, Robert O., and Gary Selden. *The Body Electric*. N.P.: Quill, 1985.

Beckerman, Joel and Tyler Gray. *The Sonic Boom*. Boston: Houghton Mifflin, 2014.

Benson, Herbert. *The Relaxation Response*. New York: William Morrow, 1975.

Bentov, Itzhak. *Stalking the Wild Pendulum*. New York: Bantam, 1977.

Bentov, Itzhak and Mirtala Bentov. *A Cosmic Book*. New York: Dutton, 1982.

Berendt, Joachim-Ernst. *Nada Brahma: The World Is Sound*. Rochester, Vt.: Destiny, 1987.

Berendt, Joachim-Ernst. *The Third Ear*. Dorset, U.K.: Element, 1988.

Berg, Richard, and David Stork. *The Physics of Sound*. Pearson, 2012.

Bernard, Patrick. *Music as Yoga*. San Rafael, Calif.: Mandala, 2004.

Bernhardt, Patrick. *The Secret Music of the Soul*. N.P.: Image, 1991.

Bernstein, Leonard. *The Unanswered Question*. Cambridge, Mass.: Harvard University Press, 1976.

Birosik, Patti Jean. *The New Age Music Guide*. New York: Collier, 1989.

Blair, Lawrence. *Rhythms of Vision*. New York: Schocken, 1976.

Bleecker, Deborah. *Acupressure Made Simple*. Dallas, Tex.: Draycott, 2018.

Blofeld, John. *Mantras: Sacred Worlds of Power*. San Rafael, Calif.: Mandala, 1981.

———. *Mantras: Secret Words of Power*. San Rafael, Calif.: Mandala, 1977.

Bonkrude, Sally. *Conscious Performing*. N.P.: Inner Source, 2008.

Bonny, Helen, and Louis Savary. *Music and Your Mind.* Port Townsend, Wash.: ICM, 1983.

Borg, Susan Gallagher. *Sing Your Body Activity Book.* N.P.: Resonant Kinesiology, 1993.

Boxhill, Edith Hillman. *Music Therapy for the Developmentally Disabled.* Rockville, Md.: Aspen, 1985.

Braden, Gregg. *Awakening to Zero Point.* Questa, N.M.: Sacred Spaces, 1994.

———. *The Divine Matrix.* Carlsbad, Calif.: Hay House, 2007.

———. *Fractal Time.* Carlsbad, Calif.: Hay House, 2009.

———. *The God Code.* Carlsbad, Calif.: Hay House, 2004.

———. *Human By Design.* Carlsbad, Calif.: Hay House, 2017.

———. *Secret of the Lost Mode of Prayer.* Carlsbad, Calif.: Hay House, 2006.

———. *The Spontaneous Healing of Belief.* Carlsbad, Calif.: Hay House, 2008.

———. *Walking Between the Worlds.* [Washington?]: Radio Bookstore, 1997.

Brennan, J. H. *Occult Tibetan.* Woodbury, Minn.: Llewellyn, 2002.

———. *Tibetan Magic and Mysticism.* Woodbury, Minn.: Llewellyn, 2006.

Brodie, Renee. *The Healing Tones of Crystal Bowls.* Canada, 1998.

Brody, Sarmad. "Healing and Music: The Viewpoint of Hazrat Inayat Khan." *Healing in Our Time* 1, no. 1 (1981).

Brown, Barbara. *Supermind.* New York: Harper & Row, 1980.

Bruce, Robert. *Energy Work.* Charlottesville, Va.: Hampton Roads, 2007.

Bruyer, Rosalyn. *Wheels of Light.* Sierra Madre, Calif.: Bon Productions, 1989.

Buckland, Raymond. *The Magick of Chant-O-Matics.* West Nyack, N.Y.: Parker, 1978.

Bunther, Emil. *Music and Your Emotions.* New York: Liveright, 1962.

Burrell, Lloyd. *Healing with Vibration.* N.P.: ElectricSense, 2021.

Byrne, David. *How Music Works.* McSweeney's, 2012.

Calais-Germain, Blandine, and Francois Germain. *Anatomy of Voice.* Rochester, Vt.: Inner Traditions, 2013.

Cameron, Julia. *The Vein of Gold.* New York: J. P. Tarcher, 1997.

Campbell, Don. *The Harmony of Health.* Carlsbad, Calif.: Hay House, 2006.

———. *Introduction to the Musical Brain.* St. Louis, Mo.: MMB, 1984.

———. *The Mozart Effect.* New York: Avon, 1997.

———. *The Mozart Effect for Children,* New York: HarperCollins, 2000.

———. *Music and Miracles.* Wheaton, Ill.: Quest, 1992.

———, ed. *Music: Physician for Times to Come.* Wheaton, Ill.: Quest, 1990 .

———. *100 Ways to Improve Teaching Using Your Voice & Music.* Tuscon, Ariz.: Zephyr, 1992.

———. *The Roar of Silence.* Wheaton, Ill.: Quest, 1989.

———. *Sound Spirit.* Carlsbad, Calif.: Hay House, 2008.

Campbell, Don G., and Chris Brewer. *Rhythms of Learning.* Tuscon, Ariz.: Zephyr, 1991.

Campbell, Don, and Alex Doman. *Healing at the Speed of Sound.* London: Penguin, 2011.

Campbell, Murray, and Clive Greated. *The Musician's Guide to Acoustics.* U.K.: Macmillan, 1987.

Carey, Donna, Ellen F. Franklin, Paul Ponton, MichelAngelo, and Judith Ponton. *Acutonics: From Galaxies to Cells.* Llano, N.M.: Devachan, 2010.

Carroll, Lee. *The New Human.* N.P.: New Leaf, 2017.

Chatwin, Bruce. *The Songlines.* New York: Viking, 1987.

Chaudhary, Kulreet. *Sound Medicine.* New York: Harper Wave, 2020.

Cheney, Margaret. *Tesla: Man Out of Time.* New York: Touchstone, 2011.

Chia, Mantak. *Taoist Ways to Transform Stress into Vitality.* Huntington, N.Y.: Healing Tao, 1985.

Chiasson, Ann Marie. *Energy Healing.* Louisville, Colo.: Sounds True, 2013.

Childress, David Hatcher, and Stephen Mehler. *The Crystal Skulls.* Kempton, Ill.: Adventures Unlimited, 2008.

Childress, David Hatcher, ed. *Anti-Gravity and the World Grid.* Kempton, Ill.: Adventures Unlimited Press, 1987.

Chinmoy, Shri. *Kundalini: The Mother Power.* New York: Agni, 1974.

Chopra, Deepak. *Quantum Healing.* New York: Bantam, 1999.

Clynes, Manfred. *Music, Mind and Brain.* New York: Plenum, 1982.

Colton, Ann Ree. *The Third Music.* Glendale, Calif.: ARC, 1982.

Cooper, Grosvenor, and Leonard B. Meyer. *The Rhythmic Structure of Music.* Chicago: University of Chicago, 1960.

Cooper, Lyz. *Sounding the Mind of God.* N.P.: O. Books, 2009.

———. *What Is Sound Healing?* London: Watkins Media, 2016.

Cope, Jonathan. *How to Khoomei.* N.P.: Wild Wind, 2003.

Cott, Jonathan. *Stockhausen.* New York: Simon & Schuster, 1973.

Cousto, Hans. *The Cosmic Octave.* Mendocino, Calif.: LifeRhythm, 1988.

Cowan, James P. *The Effects of Sound on People.* Chichester, West Sussex, U.K.: John Wiley & Sons, 2016.

Crandall, Joanne, *Self-Transformation through Music.* Wheaton, Ill.: Quest, 1986.

Cromwell, Mandara. *Soundflower.* Augusta, Ga.: CymaTechnologies, 2019.

Crowe, Barbara. *Music and Soul Making.* Lanham, Md.: Scarecrow 2004.

Crowley, Brian, and Esther Crowley. *Mantras and Chants.* Woodbury, Minn.: Llewelyn, 2010.

Dalai Lama, The. *The Compassionate Life.* Boston: Wisdom, 2001.

D'Angelo, James. *Healing with the Voice.* New York: HarperCollins, 2000.

———. *Seed Sounds for Tuning the Chakras.* Rochester, Vt.: Inner Traditions 2012.

Daniélou, Alain. *Music and the Power of Sound.* Rochester, Vt.: Inner Traditions, 1995.

Das, Krishna. *Chants of a Lifetime.* Carlsbad, Calif.: Hay House 2010.

David, William. *The Harmonics of Sound, Color and Vibration.* Marina del Ray, Calif.: DeVorss, 1980.

David-Neel, Alexandra. *Magic and Mystery in Tibet.* New York: Dover, 1971.

Davidson, Gustav. *A Dictionary of Angels.* U.K.: Macmillan, 1967.

Davis, Dorrine S. *Sound Bodies through Sound Therapy.* Budd Lake, N.J.: Kalco, 2004.

Deighton, Hilda, Gina Palermo, and Dina Soresi Winter. *Singing and the Etheric Tone.* Hudson, N.Y.: Anthroposophic, 1991.

Devananda, Swami Vishu. *Meditation and Mantras.* New York: Om Lotus, 1978.

Dewhurst-Maddock, Olivea. *The Book of Sound Therapy.* New York: Simon and Schuster, 1993.

Diallo, Yaya, and Mitchell Hall. *The Healing Drum.* New York: Destiny Books, 1989.

Diamond, John. *The Life Energy in Music.* Volume I. Valley Cottage, N.Y.: Archaeus, 1981.

———. *The Life Energy in Music.* Volume II. Valley Cottage, N.Y.: Archaeus, 1983.

———. *The Life Energy in Music.* Volume III. Valley Cottage, N.Y.: Archaeus, 1986.

———. *Your Body Doesn't Lie.* New York: Warner, 1980.

Dickinson, Bob. *Music and the Earth Spirit.* U.K.: Capall Bann, 2001.

Dispenza, Joe. *You Are the Placebo.* Carlsbad, Calif.: Hay House 2015.

Dmitriev, L. B., B. P. Chernov, and V. T. Maslov. "Functioning of the Voice Mechanism in Double Voice Touvian Singing." *Folia Phoniat* 35 (1983).

Doczi, Gyorgy. *The Power of Limits.* Boulder, Colo: Shambhala, 1981.

Dodd, Vickie. *Tuning the Blues to Gold.* Boulder, Colo.: Woveword, 1999.

D'Olivet, Fabre. *The Secret Lore of Music.* Rochester, Vt.: Inner Traditions, 1987.

Dossey, Larry. *Healing Words.* New York: HarperCollins, 1993.

Douglas-Klotz, Neil. *Prayers of the Cosmos* New York: HarperCollins, 1990.

Dow, Mike. *Heal Your Drained Brain.* Carlsbad, Calif.: Hay House, 2018.

Drake, Michael. *The Shamanic Drum.* Bend, Ore.: Talking Drum, 1991.

Duffin, Ross W. *How Equal Temperament Ruined Harmony.* New York: Norton, 2007.

Duquette, Lon Milo. *The Chicken Qabalah.* York, Maine: Weiser, 2001.

Dyer, Wayne. *The Power of Intention.* Carlsbad, Calif.: Hay House, 2004.

Eden, Donna, and David Feinstein. *Energy Medicine.* New York: J. P. Tarcher, 2008.

Elkington, David, *The Ancient Language of Sacred Sound.* Rochester, Vt.: Inner Traditions, 2021.

Ellingson, Terry Jay. *The Mandala of Sound: Concepts and Sound Structures in Tibetan Ritual Music.* N.P.: University Microfilms, 1979.

Emoto, Masaru. *The Hidden Messages in Water.* Hillsboro, Ore.: Beyond Words, 2004.

———. *Messages from Water.* N.P.: Hado, 1999.

Faeth, Laura. *I Found All the Parts: Healing the Soul through Rock 'n' Roll.* Deadwood, Ore.: Sounds of Your Soul, 2008.

Feder, Elaine, and Bernard Feder. *The Expressive Arts Therapies.* Hoboken, N.J.: Prentice Hall, 1981.

Ferguson, Marilyn, ed. "Melanin as Key Organizing Molecule." *Brain/Mind Bulletin* 8 no. 12/13 (August 1, 1983).

Finney, Shan. *Noise Pollution.* New York: Franklin Watts, 1984.

Flatischler, Reinhard. *The Forgotten Power of Rhythm.* Mendocino, Calif.: LifeRhythm, 1992.

Frawley, David. *Mantra Yoga and Primal Sound.* Twin Lakes, Wisc.: Lotus, 2010.

———. *Tantric Yoga and the Wisdom Goddesses.* Salt Lake City, Utah: Passage Press, 1994.

Freeman, Ira M. *All About Sound and Ultrasonics.* New York: Random House, 1961.

Gach, Michael Reed. *Acupressure's Potent Points.* New York: Bantam, 1990.

Gadalla, Moustafa. *Egyptian Rhythm.* Greensboro, N.C.: Tehuti Research Foundation, 2002.

Galgut, Peter. *Humming Your Way to Happiness.* N.P.: O. Books, 2005.

Gardner, Kay. *Sounding the Inner Landscape.* Stonington, Maine: Caduceus, 1990.

Gardner-Gordon, Joy. *Color and Crystals.* N.P.: Crossing, 1983.

———. *The Healing Voice.* N.P.: Crossing, 1993.

Garfield, Laeh Maggie. *Sound Medicine.* Berkeley, Calif.: Celestial Arts, 1987.

Gass, Robert, with Kathleen Brehony. *Chanting.* New York: Broadway, 1999.

Gaynor, Mitchell L. *Sounds of Healing* .New York: Broadway, 1999.

Gerard, Robert V. *Change Your DNA, Change Your Life.* Coarsegold, Calif.: Oughten House, 2000.

Gerber, Richard. *Vibrational Medicine.* Rochester, Vt.: Bear & Co., 1988.

Getty, Alice. *The Gods of Northern Buddhism.* New York: Dover, 1988.

Gibson, David. *The Complete Guide to Sound Healing.* N.P.: Globe Institute of Recording and Production, 2013.

Gilmour, Timothy M., Paul Madaule, and Billie Thompson, eds. *About the Tomatis Method.* Toronto: Listening Center, 1988.

Gimbel, Theo. *Form, Sound, Colour and Healing.* U.K.: C. W. Daniel, 1987.

Gioia, Ted. *Healing Songs.* Durham, N.C.: Duke University Press, 2006.

Godwin, David. *Caballistic Encyclopedia.* Woodbury, Minn.: Llewellyn, 1994.

Godwin, Joscelyn. *Harmonies of Heaven and Earth.* Rochester, Vt.: Inner Traditions, 1987.

———. *The Mystery of the Seven Vowels.* Grand Rapids, Mich.: Phanes, 1991.

Goldman, Jonathan. *The Divine Name.* Carlsbad, Calif.: Hay House, 2015.

———. *Forbidden Frequencies: The Lost Chord.* Pennsauken, N.J.: Book Baby, 2013.

———. *The Lost Chord.* Boulder, Colo.: Spirit Music, 1999.

———. *The Power of Sound Healing.* Carlsbad, Calif.: Hay House, 2017.

———. *The 7 Secrets of Sound Healing.* Carlsbad, Calif.: Hay House, 2017.

———. *Shifting Frequencies.* Flagstaff, Ariz.: Light, Technology, 1998.

Goldman, Jonathan, and Andi Goldman. *Chakra Frequencies.* Rochester, Vt.: Inner Traditions, 2011.

———. *The Humming Effect.* Rochester, Vt.: Inner Traditions, 2017.

Goldman, Joshua, and Alec Sims. *Sound Healing for Beginners.* Woodbury, Minn.: Llewellyn, 2015.

Goldstein, Barry. *The Secret Language of the Heart.* San Antonio, Tex.: Hierophant, 2016.

Good, Bob. *The Science of Reincarnation.* N.P.: CreateSpace, 2012.

Goodchild, Chloe. *The Naked Voice.* Berkeley, Calif.: North Atlantic, 2015.

Gore, Belinda. *Ecstatic Body Postures.* Rochester, Vt.: Bear & Co., 1995.

Govinda, Lama Anagarika. *Foundations of Tibetan Mysticism.* New York: Samuel Weiser, 1960.

———. *Creative Meditation and Multi-Dimensional Consciousness.* Wheaton, Ill.: Quest, 1976.

Graham, F. Lanier (ed.). *The Rainbow Book.* New York: Vintage, 1979.

Gray, William. *The Talking Tree.* New York: Weiser, 1977.

Green, Barry, and Gallwey, Timothy W. *The Inner Game of Music.* Garden City, N.Y.: Doubleday,1986.

Gunther, Bernard. *Energy, Ecstasy and Your Seven Vital Chakras.* San Bernadino, Calif.: Newcastle, 1983.

Gustafson, Eric. A. *The Ringing Sound.* Austin, Tex.: Conscious Living, 2000.

Gutheil, Emil A. *Music and Your Emotions.* New York: Music Research, 1952.

Guthrie, Kenneth Slyvan. *The Pythagorean Sourcebook & Library.* Grand Rapids, Mich.: Phanes, 1988.

Hale, Susan Elizabeth. *Sacred Spaces, Sacred Sounds,* Wheaton, Ill.: Quest, 2007.

———. *Song and Silence.* Albuquerque, N.M.: La Alameda, 1995.

Halevi, Z'ev ben Shimon. *Adam and the Kabbalistic Tree.* New York: Weiser, 1974.

Hall, Manly P. *The Secrets Teachings of All Ages.* N.P.: Masonica, 2020.

———. *The Therapeutic Value of Music.* N.P.: Philosophical Research, 1982.

Halpern, Steven, *Tuning the Human Instrument.* N.P.: Spectrum, 1980.

Halpern, Steven, and Louis Savary. *Sound Health.* New York: Harper & Row, 1985.

Hamel, Peter Michael. *Through Music to the Self.* Dorset, U.K.: Element, 1984.

Hammerschlag, Carl A. *The Dancing Healers.* New York: Harper & Row, 1988.

Harner, Michael. *The Way of the Shaman.* New York: Bantam, 1980.

Harris, Lee. *Energy Speaks.* Novato, Calif.: New World Library, 2019.

Harrison, R. K. *Biblical Hebrew.* Chicago: NTC, 1993.

Hart, Mickey, Fredric Lieberman, and Jay Stevens. *Drumming at the Edge of Magic.* New York: Harper Collins, 1990.

———. *Planet Drum.* New York: Harper Collins, 1991.

———. *Spirit into Sound.* Petaluma, Calif.: Grateful Dead Books, 1999.

Harvey, Arthur, ed. *Music and Health Sourcebook of Readings.* Richmond: Eastern Kentucky University, 1989.

Hayes, Michael. *The Hermetic Code in DNA.* Rochester, Vt.: Inner Traditions, 2008.

Heline, Corinne. *Color and Music in the New Age.* Los Angeles: New Age, 1985.

———. *Music: The Keynote of Human Evolution.* Santa Barbara, Calif.: J. F. Rowny, 1965.

Helmholtz, Hermann. *On the Sensations of Tone.* New York: Dover, 1954.

Hero, Barbara. *Lambdoma Unveiled.* N.P.: Strawberry Hill, 1990.

Hersey, Baird. *The Practice of Nada Yoga.* Rochester, Vt.: Inner Traditions, 2014.

Hicks, Esther, and Jerry Hicks, *The Law of Attraction.* Carlsbad, Calif.: Hay House 2006.

Hill, Ann. *A Visual Encyclopedia of Unconventional Medicine.* New York: Crown, 1979.

Hills, Christopher. *Nuclear Evolution: Discovery of the Rainbow Body.* Boulder Creek, Calif.: University of the Trees, 1972.

———. *Supersensonics.* Boulder Creek, Calif.: University of the Trees, 1978.

Holecek, Andrew. *Dream Yoga.* Louisville, Colo.: Sounds True, 2016.

Horowitz, Leonard. *Walk on Water.* Las Vegas: Tetrahedron, 2006.

Horowitz, Leonard, and Joseph Puleo. *Healing Codes for the Biological Apocalypse.* Las Vegas: Tetrahedron, 1999.

Horowitz, Mitch. *The Seekers Guide to the Secret Teachings of All Ages.* N.P.: G & D, 2020.

Hulse, David Allen. *The Key of It All: The Eastern Mysteries.* Woodbury, Minn.: Llewellyn, 1996.

———. *The Key of It All: The Western Mysteries* Woodbury, Minn.: Llewellyn, 1996.

Hunt, Roland. *Fragrant and Radiant Healing Symphony.* First published in London by C. W. Daniel, 1937.

Hunt, Valerie. *Infinite Mind.* Malibu, Calif.: Malibu, 1989.

Hurtak, J. J. *The Book of Knowledge: The Keys of Enoch.* Los Gatos, Calif.: Academy for Future Science, 1977.

———. *72 Divine Names.* Los Gatos, Calif.: Academy for Future Sciences, 1989.

Hutchinson, Michael. *Megabrain.* New York: Ballantine, 1986.

Huyser, Anneke. *Singing Bowl Exercises.* San Francisco, Calif.: Red Wheel/Weiser, 2006.

Hykes, David. *Sonnez Fort: Better Listening and Some Leading Unspoken Questions.* N.P.: Harmonic Arts, 1984.

James, Chris. *Sound Wisdom.* Australia: Sounds Wonderful, 1999.

James, R. S. *Music Spirit and the Keys to Prophecy.* N.P.: Sacred Scales, 2001.

Janowitz, Naomi. *The Poetics of Assent.* Albany: State University of New York Press, 1989.

Jansen, Eva Rudy. *Singing Bowls.* York, Maine: Weiser, 1990.

Jansen, Gerd. *Effects of Noise on Psychological States.* Speech and Hearing Association Report no. 4, 89–98, February, 1969.

Jean, James. *Science & Music.* New York: Dover, 1976.

Jenny, Hans. *Cymatics.* Vols. I and II. Basel: Basilius Presse, 1974.

Johns, Glyn, *Sound Man.* London: Penguin, 2015.

Johnson, Beth. *First You Sigh.* N.P.: Millenia, 2000.

Johnson, Julian. *The Path of the Masters.* India: Radha Soami Satsang Beas Publications Committee, 1974.

Jones, Gene S. *Younger and Wiser.* N.P.: Dreamquest, 2021.q

Joseph, Arthur Samuel. *The Sound of the Soul.* Encino, Calif.: Vocal Awareness, 1996.

———. *Vocal Power.* Encino, Calif.: Vocal Awareness, 2003.

Joslow-Rodewalk, and Patricia West-Barker. *Healing Spirits.* Freedom, Calif.: Crossing, 2001.

Joudry, Patricia. *Sound Therapy for the Walk Man.* Mansfield, Mass. (?): Steel & Steel, 1989.

Judith, Anodea. *Wheels of Life.* Woodbury, Minn.: Llewellyn, 2007.

Kaku, Michio. *The God Equation.* New York: Doubleday, 2021.

Kamenetz, Roger. *The Jew in the Lotus.* New York: Harper, 1994.

Kaplan, Aryeh. *Meditation and Kabbalah.* York, Maine: Weiser, 1982.

Karpf, Anne. *The Human Voice.* New York: Bloomsbury, 2006.

Katsch, Shelley, and Carol Merle-Fishman. *The Music Within You.* New York: Simon & Schuster, 1985.

Kayser, Hans. *Akroasis: The Theory of World Harmonics.* Boston: Plowshare, 1970.

Kenyon, Tom, and Virginia Essen. *The Hathor Material.* Santa Clara, Calif.: S.E.E., 1996.

Keyes, Laurel Elizabeth. *Toning: The Creative Power of the Voice.* Marina del Ray, Calif.: DeVorss, 1973.

Keys, Laurel Elizabeth, and Don Campbell. *Toning.* Marina del Ray, Calif.: DeVorss, 2008.

Khan, Hazrat Inayat. *The Music of Life.* New Lebanon, N.Y.: Omega, 2005.

———. *The Mysticism of Sound; Music; The Power of the Word; Cosmic Language.* London: Barry & Rockcliff, 1962.

Khan, Pir Vilayat. "Healing with Light and Sound." Lecture presented at Healing in Our Time, November 6, 1981.

———. *Toward the One.* New York: Harper, 1974.

Khanna, Madhu. *Yantra: Tantric Symbol of Cosmic Unity.* London: Thames & Hudson, 2003.

Knight, Christopher, and Robert Lomas. *The Hiram Key.* N.P.: Barnes & Noble, 1996.

Kobialka, Daniel. *The Wonders of Sound.* San Antonio, Tex.: Wonders of Sound, 2009.

Koldenhoven, Darlene. *Tune Your Voice.* N.P.: TimeArt, 2007.

Kushner, Lawrence. *The Book of Letters.* Woodstock, Vt.: Jewish Lights, 1990.

Le Meg, Katharine. *Chant.* New York: Random House, 1994.

Leadbetter, C. W. *The Chakras.* Wheaton, Ill.: Quest, 1997.

Leeds, Joshua. *The Power of Sound.* Rochester, Vt.: Inner Traditions, 2001.

———. *Sonic Alchemy.* Sausalito, Calif.: InnerSong, 1999.

———. *Through A Dog's Ear.* Louisville, Colo.: Sounds True, 2008.

Leet, Leonara. *The Secret Doctrine of Kabbalah.* Rochester, Vt.: Inner Traditions, 1999.

Leonard, George. *The Silent Pulse.* New York: E. P. Dutton, 1978.

Levarie, Siegmund, and Ernst Levy, *Tone.* Cleveland, Ohio: Kent State, 1968.

Levin, Flora R. *Manual of Harmonics.* Grand Rapids, Mich.: Phanes, 1994.

Levin, Ted. *A Note about Harmonic Music.* N.P.: Harmonic Arts, 1984.

Levine, Peter A. *In an Unspoken Voice.* Berkeley, Calif.: North Atlantic, 2012.

Levitin, Daniel J. *Successful Aging.* New York: Dutton, 2020.

———. *This Is Your Brain on Music.* New York: Dutton, 2006.

———. *The World in Six Songs.* New York: Dutton, 2008.

Lewis, Robert C. *The Sacred Word and Its Creative Overtones.* Oceanside, Calif.: Rosicrucian Fellowship, 1986.

Liberman, Jacob. *Light: Medicine of the Future.* Rochester, Vt.: Bear & Co., 1991.

Lindahl, Kay. *The Sacred Art of Listening.* Woodstock, Vt.: Skylight Paths, 2002.

Lindenfeld, George L. *The Treatment of PTSD Comorbid Conditions.* N.P.: Lindenfeld, 2016.

Lingerman, Hal A. *The Healing Energies of Music.* Wheaton, Ill.: Quest, 1983.

Lipton, Bruce. *The Biology of Belief.* Carlsbad, Calif.: Hay House, 2015.

Lipton, Bruce H., and Steve Bhaerman. *Spontaneous Evolution.* Carlsbad, Calif.: Hay House, 2009.

Lloyd, Llewellyn S., and Hugh Boyle. *Intervals, Scales and Temperament.* New York: St. Martin's, 1978.

London, Erica. *Vibrational Sound Healing.* Rochester, Vt.: Inner Traditions, 2020.

Love, Roger. *Love Your Voice.* Carlsbad, Calif.: Hay House 2007.

Lyle, Heather. *Vocal Yoga.* Pacific Palisades, Calif.: Bluecat Music, 2014.

Lyons, Lawrence William. *The Language Crystal.* N.P.: Grammar, 1988.

Madagan, David. *Creation Myths.* London: Thames & Hudson, 1977.

Madaukem, Paul. *When Listening Comes Alive.* Norval, Canada: Moulin, 1993.

Maharshi, Ramana. *Who Am I?* India: Ramanasramam, 2013.

Maman, Fabien. *Healing with Sound, Color and Movement.* N.P.: Tama-Do, 1997.

———. *The Role of Music in the Twenty-First Century.* N.P.: Tama-Do, 1997.

———. *Sound and Acupuncture.* N.P.: Tama-Do, 1997.

———. *The Tao of Sound.* N.P.: Tama-Do, 2008.

Maniscalo, Maurice. *Humming, Nitric Oxide and Paranasal Sinus Ventilation.* Stockholm: Karolinska University Press, 2006.

Mannes, Elena. *The Power of Music.* New York: Walker & Co., 2011.

Manners, Peter Guy. *Cymatic Therapy.* Bretforton, 1976.

———. *The Future of Cymatic Therapy: Sound and Vibratory Pattern Research.* Bretforton, 1976.

Maple, Eric. *Incantations and Words of Power.* New York: Samuel Weiser, 1974.

Marciniak, Barbara. *Bringers of the Dawn.* Rochester, Vt.: Bear & Co., 1992.

Mathieu, W. A. *Harmonic Experience.* Rochester, Vt.: Inner Traditions, 1997.

———. *The Musical Life.* Boulder, Colo.: Shambhala, 1994.

Mattson, Jill. *Ancient Sounds, Modern Healing.* N.P.: Wings of Light. 2008.

McClain, Ernest G. *The Myth of Invariance.* New York: Nicolas Hays, 1976.

———. *The Pythagorean Plato.* Stony Brook, N.Y.: Nicolas Hays, 1978.

McClellan, Randall. *The Healing Forces of Music: History, Theory and Practice.* Amity, N.Y.: Amity House, 1988.

McKusick, Eileen Day. *Electric Body, Electric Health.* New York: St. Martin's, 2021.

———. *Tuning the Human Biofield.* Rochester, Vt.: Healing Arts Press, 2014.

McMakin, Carolyn. *The Resonance Effect.* Berkeley, Calif.: North Atlantic, 2017.

McTaggart, Lynne. *The Field.* N.P.: Quill, 2001.

———. *The Intention Experiment.* New York: Simon & Schuster, 2013.

Mehler, Stephen S. *From Light into Darkness.* Kempton, Ill.: Adventures Unlimited, 2005.

Merrit, Stephanie. *Mind, Music and Imagery.* London: Penguin, 1990.

Metzner, Jim. *Chanted Blessings in Disguise.* N.P.: Parabola, 1989.

Meyers, John. *Human Rhythms and the Psychobiology of Entrainment.* N.P.: Bell Communication, 1987.

Michael, Salim Edward. *The Law of Attention.* Rochester, Vt.: Inner Traditions, 2010.

Miles, Elizabeth. *Tune Your Brain.* New York: Berkley, 1997.

Mishra, Ramamurti, S. *Nada Yoga.* Monroe, N.Y.: Baba Bhagavanda, 2007.

Mitchell, Thomas J. *Rosslyn Chapel: The Music of the Cubes.* U.K.: Diversions, 2006.

Montello, Louise. *Essential Musical Intelligence.* Wheaton, Ill.: Quest, 2002.

Mora, Kay. *The Kay Mora Sound Trance.* N.P.: Spirit, 1983.

Morales, Jay Emmanuel. *The Healing Forces of Harmonic Sounds and Vibrations.* New York: JEM, 2017.

Motoyama, Hiroshi. *Theories of Chakras: Bridge to Higher Consciousness.* Wheaton, Ill.: Quest, 1981.

Mulder, Evelyn. *The Essence of Sound.* Palmer Lake, Colo.: Satiama Publishing, 2020.

Muranyi, Monika, and Amber Wolf. *The Women of Lemuria.* Montreal: Ariane, 2018.

Murchie, Guy. *Music of the Spheres.* Boston: Houghton Mifflin, 1961.

Murthy, Padma. "Therapeutic Value of South Indian Music." *International Journal of Music, Dance and Art Therapy* (April 1988).

Nakazono, Mikoto Masahilo. *Inochi: The Book of Life.* Santa Fe, Kototama, 1984.

Neal, Viola Petitt, and Shafica Karagulla. *Through the Curtain.* Marina del Ray, Calif.: DeVorss, 1983.

Nelson, Roger, D. *Connected.* Princeton, N. J.: ICRL, 2019.

Newby, Hayes A. *Audiology.* New York: Meredith, 1964.

Newham, Paul. *The Singing Cure.* Boulder, Colo.: Shambhala, 1993.

Newman, Frederick R. *Mouth Sounds.* New York: Workman, 1980.

Nichols, Preston B. *The Music of Time.* N.P.: Sky Books, 2000.

Nielsen, Linda. *Microtonal Healing.* Marina del Ray, Calif.: DeVorss, 2004.

Oates, David John. *Reverse Speech.* Indianapolis: Knowledge Systems, Inc., 1991.

O'Brien, Christopher. *Secrets of the Mysterious Valley.* Kempton, Ill.: Adventures Unlimited, 2007.

Olson, Harry F. *Music, Physics and Engineering.* New York: Dover, 1967.

Palombo, Anthony J. *Attunement with Sacred Sound.* St. Augustine, Fla.: Health Light, 2015.

Patel, Aniruddh D. *Music, Language and the Brain.* Houston, Tex.: Rice University Press, 2010.

Paul, Russell. *The Yoga of Sound.* Novato, Calif.: New World Library, 2004.

Pauwels, Louis, and Jacques Bergier. *The Morning of the Magician.* London: Souvenir, 2007.

Peirce, Penny. *Frequency.* Hillsboro, Ore.: Beyond Words, 2009.

Perret, Daniel. *Sound Healing with the Five Elements.* N.P.: Binkey Kok, 2005.

Perry, Wayne. *Overtoning.* Los Angeles: Musikarma, 2005.

Phillips, Jan. *Marry Your Muse: Making a Lasting Commitment to Your Creativity.* Wheaton, Ill.: Theosophical, 1997.

Pierce, John R. *The Science of Musical Sound.* New York: Scientific Books, 1983.

Ponce, Charles. *The Kabbalah.* Wheaton, Ill.: Quest, 1972.

Pond, Dale. *Universal Law: Keely's Secrets.* Santa Fe, N.M.: The Message Company, 2000.

Porté, Sylvain. *The Singing Bowl Manual.* N.P.: independently published, 2020.

Purce, Jill. "Sound in Mind and Body." *Resurgence,* no. 115 (March/April. 1986).

Rachele, Rollin. *Overtone Singing Study Guide.* Amsterdam: Cryptic Voices, 1996.

Radha, Swami Sivananda. *Mantras: Words of Power.* Spokane, Wash.: Timeless, 1980.

Rael, Joseph. *Being and Vibration.* Tulsa, Okla.: Council Oak Books, 1993.

Rael, Joseph, and Lindsay Sutton. *Tracks of Dancing Light.* Dorset, U.K.: Element 1993.

Rama, Rudolph Ballentine, and Allen Hymes. *Science of Breath.* Honesdale, Penn.: Himalayan Institute, 1979.

Redmond, Layne. *When Women Were Drummers.* Brattleboro, Vt.: Echo Point, 2018.

Regardie, Israel. *Eye in the Triangle.* France: Camion Blanc, 2015.

Retallack, Dorothy. *The Sound of Music and Plants.* Marina del Ray, Calif.: DeVorss, 1973.

Rigby, Dick. *Holistic Singing and Toning.* Australia: Kenmore Specialist, 1998.

Riley, Laurie. *Body, Mind and Music.* St. Louis, Mo.: MMB, 1999.

Ristad, Eloise. *A Soprano on Her Head.* Boulder, Colo.: Real People, 1982.

Rogers, Clint. *Ancient Secrets of a Master Healer.* N.P.: Wisdom of the World, 2021.

Rosen, Richard. *The Yoga of Breath.* Boulder, Colo.: Shambhala, 2002.

Rouget, Gilbert. *Music and Trance.* Chicago: University of Chicago Press, 1985.

Rudyhar, Dane. *The Magic of Tone and the Art of Music.* Boulder, Colo.: Shambhala, 1983.

———. *The Rebirth of Hindu Music.* New York: Samuel Weiser, 1979.

Sachs, Oliver. *Musicophilia.* New York: Vintage, 2008.

Sandzer-Bell, Ezra. *Astromusik.* N.P.: Sync, 2014.

Santana, Carlos. *The Universal Tone.* New York: Little Brown, 2014.

Saraswati, Swami Yogeshwaranand. *Science of Divine Sound.* India: Yog Niketan Trust, 1984.

Sawyer, Karen. *The Dangerous Man.* N.P.: O. Books, 2010.

Scarantino, Barbara Ann. *Music Power.* New York: Dodd, Mead & Co, 1987.

Schachter-Shalomi, Zalman, *Davening.* Woodstock, Vt.: Jewish Lights, 2012.

Schafer, R. Murray. *The Soundscape: Tuning of the World.* Rochester, Vt.: Destiny, 1994.

Schneider, Michael S. *A Beginner's Guide to Constructing the Universe.* New York: Harper 1995.

Schwartz, Jack, *Voluntary Controls.* New York: Dutton, 1978.

Scott, Cyril. *Music: Its Secret Influence through the Ages.* U.K.: Aquarian, 1982.

SCWL Research Report. *Comparative Studies and Other Documentation on the Effect of Subliminal Suggestion.* N.P.: Joe Land, 1985.

Seashore, Carl E. *Psychology of Music.* New York: Dover, 1938.

Seeger, Anthony. *Why Suya Sing.* Cambridge: Cambridge University Press, 2004.

Seifer, Marc J. *Wizard: The Life & Times of Nikolai Tesla.* New York: Citadel, 2011.

Serjak, Cynthia. *Music and the Cosmic Dance.* Washington, D.C.: Pastoral, 1987.

Sha, Zhi Gang. *Tao Song and Tao Dance.* New York: Simon & Schuster, 2011.

Shannanoff-Khalsa, D. S., and Yogi Bhajan. "Sound Current Therapy and Self-Healing: The Ancient Science of Nada and Mantra Yoga." *International Journal of Music, Dance and Art Therapy* (April 1988).

Shapiro, Eddie. *Inner Conscious Relaxation.* Dorset, U.K.: Element, 1990.

Shesso, Rhenna. *Math for Mystics.* San Francisco, Calif.: RedWheel/Weiser, 2007.

Shirlie Roden. *Sound Healing.* U.K.: Piakus, 1999.

Shrestha, Suren. *How to Heal with Singing Bowls.* Boulder, Colo.: Sentient, 2013.

Shulman, Lee, Joyce Shulman, and Gerald Rafferty. *Subliminal.* Santa Monica, Calif.: InfoBooks, 1991.

Siegel, Bernie. *Peace, Love and Healing.* U.K.: Ebury, 1998.

Singh, Kirpal. *Crown of Life.* India: Ruhani Satsang, 1970.

———. *Naam or Word.* India: Ruhani Satsang, 1960.

Singh, Ranje N. *Self Healing: Powerful Techniques.* N.P.: Health Psychology, 1997.

Smith, Huston, narr., and Elda Hartley, dir. *Requiem for a Faith.* Westport, Conn.: Hartley Film Foundation, 1980.

Snow, Shelley, Nicolò Francesco Bernadi, Sabet-Kassouf, Moran Daniel, and Alexandre Lehmann. "Exploring the Experience and Effects of Vocal Toning." *Journal of Music Therapy* 55 no. 2 (2018): 221–50.

Spintge, Ralph, and Roland Droh. *MusicMedicine.* St. Louis, Mo.: MMB, 1992.

St. Vincent, Justin. *The Spiritual Signficance of Music.* N.P.: Xtreme Music, 2009.

Statnekov, Daniel K. *Animated Earth.* Berkeley, Calif.: North Atlantic, 1987.

Stearns, Jess. *Edgar Cayce, The Sleeping Prophet.* New York: Doubleday, 1967.

Steiger, Brad. *Charms: Chants and Crystal Magic for the New Age.* New Brunswick, N.J.: Inner Light, 1987.

Steiner, Rudolph. *The Inner Nature of Music and the Experience of Tone.* Hudson, N.Y.: Anthroposophic, 1983.

Steven, Christine. *Music Medicine.* Louisville, Colo.: Sounds True, 2012.

Stewart, R. J. *Music and the Elemental Psyche.* Rochester, Vt.: Destiny, 1987.

———. *The Spiritual Dimensions of Music.* Rochester, Vt.: Destiny, 1987.

Stockhausen, Karl Heinz. *Towards a Cosmic Music.* U.K.: Element, 1989.

Storr, Anthony. *Music and the Mind.* New York: Ballantine, 1992.

Sullivan, Anita T. *The Seventh Dragon: The Riddle of Equal Temperament.* Lake Oswego, Ore.: Metamorphous, 1985.

Tame, David. *The Secret Power of Music.* New York: Destiny, 1984.

Tansley, David V. *Radionics and the Subtle Anatomy of Man.* Rustington, U.K.: Health Science, 1972.

Taylor, Dale B. *Biomedical Foundations of Music as Therapy.* St. Louis, Mo.: MMB, 1997.

Taylor, Thomas. *Life of Pythagoras.* Rochester, Vt.: Inner Traditions, 1986.

Teeguarden, Iona Marsaa. *Acupressure Way of Health.* Tokyo: Japan Publications, 1978.

Thaut, Michael H. *A Scientific Model of Music in Therapy and Medicine.* St. Louis, Mo.: MMB, 2000.

Todeschi, Kevin J. *Edgar Cayce on Vibrations.* Virginia Beach, Va.: A.R.E., 2007.

Tokar, David A. *Hans Kayser's Lehrbuch Der Harmonik.* New Brunswick, N.J.: Rutgers, 2002.

Tomatis, Alfred A. *The Conscious Ear.* Barrytown, N.Y.: Station Hill, 1991.

———. *The Ear and Language.* Norval, Canada: Moulin, 1996.

———. *Education and Dyslexia.* Fribourg, Switzerland: A.I.A.P.P., 1978.

Tompkins, Peter, and Christopher Bird. *Secrets of the Soil.* New York: Harper, 1989.

Twitchell, Paul. *The Spiritual Notebook.* Menlo Park, Calif.: Illuminated Way, 1971.

Twyman, James F. *The Moses Code.* Carlsbad, Calif.: Hay House, 2008.

Van Heerden, Derrick Scott. *Mathemagical Music Production.* N.P.: CreateSpace, 2016.

Vennard, William. *Singing.* New York: Carl Fischer, 1967.

Wade-Mathews, Max, and Wendy Thompson. *The Encyclopedia of Music.* U.K.: Hermes, 2002.

Walcott, Ronald. "The Choomij of Mongolia: A Spectral Analysis of Overtone Singing," *Selected Reports in Ethnomusicology* II, no. 1, 1974.

Wangyal, Tenzin. *Healing with Form, Energy and Light.* Ithaca, N.Y.: Snow Lion, 2002.

———. *Tibetan Sound Healing.* Louisville, Colo.: Sounds True, 2006.

———. *The Tibetan Yogas of Dream and Sleep.* Ithaca, N.Y.: Snow Lion, 1998.

Washington, Peter. *Madame Blavatsky's Baboon.* New York: Schocken, 1995.

Watson, Andrew, and Nevill Drury. *Healing Music.* Chatswood, N.S.W. Australia: Nature & Health, 1987.

Weed, Joseph, J. *Wisdom of the Mystic Masters.* West Nyack, N.Y.: Parker, 1973.

West, John Anthony. *Serpent in the Sky.* Wheaton, Ill.: Quest, 1993.

White, Gary, David Stuart, and Elyn Aviva. *Music in Our World.* New York: McGraw-Hill, 2001.

White, Harvey, and Donald White, *Physics of Music.* Philadelphia: Holt, Rinehart & Winston, 1980.

Wieder, June Leslie. *The Human Symphony.* N.P.: CreateSpace, 2019.

———. *Song of the Spine.* North Charleston, S.C.: Booksurge, 2004.

Wier, Dennis R. *Trance.* Ann Arbor, Mich.: Trans Media, 1996.

Wilson, Robert Anton. *Cosmic Trigger I, II, and III.* Grand Junction, Colo.: Hilaritas, 2016–19.

Winn, James Anderson. *Unsuspected Eloquence.* New Haven, Conn.: Yale University Press, 1981.

Winnston, Shirley Rabb. *Music as the Bridge.* Virginia Beach, Va.: A.R.E., 1972.

Winston, Judith Diana. *Meditative Magic: The Pleiadean Glyphs.* Santa Monica, Calif.: Chewut, 1994.

Winter, Dan. *Sacred Geometry: The Alphabet of the Heart.* Eden, N.Y.: Crystal Hill, 1992.

Wolf, Fred Alan. *The Yoga of Time Travel.* Wheaton, Ill.: Quest, 2004.

Wood, Alexander. *The Physics of Music.* London: Methuen, 1961.

Woods, Alana. *The Healing Touch of Music.* Albuquerque, N.M.: Sound Vistas, 2003.

Wooten, Victor. *The Music Lesson.* New York: Berkley Books, 2006.

Wyatt, Keith, and Carl Schroeder. *Harmony and Theory.* Milwaukee, Wisc.: Hal Leonard, 1998.

Zukav, Gary. *The Dancing Wu Li Masters.* New York: Bantam, 1979.

Discography

Christian Bollmann and the Düsseldorf Overtone Choir. 1988. *Rise My Soul* (Network). There are eight pieces on this recording, which at times resemble David Hykes with the Harmonic Choir and, at other times, Michael Vetter's work. Along with pure overtone singing, there is choral chanting, as well as instrumentation including flute and tambura. A very interesting and soothing recording from a harmonic vocalist who was influenced by Stockhausen.

Christian Bollmann. 1990. *Drehmomente* (Network). Bollmann, the director of the Düsseldorf Overtone Choir, sets out solo on this recording. Much like his previous recording, there is solo and choral overtone work, as well as some instrumentals with flute, tambura, and gong. The last piece is a wonderful version of "Amazing Grace" created solely through overtones.

Christian Bollmann. 1991. *Spirit Come* (Network). Solo and group overtone singing by the Düsseldorf Overtone Choir with instruments such as monochord, Tibetan bowls, and horns create a beautifully textured journey into sacred sound. Certain selections on this recording sound like the Harmonic Choir.

Christian Bollmann. 1992. *Akasha* (Lichthaus). An environmental soundscape to experience meditation and movement. There are solo and group vocal harmonics by Bollmann and the Düsseldorf Overtone Choir. Instrumentation includes bowls, gongs, waterhorn, synthesizer, and percussion.

Christian Bollmann and Michael Reimann. 1993. *Evolution* (Fonix). Further exploration into overtone music with ancient instruments and voice. Bollmann is a fine vocalist who utilizes many different styles of overtone chanting. Instrumentation includes didjeridoo, kalimba, frame drum, and shakuhachi.

Drepung Loseling Monks. 1992. *Sacred Tibetan Chants* (Music Arts). An exceptional recording of Tibetan Buddhist chanting that features three chant masters from the Drepung Loseling Monastery creating the "Deep Voice" with five other monks. Very powerful and hypnotic.

Drepung Loseling Monks. 1993. *The Sound of the Voice* (Telluride Bluegrass). Recorded at the Telluride Bluegrass Festival in Colorado, the Drepung Loseling monks chant their "Deep Voice" as well as give an example of Tibetan debating and dance. There is audience applause after the chants.

Eight Lamas from Drepung. 1988. *Tibetan Sacred Temple Music* (Shining Star). There are six different pieces on this recording. It seems that only one of the chanting lamas is truly a master of the One Voice Chord, and his vocals are predominantly featured. This is a most interesting release that is very different from the majority of other Tibetan chanting on record. At times it almost seems as though there is a Gregorian or a Hebrew flavor to the chanting style of these monks.

Gaden Shartse Monastery. 1989. *Sacred Healing Chants of Tibet* (East West Music). A wonderful recording of healing and purification chants to the Medicine Buddha and the environment. The invocations of this recording seem to be more melodic than those on the Gyuto or Gyume releases while incorporating the One Voice Chord.

Jonathan Goldman. 1991. *Gateways: Men's Drumming and Chanting* (Spirit Music). Thirty men contributed to this recording that features sacred chants with drumming from different traditions including Native American, Hindu, Tibetan, Hebrew, and others. "Om Mani Padme Hum" features Goldman using the Tibetan Deep Voice. "Kodosh/Allahu" has Middle Eastern overtone singing.

Jonathan Goldman. 1992. *Healing Sounds Intructional* (Spirit Music). This recording was created as an accompaniment to *Healing Sounds* and is an extremely efficient aid to learning some of the sonic techniques in this book. Designed to let the reader listen and sound with Goldman. On track one, "Vowels as Mantras," listeners learn to create resonance to balance their chakras. On track two, "The Fundamentals of Vocal Harmonics," they can learn to create vocal harmonics. (Also included as a download with this edition.)

Jonathan Goldman. 1993. *Angel of Sound* (Spirit Music). An invocation to Shamael, the angel of sound, this richly layered extended play recording features Goldman creating vocal harmonics with mantric chanting and Tibetan overtone chanting. Instrumentation includes Native American flute, and drums and Tibetan singing bowls and bells. Very powerful!

Jonathan Goldman. 1994. *Song of Saraswati* (Spirit Music). A sonic environment of chanting to honor the Hindu goddess of sound and science. Ideal for ritual and trance, it features male and female voices, vocal harmonics, tambura, monochord, Tibetan bells, whale sounds, and sitar. Beautiful and relaxing.

Jonathan Goldman. 1995. *Hermetic Harmonics* (Spirit Music). A sonic environment to create interdimensional fields of sound. With vocal harmonics, Tibetan bowls, and bells processed, looped together, and multi-tracked to create a pulsing waveform. Designed for deep meditation, channeling, ritual, and healing. Trance inducing!

Jonathan Goldman. 1996. *Trance Tara* (Spirit Music). An extended chant to the Tibetan goddess of compassion, this is an extraordinary recording featuring lush choral vocals, Tibetan overtone chanting and singing bowls on top of a pulsating layer of drums. Excellent for deep inner traveling as well as movement and dance.

Jonathan Goldman. 1997. *Chant Masters* (Spirit Music). A historic recording featuring Jonathan Goldman and Tibetan chant master Ngawang Tashi Bapu as they explore the depths of the Sound Current. These sonics include Tibetan "Deep Voice" chanting, vocal harmonics, toning, drums, Tibetan bowls, and bells.

Jonathan Goldman. 1999. *Chakra Chants* (Spirit Music). Designed for meditation and deep sound healing, this recording initiates a new level of the therapeutic uses of sound. Combines many different systems of chakra resonance including the seven sacred vowels, bija mantras, Pythagorean tunings, Shabda Yoga sounds, choral voices, and toning for an extraordinary hour-long transformational experience. Winner of the 1999 Visionary Award for "Best Healing/Meditation Album" and "Album of the Year."

Jonathan Goldman. 2000. *The Lost Chord* (Spirit Music). A new sonic experience that is both a journey through the chakras and the Kabbalistic Tree of Life. It features vocal harmonics, sacred mantras, and tones sounded by extraordinary chant masters from the Hindu, Tibetan, and Hebrew traditions. Includes bija and god/goddess mantras from the Hindu and Tibetan tradition, Hebrew chants of the Angelic and God Names, sacred vowel sounds, as well as psychoacoustic frequencies and sacred ratios.

Jonathan Goldman. 2001. *Medicine Buddha* (Spirit Music). Created for H. H. the Dalai Lama, this recording contains two powerful mantras, designed to invoke divine energies for healing and meditation: Medicine Buddha and the Heart of Wisdom Sutra. Each piece begins with the

Tibetan "Deep Voice" chanting of the Ven. Tashi, Tibetan chant master. Features vocal harmonics, choral voices, Tibetan singing bowls and bells, Native flute, guitars, drums, and whale sounds.

Jonathan Goldman. 2002. *Ultimate Om* (Spirit Music). A beautiful, transcendent sound as hundreds of voices chant a continuous "OM." It is like the original sacred sound source of the universe—the Divine sound of the cosmos that manifested all. These voices are singing the "OM" in the sacred Pythagorean ratio of 2:3, the perfect fifth. In addition, Jonathan Goldman and Alec Sims contribute beautiful vocal harmonics that float upon the lush choral sounds.

Jonathan Goldman. 2003. *Chakra Chants II* (Spirit Music). The long awaited follow up to *Chakra Chants*, this recording features Jonathan Goldman's amazing chakra chanting and sound healing expertise coupled with the toning and flute of Sarah "Saruah" Benson—the Divine Mother of Sound. It goes through the seven chakras featuring vocals using sacred vowels, bija mantras, toning and overtoning, with: elemental and Shabda sound, Tibetan bowls, Pythagorean tuning forks, conch shell, clay flutes, Native American flutes, and silver flutes.

Jonathan Goldman. 2004. *The Divine Name: Sounds of the God Code* (Spirit Music). This recording features the rediscovered universal vocal sound that many understand to be the personal name of the Divine as revealed in the Old Testament. Created through the harmonics of a unique series of sacred vowel sounds, the Divine Name is reproduced in its original form by Jonathan Goldman with his vocal overtones and sacred sound techniques. A unique, lush choral experience that is beautiful and enchanting. It is unlike anything that you have ever heard.

Jonathan Goldman. 2006. *The Angel and The Goddess* (Spirit Music). This recording features two very different sonic compositions that invoke and honor Shamael and Saraswati. These two releases, "Angel of Sound" and "Song of Saraswati," are divine invocations of celestial beings of sound. Both tracks feature vocal harmonics. "Angel of Sound" features Jonathan Goldman using numerous techniques of overtone chanting, including the Tibetan "Deep Voice" as well as vocal harmonics in a Middle Eastern style.

Jonathan Goldman. 2013. *Ascension Harmonics* (Spirit Music). Designed to help awaken listeners through enhancing altered states of consciousness and heightened awareness. Composed of overtone chanting and Tibetan bowls and bells, these undulating waves of healing sounds will transform you. Ascension Harmonics assist vibrational activation and frequency shifts. The sacred, multidimensional harmonic sounds are excellent for enhancing deep states of meditation as well as for shamanic journeys, rituals, and the ascension process. 2008 Visionary Award "Best Meditation/Healing Music."

Jonathan Goldman. 2012. *Cosmic Hum* (Spirit Music). Many ancient traditions suggest that the original sound of creation was the humming of prana—the energy of life. This recording features the sound of thousands of people toning the hum together, along with many different frequencies embedded into the sounds for healing and transformation. Sounds include cymatic frequencies for vital health energy and binaural beat frequencies for creating coherence and amplifying the human energy field. This hour-long recording is a unique and transcendent sonic experience with extraordinary energy and power!

Jonathan Goldman. 2013. *The Divine Name: I Am* (Spirit Music). This recording explores two sonic discoveries by Jonathan Goldman: the Divine Name, a universal sound for the lost name of God, and the Moses Code Frequencies, the numerical frequencies of the "I Am." It features the Moses Code Tuning Forks, Jonathan Goldman's intoning of the Divine Name in the frequencies of the Moses Code and the beautiful sacred toning of extraordinary vocalist Tina Malia. Together, the overall sounds are like ancient Gregorian monks chanting in a sacred temple as an enchanting priestess tones along.

Jonathan Goldman. 2014. *Merkaba of Sound* (Spirit Music). The word "Merkaba" is an ancient Middle Eastern term—found in both the Hebrew and Egyptian traditions—referring to a vehicle of inter-dimensional travel for body, mind, and spirit. This recording weaves a spiraling vortex of inter-dimensional Phi Sonics featuring a masterful blend of the Divine Name chanting and toning of Jonathan Goldman with the "Deep Voice" intonations of master Tibetan chanter Lama Tashi. 2014 Visionary Award Winner, "Best Frequency and Sound Healing" Music of the Year.

Jonathan Goldman. 2018. *Global Ah* (Spirit Music). In the tradition of the *Ultimate Om,* this piece consists of a composite of a large number of people toning the "AH" syllable—a universal sound of love and the heart chakra. Created to enhance World Sound Healing Day, this hour-long recording is a beautiful sonic soundscape to enhance tranquility, peace, and compassion. It is wonderful to listen to and can also be used as a musical accompaniment for your own toning practice.

Jonathan Goldman. 2021. *Colors of Sound* (Spirit Music). This recording features ten enchanting environments of sacred flowing sounds featuring

Jonathan Goldman working with some of the great sound healing luminaries of all time, including Lama Tashi, world renowned Tibetan chant master; Sarah Benson, Divine Mother of sound healing; Laraaji, godfather of ambient music; and Christian Bollmann, German overtone singing maestro. Instrumentation includes vocal toning and harmonics, Tibetan "Deep Voice" chanting, synthesizer, guitars, tambura, Tibetan bowls, zither, flute, trumpet, and tuning forks.

The Gyume Tibetan Monks. 1986. *Tantric Harmonics* (Spirit Music). This is a different Tantric college than the Gyuto and they create a different kind of One Voice Chord, stressing the overtone two octaves and a fifth above the fundamental. This was the first time the monks went into a modern recording studio to share their sacred chants and create a transcendent experience.

The Gyuto Monks. 1981. *Tantras of Gyuto* (Folkways). This is the first field recording of the Gyuto monks made in the 1970s. The fidelity is adequate and features the chanting of dozens of the Gyuto monks at their monastery.

The Gyuto Monks. 1987. *Tibetan Tantric Choir* (Windham Hill). This recording features the One Voice Chord of these Tibetan monks. Their distinct overtone, two octaves and a third above the fundamental, sounds like there is a children's choir singing along with the growl-like voices of the monks. The chants are hypnotic and the Tibetan cymbals and horns are quite awe-inspiring. There are other recordings of the Gyuto monks, but this is the best.

The Gyuto Monks. 1989. *Freedom Chants from the Roof of the World* (RykoDisc). This is a live recording of the sacred chants of the Gyuto monks. Kitaro, Philip Glass and Mickey Hart also appear on one cut (not with the monks).

Gyuto Tantric University. 1986. *Chants Secrets des Lamas Tibetan* (Dewatshang). This recording features shorter chants by the Gyuto monks. Available from France, this is a fairly rare and interesting release without instruments.

The Gyuto and the Gyume Tantric Monks. 1983. *Chog-Ga Tantric and Ritual Music of Tibet* (Dorje Ling). Field recordings from 1970 featuring both the Gyuto and the Gyume Tantric monks as well as other Tibetan chanting. At times the fidelity is less than adequate. On some of the tracks, there are over six hundred monks chanting together.

Nigel Charles Halfhide. 1986. *Movements of Mind* (Jecklin). Halfhide is a British overtone singer who now resides in Switzerland. A classical musician, music therapist, and student of meditation, he has been pursuing overtone singing as an intercultural music. There are five pieces on this recording featuring Halfhide doing overtone singing, accompanied by tambura or harmonium.

Nigel Charles Halfhide. 1989. *Colours of Silence* (Jecklin). There are three very beautiful pieces on this recording. Halfhide sings beautiful overtones while accompanying himself on tambura or harmonium. This is my favorite of the two available recordings and among my favorite releases that feature overtone singing. Very meditative and entrancing.

Harmonic Voices. 1995. *Whistling in the Temple* (Simone). This choral group creates experimental sounds that center around vocal harmonics. Sonics include Tibetan overtone chanting, solo and choral overtone chanting, monochord, Tibetan bowls, and waterphone.

Hartyga. 2018. *Amyrsanaa* (Hevhetia). They have been called Tuvan psychedelic ethno rock, and indeed with their electric guitars and musical arrangements they are far from what is thought of as traditional hoomi. But the incorporation of different overtone styles into rock music is quite interesting and unique. It represents the beginning of a new evolution of hoomi.

Anna-Maria Hefele. 2015. *Sweven* (Amazon). One of the finest of a new generation of overtone singers, Anna-Maria Hefel takes the genre of vocal harmonics into new directions, including jazz and unique world music. This recording has only four tracks and is less than twenty minutes in length, but it demonstrates her uncanny ability to manifest and manipulate harmonics. On October 2014, she was number two on the *Guardian*'s Viral Video Chart, with the online video titled *Polyphonic Overtone Singing.*

The Hu. 2019. *The Gereg* (Better Noise Music). This is a metal group from Mongolia that utilized hoomi throat-singing techniques in their rock music. This music works really well on many levels. For those who thought that hoomi techniques would only be limited to traditional folk music from Asia, this group shows you the pop music possibilities.

Huun-Huur-Tu. 1994. *60 Horses in My Heard* (Shanachie). Three Tuvan singers and one percussionist perform traditional Tuvan folk songs, using Indigenous instruments. The singers are masters of the different styles of hoomi. This is a very accessible recording of vocal harmonics and Tuvan songs.

David Hykes and the Harmonic Choir. 1982. *Hearing Solar Winds* (Ocora). Beautiful and transformative, this music is cloudlike and very hypnotic. The opening eight-minute "Rainbow Voice" features the first solo Western hoomi on record. Hykes is a fine singer as well as an extraordinary harmonic vocalist. His work with the choir is fascinating. Together they build chords based upon the harmonics in each others' tones and create Pythagorean tuned chords. The results are hypnotic and enchanting.

David Hykes and the Harmonic Choir. 1983. *Current Circulation* (Celestial

Harmonies). This is Hykes's second release. Very similar to *Hearing Solar Winds* in its texture and content.

David Hykes and the Harmonic Choir. 1986. *Harmonic Meetings* (Celestial Harmonies). On this release, Hykes steps from the wordless, drone-like pieces on his first two recordings, using sacred words such as "Halleluyah" and "Kyrie." Tim Hill contributes some nice Tibetan chanting as well. The unreleased "Harmonic Mass" is mentioned in the notes.

David Hykes and Djamchid Chemirani. 1989. *Windhorse Rider* (New Albion). Hykes contributes further vocal harmonic innovations to the musical world, this time with master Middle Eastern drummers. The music is fast and moving, with Arabian and Hindu tonal scales and excellent harmonic singing from Hykes.

David Hykes. 1991. *Let The Lover Be* (Auvidis). Hykes continued to branch out and experiment with sacred sounds. He sings songs from the Persian poet Rumi, plays synthesizer, and often is accompanied by a drummer. There are beautiful vocals and instrumentals, though less harmonic singing than on Hykes's other works.

David Hykes. 1993. *True to the Times (How to Be)* (New Albion). Further exploration in harmonics features Hykes working with drummers who rhythmically play the harmonic intervals he is singing. He is often accompanied by zard and other drums as well as synthesizer. A very interesting and beautiful recording.

Khusugtun. 2009. *Khusugtun Ethnic Ballad Group* (Khusugtun) This group uses traditional Mongolian music as well as Western classical musical styles to create unique ensemble arrangements featuring hoomi vocal techniques. It is some of the more advanced stylistic recordings, featuring harmonized overtone melodies and Western four-part, throat-singing harmonics.

Kitaro. 1993. *Dream* (Geffen). A symphonic recording of keyboard wizard Kitaro. "Dream of Chant" features Jonathan Goldman's Tibetan overtone chanting coupled with unique studio effects.

Mongolian Traditional Folk Groups. 1992. *Sounds of Mongolia* (Tibet Foundation). Mongolian hoomi overtone singing performed by traditional folk groups. There are instrumentals as well as singing in different hoomi styles. An interesting version of the Buddhist "Om Mani Padme Hum" performed using the Mongolian overtone voice.

Kongar-ol Ondar. 2012. *Back Tuva Future* (Warner Nashville). The ancient, multitone singing technique from Tuva is relocated to the heartland of America. This CD features Nashville musicians. With guest appearances from Willie Nelson, Randy Scruggs, and Bill Miller, these ten tracks take on the shape of a multicultural hoedown. The combination of hoomi master Kongar-ol Ondar hoomi singing and country music is truly unique.

Paul Pena and Kongar-ol Ondar. 2000. *Genghis Blues* (Six Degrees Records). This is the soundtrack from an astounding documentary about Paul Pena, a blind, black, blues singer from the United States who traveled to Tuva to win an award at a throat-singing contest. The music features both Paul and hoomi legend Kongar-ol Ondar singing separately and together creating an astounding fusion of sound—truly global music. Paul's story and his music are amazing and inspiring!

Frank Perry. 1988. *Infinite Peace* (Mountain Bell). The sounds of bells and gongs make up a majority of the sonics on this calming and tranquil recording. There is fine overtone singing with instruments on the second side.

Wayne Perry. 1994. *Sounds for Self-Healing* (Musikarma). This is a musical journey designed to tone and tune the physical and emotional body using the vocal harmonics. There are twelve pieces on this recording, which chromatically go up the scale from the note C.

Bojidar Pinek. 1988. *Vocal Spaces* (Hoomi). Several of the cuts on this release feature overtone chanting. Pinek is quite a fine choral master working with some talented vocalists. Together they create some very interesting modal vocal music in which he incorporates overtone chanting.

Iegor Reznikoff. 1989. *Le Chant de Fontenay* (SM). Reznikoff combines Gregorian chant with vocal overtones to create a remarkably tranquil recording of sacred sounds. He sings solo in the Cathedral of Fontenay, often accompanying himself on tambura.

Wolfgang Saus and Michael Reisman. 2012. *Harmoniversum* (Acorn Music). A very interesting and pleasant combination of the improvisational piano of Wolfgang Saus and the overtone singing of Michael Reisman. Reisman has recorded with Christian Bollmann and made numerous recordings on his own. He is a fine overtone singer. Working with Saus, the resulting music is works surprising well and continues to expand the parameters of vocal harmonic music.

StarScape Singers. 1989. *Fire Mass* (Sun-Scape). This music has been described as twenty-first-century choral music. It certainly is something different and most interesting. A readaptation of the Catholic Mass, with the singers creating some amazing sounds that at times incorporate both Mongolian and Tibetan overtone chanting. Kenneth Mills wrote the words and directed this choir in their endeavors.

Shu-De. 1994. *Voices from the Distant Steppe* (Real World). The different styles of Tuvan throat singing are displayed on this recording as well as other examples of Tuvan music. The hoomi vocalists are all excellent, and this disc is a fine addition to any musical library.

Lama Tashi. 2005. *Tibetan Master Chants* (Spirit Music). This is the Grammy nominated recording. It features the sacred "Deep Voice" chanting of Lama Tashi, one of the world's foremost Tibetan chant masters, chanting twelve well-known Tibetan mantras. Produced by Healing Sounds pioneer Jonathan Goldman, this CD was created for listening pleasure, to create sacred space and vibrational shifts and to learn the sacred Tibetan mantras. There is a specific order and function for each of the chants on this recording, which work together in order to assist personal and planetary consciousness.

Lama Tashi. 2015. *Chen Dren* (Spirit Music). This recording features the never before realized sound experience of a powerful mantra chanted in many different Tibetan multiphonic One Voice Chord styles by Chant Master Lama Tashi. It was edited, layered, and engineered using powerful, psychoacoustic techniques by Jonathan Goldman. "Chen Dren" is a Tibetan term meaning "invocation." The primary verse on this recording is considered to be an extraordinarily sacred Buddhist invocation—perhaps the most powerful and blessed ever created. This mantra is an invitation to all the benevolent energies and entities in the Buddhist pantheon to come into your sacred space and be with you.

Tyva Kyzy. 2020. *Ayalgalar: Melodies* (Pan Records). Tyva Kyzy are the only all-female group that is able to sing all the different styles of hoomi. They are able to do this as well as any of their male counterparts. The singing is extraordinary, with beautiful arrangements. Instrumentation includes zither and other traditional instruments.

Various Artists. 1989. *Tuva—Voices from the Center of Asia* (Rounder). Founding Harmonic Choir Member Ted Levin traveled to Mongolia to make field recordings of the extraordinary sounds on this release. There are about thirty pieces on this recording, featuring masters of the hoomi technique. Most of the pieces are about a minute and a half long, but they are among the most unique sounds on the planet.

Various Artists. 1992. *Tuva: Echoes from the Spirit World* (Pan). Recordings of the music of Tuva from folk ensembles whose soloists perform the hoomi technique of throat singing. One of the most interesting selections is a Buddhist lama chanting a prayer using the vocal styles of Tuva.

Various Artists. 1993. *Tuva: Voices from the Land of the Eagles* (Pan). Three master soloists from the folk ensemble Tuva create extraordinary vocal harmonics with the hoomi technique. They sing folk songs from their homeland, often accompanying themselves on Indigenous instruments.

Glen Velez. 1991. *Ramana* (Music of the World). Glen is an exceptional percussionist, using a wide variety of handheld drums. He is also a fine harmonic singer who can accompany himself while drumming. On this recording, three of the eight cuts feature overtone singing.

Michael Vetter. 1982. *Overtones and Tambura* (Wergo). There are two pieces on this release. Side one features Vetter doing overtone chanting while strumming the tambura, a northern Indian instrument. There are some excellent vocal harmonics with Vetter using a technique of overtone chanting by opening and closing the back of his throat to create harmonic melodies. The sounds on side two are tambura instrumental music without overtone singing.

Michael Vetter. 1985. *Missa Universalis: (Obertonmesse)* (Wergo). The *Overtone Mass* has six movements utilizing the traditional names of the Mass: "Kyrie," "Gloria," "Credo," "Sanctus," and "Agnus Dei." Vetter sings the single-word names using some overtones, creating what he calls a "transverbal" language.

Michael Vetter. 1987. *Overtones in Old European Cathedrals: Senanque* (Wergo). Two movements. Vetter accompanies himself on tambura while he creates beautifully distinct vocal harmonics. In many of the follow-up releases after *Overtones and Tambura* he spent much time experimenting with different sounds but did not focus his attention specifically on the creation of vocal harmonics. On this recording, his overtoning singing is splendid. This is my favorite recording from this German overtone singer.

Michael Vetter. 1987. *Overtones in Old European Cathedrals: Thoronet* (Wergo). Two movements. Vetter accompanies himself on tambura and sings well. However, he does not utilize vocal harmonics as much as he does on the recording in *Senanque.*

Michael Vetter. 1987. *Overtones—Instrumental: Wind* (Jecklin). Music for flutes, voice, and gongs. Three movements. Meditational music with more instrumental music than overtone singing.

Michael Vetter. 1989. *Overtones—Instrumental: Flowers* (Jecklin). Music for piano and voice. One movement. Meditational music with more instrumental music than overtone singing.

Michael Vetter. 1989. *Overtones—Instrumental: Light* (Jecklin). Music for tamburas and voice. One movement. Meditational music with more instrumental music than overtone singing.

Michael Vetter. 1989. *Overtones—Instrumental: Silence* (Jecklin). Music for singing bowls, cymbals, and voice. One movement. Meditational music with more instrumental music than overtone singing.

Michael Vetter. 1989. *Overtones—Instrumental: Spaces* (Jecklin). Music for gong and voice. One movement. Meditational music with more instrumental music than overtone singing.

Michael Vetter. 1990. *Overtones—Instrumental: Clouds* (Jecklin). Music for Koto harp and voice. Three movements. Meditational music with more instrumental music than overtone singing.

On Wings of Song. 1991. *Heart of Perfect Wisdom* (SpringHill). This is a lush choral rendition of the Tibetan Buddhist Heart Sutra. Jonathan Goldman contributes Tibetan overtone chanting and Tibetan singing bowls and bells.

Index

About the Author

Photo by John Daniels

Jonathan Goldman, M.A., is an international authority and pioneer in the field of sound healing. He is author of numerous books including *Healing Sounds, The 7 Secrets of Sound Healing, The Divine Name,* and his latest, the best-selling *The Humming Effect* (co-authored with his wife Andi Goldman), which won the 2018 Gold Visionary Award for "Health Books." Jonathan is the director of the Sound Healers Association and president of Spirit Music, Inc. in Boulder, Colorado. A Grammy nominee, he has created over thirty best-selling, award-winning recordings including *Chakra Chants, The Divine Name, Ascension Harmonics,* and *Reiki Chants.* Jonathan has been named one of *Watkins' Mind Body Spirit* magazine's "100 Most Spiritually Influential Living People." Jonathan lectures and gives workshops and online courses on the therapeutic and transformational use of sound throughout the world.

www.healingsounds.com